D1345159

MATTHEW McCONAUGHEY

MATTHEW McCONAUGHEY

THE BIOGRAPHY

NEIL DANIELS

Published by John Blake Publishing Ltd,
3 Bramber Court, 2 Bramber Road,
London W14 9PB, England

www.johnblakepublishing.co.uk

www.facebook.com/johnblakebooks 🔲
twitter.com/jblakebooks 🔲

This edition published in 2014

ISBN: 978 1 78418 027 0

British Library Cataloguing-in-Publication Data:

A catalogue record for this book is available from the British Library.

Design by www.envydesign.co.uk

Printed in Great Britain by CPI Group (UK) Ltd

1 3 5 7 9 10 8 6 4 2

Papers used by John Blake Publishing are natural, recyclable products made from
wood grown in sustainable forests. The manufacturing processes conform to the
environmental regulations of the country of origin.

Every attempt has been made to contact the relevant copyright-holders, but some
were unobtainable. We would be grateful if the appropriate people could contact us.

ABOUT THE AUTHOR

Neil Daniels is the author of numerous books on music and pop culture, including biographies of Metallica, AC/DC, Iron Maiden, Bon Jovi and Journey. His books have also been translated into over a dozen languages. His reviews, articles and interviews on music and pop culture have been published in *The Guardian*, *Record Collector*, *Rock Sound*, *Media Magazine* and *musicOMH*. He has also written several sets of sleeve notes for various record labels.

Neil lives in the northwest of England.

His official website is www.neildanielsbooks.com.

CONTENTS

CONTENTS

CHAPTER ONE

GROWING UP
IN TEXAS

'I am from Texas and love Texas.'
Matthew McConaughey, *Daily Express*, 2014

Matthew McConaughey and Texas are inextricably intertwined. Wherever McConaughey goes Texas is always in his heart. He's your typical Southern American charmer – he has the Texan drawl, the humble attitude, the pious zeal and the archaic sense of humour.

Texas is the largest of the Lower 48 contiguous states (only Alaska is bigger). As someone once said, 'The sun has riz, the sun has set, and here we is in Texas yet.' Texas is nearly three times the size of the United Kingdom, but with only 25 million inhabitants has well under half the population, which explains why most Texans prefer to celebrate the sprawling open spaces and the freedom they bring, particularly in film and music.

Texans have a reputation for being larger than life too, a notion Matthew McConaughey has done nothing to dispel throughout his illustrious career through all sorts of film roles and a healthy attitude towards travel and culture in his personal life. It is wrong to generalise, of course, but, down the years, Texas does seem to have produced more than its fair share of genuine characters, from Hondo Crouch, Mayor of Luckenbach (Population 3!), through to great storytellers such as novelist Larry McMurtry, comedian Bill Hicks, rock band ZZ Top, to say nothing of a raft of fellow thespians, including Larry 'JR' Hagman and Tommy Lee Jones, or even disgraced cyclist Lance Armstrong, who is one of McConaughey's pals. Depending on which side of the political fence you sit, you can claim four presidents as Texan, or only two if you aren't a fan of former US presidents George Bush Senior and his equally controversial son George Bush Junior, neither of whom were actually born in the state. This is just the tip of the Texan iceberg, of course.

While the majority of Texans speak English as their first language, Spanish is spoken by about a third — after all, it borders Mexico and was once ruled by her — and the language is taught in schools. Remember the Alamo? Texans do! Matthew McConaughey has, of course, celebrated the Texan influences and culture in his films, from *Dazed and Confused* right up to *Killer Joe* and *Dallas Buyers Club*. Let's not mention *Texas Chainsaw Massacre: The Next Generation*, though.

In fact, six countries have had control of Texas at one time or another (Spain, France, Mexico, Republic of Texas, the Confederate States and the United States). Texas is the only US State with the right to secede from the union, and a minority of Texans want to do just that (though whether Washington would allow it, if push came to shove, is a moot point). It does, however, show an independent, free spirit. Matthew McConaughey is certainly a free spirit; often getting into one of his Airstreams or a car and driving off anywhere that takes his fancy, or even hopping on a plane and flying to somewhere faraway. Gun control laws are amongst the most relaxed in the country, and concealed handguns can be carried legally in many circumstances.

In addition to the Spanish influence, Texas was settled by, amongst others, many Czechs and Germans, who brought with them their own traditions including music, literature and film. Perhaps this explains McConaughey's love of travel, the arts and culture.

In fact, Texas has an astonishing musical heritage, where different cultural groups have melded their music into something unique. It has spawned many notable musicians, including, but certainly not limited to: T-Bone Walker, Freddie King, Blind Willie Johnson, Blind Lemon Jefferson, Mance Lipscomb, Lightnin' Hopkins, Albert Collins and Big Mama Thornton. More recent Texan blues players include Stevie Ray Vaughan and older brother Jimmie, Willie Nelson, Janis Joplin, Edgar and Johnny Winter, ZZ Top, and many more. All these musicians are Texan born and bred. McConaughey loves music so much that he founded his own independent record label. Before it sounds like things are getting a little bit Texas-centric around here, it should be pointed out that Matthew McConaughey has been generous in his praise of Texan blues players and local musicians – Willie Nelson being a personal friend and one-time acting colleague in the movie *Surfer, Dude.*

Not to forget Texas had spawned some of McConaughey's acting peers, including Woody Harrelson, Jennifer Garner, Jennifer Love Hewitt, Renée Zellweger and Jamie Foxx, and not forgetting such popular actors as Owen Wilson, Hilary Duff and the late Patrick Swayze.

To sum it up, Texas is a huge melting pot of creativity and achievements in the arts and entertainment from country to folk by the way of blues, rock and even metal and punk, and masterful westerns in literature and film as well as irreverent comedians and actors. There has been such a variety of talent to come out of Texas. However, if you want a modern day actor who personifies the true Texan spirit, look no further than Matthew McConaughey. In fact, McConaughey was ranked as the most popular male actor to come from Texas on IMDB (International Movie Data Base) recently.

How Texas has influenced him is perhaps a matter for debate, but that it has isn't up for grabs. Even when he moved to LA in the mid-1990s he took pieces of home with him.

Y'all have gotta understand that Matthew McConaughey is a Texan through and through.

*****

Matthew McConaughey was the surprise baby, the one that was not planned. His parents were unable to conceive a second child and adopted a son, Pat, as a tenth birthday present for their eldest boy, Rooster (real name Michael). Matthew came along six years later as a total surprise. He was born Matthew David McConaughey on 4 November 1969 in Uvalde, Texas to Mary Kathleen (née McCabe) and James 'Big Jim' Donald McConaughey. Michael McConaughey is seventeen years older than Matthew, and Pat is seven years his senior.

Trenton, New Jersey-born Mary Kathleen, nicknamed 'K-Mac' but regularly called Kay for short, was a kindergarten teacher and later published author while her husband James, whom everyone called Pop or 'Big Jim', ran a Texaco station in Uvalde. In 1980, however, he upped sticks and moved the family to Longview, a couple hours east of Dallas, where he worked in the oil pipe business. Theirs was a tough love, but their love for their boys was immeasurable.

'She also taught me to look at life as if it were a rose in a vase, something beautiful. If I woke in a grumpy mood she'd come up and hit me on the side of the head,' McConaughey said of Kay to Garth Pearce of the *Daily Express* in 2014. 'She would say, "You can go back down that hallway and start over." I would have to go back to my room and begin the day again. My dad also had simple rules. He would say, "Don't lie and don't say 'I can't.'" We had tough love in our family.'

Pop was forty-one years old when Matthew was born. He loved sports and beer like any other lower middle class Texan male. 'He was a salesman and really pretty carny, man, in on a diamond mine in Ecuador and stuff that turned out to be bullshit. He'd take me on Saturdays to meet somebody, Chicago John, behind the strip mall who's got a dishwasher and stuff in the back of his truck,' Matthew told *Texas Monthly*'s John Spong in 2008. '"But wait," he whispered. "There's a platinum watch wrapped up in a paper towel." Pop says to me, "Put it in the glove box, buddy." Five minutes down the road and he goes, "Check and make sure it's still there." And it's just him and me in the car. He loved that. He'd go, "Open up that paper. Goddam, that's a good-looking watch."'

Matthew and his mum often talk in interviews about Pop's hands. Pop knew how to rub Kay's temples to help her sleep if her headache tablets did not work. Pop also rubbed Matthew's head if his childhood ear infections kept him awake at night.

Pop would also give foot rubs to beautiful women. He'd even rub the feet of his oldest boys' girlfriends if ever they came to the house for a date. There was nothing weird about it; Pop was just a nice fella.

Kay and Pop divorced twice and married three times, though, unbelievably, the boys didn't find out until 1992 when their father died of a heart attack. They had a wild and passionate relationship throughout their thirty-nine years together. Whenever Mrs McConaughey left the house her husband would tell the boys that she was on vacation. His older brothers understood what was happening, though. It wasn't confusing for the three lads. They didn't wonder where their mother was because in the summer they had their dad to look after them and keep them entertained when their mum was away. There were not questions about which parent loved the children more or which child loved which parent the most; the love was equal. Pop and Kay would remarry and Kay would return to the house as though nothing happened.

'[There was] a lot of love in our family,' Matthew told *The Scotsman*. 'That was the one thing. You'd get in trouble in our family and you'd hear, "I don't like you right now but I love you." It didn't matter, even if you were in trouble, you knew you were loved. And that was a big thing.'

Pop, who was originally from Louisiana, once played NFL football for the Green Bay Packers after playing college ball at the University of Houston and (for one year) at Kentucky for Bear Bryant. He was a strong man and often walked around the house with his shirt off, showing off his muscles and commenting that his strong manly arms put food on the table.

Matthew and his brothers had a Methodist upbringing and his

ancestry includes English, Irish, Scottish, Swedish and German, and he is a relative of Brigadier General Dandridge McRae. 'My last name is originally Irish,' McConaughey said to *Metro* in 2006. 'I am not exactly sure whereabouts it's from but I've got family branches that were traced back there.'

Kay purposefully chose a Biblical first name. 'When I was in kindergarten a boy came up and said: "Hey Matt let's go play." My mom overheard him and told me never to answer to Matt again in my life. And I never have,' Matthew said in an interview with *Cinema.com*, 'because Mom wouldn't like it.'

It was a loving family but hardly conventional. Mrs McConaughey had a family rule – if it's daylight, go outside. It was a no-nonsense, time-wasting sort of family. 'It was a do it, do it lifestyle,' Matthew told *The Daily Telegraph*'s Tom Shone. 'A great family of bullshitters. Oh yeah, great stories that still get rehashed every Christmas when we get together and someone puts a new tweak on 'em, just to make 'em interesting and goad the others. It's entertainment. That's how we entertained ourselves and how we still entertain ourselves.'

There was a lot of respect in the McConaughey household; respect for each other and for elders. Matthew and his siblings also grew up with a can-do attitude. Their parents taught them that there was no such word as 'can't'. On the contrary, they were taught that they could do anything in life, which would be important for Matthew down the road. They were taught about basic pleasantries such as 'please' and 'thank you', and 'pardon' and 'excuse me'. The boys were taught to address their elders as either Sir or Miss and were also taught how to be polite to people in general. 'You could maybe get away with saying a cuss word,' Matthew told *IndieLondon*, 'but the day I came home after hearing the word "hate" at school, and told my brother: "I hate you!" Well, time stopped. My Mom said: "You said WHAT!?" That was a good butt-whupping [for me].'

They had dinner together every night and told stories. Entertainment wasn't the usual trashy TV and hip chart music; it just wasn't something that was embedded in their lower middle class family roots. 'We weren't allowed to watch much TV,' Matthew said to *Texas Monthly*'s Jason Cohen in 1996. 'The rule was, if there was daylight, you were outside, building tree houses, frog gigging, riding bike trails, stuff like that. At night, okay, an hour of TV, then let's play a board game.'

Kay often reminded the McConaugheys of the stark realities of life and that they should be thankful for what they have. There are always kids worse off than they are. 'When we were raised, [when] we got out of bed in the morning, we'd come out for breakfast in the morning and be in a crappy mood,' McConaughey recalled to Josh Elliott of ABC News. 'She'd just grab us and run us back to the bed and throw us back in and say, "Don't you come back to my breakfast table where I cooked you breakfast and see the dust on the table instead of the rose in the vase, buddy."'

The McConaugheys moved to Longview from Uvalde where Matthew attended Longview High School. Something of a high school stud, he was voted most handsome in the Longview Lobo Yearbook. However, the accolade cost him a small fortune. Well, more like $35,000 as he told popular late night US talk show host Jimmy Fallon. 'Winning this award cost my family some money, though,' Matthew said. 'Cut back three years before I got this award for "Most Handsome", I'm a teenager, I'm fifteen years old. Oily skin, you got a few pimples and stuff. Well, my mom is peddling this stuff, the oil of mink.'

He got full blown acne by putting mink oil on his face. It was a dumb move because using oil on a teenager's oily face is counterproductive to pulling out impurities such as spots, zits and acne. He saw a dermatologist who informed him that it was a daft idea to use an oil-based product. 'I mean you are emotionally pounded,' Matthew explained to Terry Gross of the NPR show *Fresh Air*, 'and psychologically this really had to hurt, and everyone started feeling all of these, you know, ideas. But, yeah, I was emotionally done. Yeah, my confidence was lower. Well, there's a lawsuit filed.'

As a consequence, Pop decided to file a $35,000 lawsuit for the pain and emotional distress his youngest son suffered while using mink oil at the recommendation of Kay's boss. As lawsuits take so long to file, by the time it reached the courts Matthew had already won the 'Most Handsome' accolade and the company Pop had sued showed the photo to the judge and it was thrown out of court.

Matthew, speaking to Terry Gross, said, 'I get called in for a deposition by the defence. And he sits me down and he goes through all this, you know, emotionally this must've been so tough for you. And look at these pictures of the acne you had. Oh my God. I mean your face is almost bleeding. You look like a monster. This is so bad. Man, it must've really been tough on you. And I'm like, yes, sir. Yes, sir. Yes, sir. And he goes through this for about forty-five minutes. And I'm thinking this is great. Man, this is the defence talking to me and he's saying all the problems that I had. And then he stops and he reaches down under the table and he pulls up this yearbook and he opens up this page, turns around to me and slides over and he goes, what's this picture here, this award you won? I looked down at it and it says "Most Handsome".'

Matthew knew as soon as the accolade was highlighted that they'd lost the lawsuit. Still, his folks and his brothers saw the funny side because for years they joked with him that he lost them a $35,000 lawsuit because he was a handsome teenager. They could have been richer if he was ugly!

His first kiss was at a school dance, in similar circumstances to the dance sequence in *Ghosts of Girlfriends Past*. He was on a high for weeks afterwards because he pulled it off without embarrassment. The kiss happened just before 'Careless Whisper' by eighties pop heartthrobs Wham! was played.

Matthew couldn't afford to buy a lot of cologne and he made sure the two bottles he bought lasted for two years each. 'My friends would ask if they could have some and they were allowed to have one mist,' he recalled to *People* magazine. 'I would spray it once on them directly or spray it and they could run into it.'

Matthew was a kid who liked to have fun just like any other teenager in the neighbourhood. 'I have seventy-eight stitches on my head where my nephew ran over me with a jet ski and cut me open pretty well when I was fourteen,' he admitted to *Phase9 TV* as an adult. 'I have another scar on top of my foot from a dog fight when I was a kid.'

His first job was raking seventy-seven sand traps on a golf course before eight in the morning. He enjoyed playing golf and would continue to play a good round well into adulthood. When he was a young kid, though, he wanted to play for the Washington Redskins. He loved American football.

Matthew was very good at getting away with stuff but he got

caught a couple of times. His parents were not fond of lies so the last thing their boys could get away with was telling fibs. If they got caught lying, they would get in more trouble for lying than the deed they were lying about. It was the only time the McConaughey boys got in serious trouble. 'When [Pop] walked down the hallway you would hear his bones cracking,' Matthew told *Phase9 TV*. 'He said if we wanted to play football – he had been a line backer – we could, but that we should remember that we could hear his legs and back. His big things were respect for elders and for women. It is something that has been ingrained in me. He said if you don't lie, you don't leave crumbs.'

Matthew was asked by Andy Warhol of *Interview Magazine* if there was anything he regrets not doing. He replied: 'In the summer of 1985, I told a lady in Navarre Beach, Florida, that I wanted to lifeguard on her beach the next summer. She had never hired a non-local and said she would reserve a spot for me if I promised I'd be there by June First the next year. I said I would. As that next summer approached, I found myself doing other things and questioning whether I would go back to Florida to be a lifeguard as I gave my word that I would. As May bled into June, I kept procrastinating and talked myself into thinking, *"She probably forgot,"* and *"It won't be a big deal if I don't show,"* and I never went. I've always regretted not letting her know that I wouldn't be coming that summer. In my mind, I know she was expecting me. I "left crumbs" with that decision, meaning, I made a decision that made me look over my shoulder because I mislead someone. I regret that.'

Matthew had a good time in high school. He got As and was socially active and popular (though he has since admitted he was perhaps a touch emotionally extroverted). His good pal Rob

Benlerph was very encouraging of Matthew's talents and would have a lot to do with Matthew's future vocation. Rob – who was a somewhat introverted teen – was the one friend who told Matthew that every Friday and Saturday night did not have to be about partying and meeting girls. So, as a result, Matthew partied on Fridays, but Saturdays were spent watching a movie and having a meal. This was when Matthew was introduced to films. Rob, who would later go to NYU, was writing scripts and teaching Matthew about storytelling. Rob suggested to Matthew that he should try to act and Matthew took the idea on board. Some of the films that Matthew liked at the time were *Angel Heart*, the Alan Parker film starring Mickey Rourke and Robert De Niro, and *Hud*, directed by Martin Ritt and starring the late Paul Newman.

Another favourite film of his was *King Kong*, which has stayed with him ever since and has perhaps impacted his life more than any other feature. It's odd that the highly derided 1976 version with Jessica Lange had such an impression on Matthew, but he absolutely loved it. 'One of my favourite movies,' McConaughey admitted to *Elle*'s Holly Milea. 'When I was eight years old watchin' that movie, I cried when they took King Kong and wouldn't let him get together with Jessica Lange, because I think they could have worked it out.'

In 1988 aged nineteen, he lived for a year as a Rotary exchange student in Warnervale, New South Wales, Australia. Matthew's first application was declined but then he met Noel Crocker, an Australian from Warnervale on the Central Coast, who was staying in Texas as part of the same exchange programme. Noel rang his dad Ray in Australia and asked him if there was anything he could do to help Matthew. Noel faxed him Matthew's details and Ray then checked with Bill Symington, the Toukley Rotary President, who granted Matthew permission so long as he stayed with the Crockers (Ray, his wife Eileen and their son Noel) at their farm in Warnervale. Matthew was there two weeks later. He lived at the family farm for five months, during which time he attended Gorokan High School and helped Ray with his horses. He then went on to stay with Bill and Val Symington and their kids for six months before flying back to Texas.

Matthew moved to Australia because he wasn't sure what he wanted to do and his mother knew he loved travelling and that he wanted to explore the world. He fell in love with Australia, a foreign, almost unheard of land to many Americans. He explored the Central Coast and cities such as Brisbane. He would revisit the country many times in adulthood and even make a film there. He absorbed the culture, the people, the dialect, and of course, coming from sunny Texas, he loved the glorious weather. His trip to Australia also tripped a nerve in him for another reason – his love of travelling. One day, with enough money, he would journey to many different countries and partake in as many adventures as possible, often on his own.

Matthew is somewhat similar to a character in a Mark Twain novel or a Woody Guthrie song; a free spirit, someone who roams the country unchained of any tangles. Back in Texas, he had to concentrate on his studies and think about career plans. Going to college remains a huge source of pride and a great achievement for many lower middle class Americans, especially for those whose parents are less educated.

Asked by a fan for his fondest memories of Australia in *Empire*'s 'Public Access Unseen' interview feature, he responded: 'Mmm, being out in the Bush. That was a really interesting year. I had a couple of different jobs, lived with different families. I'd say my most satisfying job was when I was a builder. I was a carpenter, with this guy I lived with called Bill. And we went out to just a derelict property and built that house from the ground up. The whole structure, and it was just really, really cool working on that, being able to see the before and after, and getting that gratification of building a small home, and then living with him and his family. He had five daughters and I'd never had sisters, so having sisters was very cool.'

Throughout his teenage years Matthew took on a series of menial and mundane jobs to get some cash together. Such tasks included washing dishes, including at the houses he lived in Down Under. By the time he moved back home it was time to get his head stuck in the study books.

In 1989 Matthew enrolled at the University of Texas at Austin College of Communication where he joined the Delta Tau Delta International Fraternity and lived at The Castilian residence hall.

He had somewhat disjointed ideas of what he wanted to do as a career. Originally, he wanted to become a lawyer (his family joked that he could get them out of trouble), a role he ended up playing in *A Time to Kill*, *Amistad*, *The Lincoln Lawyer* and *Bernie*. Law, however, wasn't tickling his gut even though he had been on that career path from the age of fourteen.

'I was headed towards law school,' he admitted to *The Film Stage*'s Caitlin Martis, 'and it wasn't until the end of my sophomore year, right about that time when your general credits are up and your new ones aren't really going to transfer if you change your course schedule. I was a little nervous about this idea of being a lawyer.'

But there was also another reason why he switched from law to film. He would have gone to SMU in Dallas to study law but as it's a private school it would have cost his parents $16,000, whereas the University of Texas fees were $6,000. He was advised of the difference in outlays in a call from his middle brother, who also told him that the oil business wasn't doing so great so his Pop would struggle to raise the finances to send him to Dallas.

Matthew didn't want to miss out on his twenties, figuring he would be twenty-eight by the time he got out of school, and thus would not be able to do all the things young people can do. 'I wanted to get out in my twenties and try and make some sort of imprint in society,' McConaughey said to *All Access Hollywood* in 2011. 'I didn't have the patience or the want to go for another six years of just education before I wanted to try out and get my own experience.'

He loves to debate and grew interested in criminal defence and law. 'When I was nineteen, twenty, twenty-one,' he explained to Eric Eisenberg of *Cinema Blend*, 'I really started to fall on the side of the defence and really felt like that I was purely built for it, and felt 100 per cent clear with being able to defend someone, if I knew they were innocent. That was a battle that I could not lose. There are certain things that you believe in and go, "That's one of those places that I'll find every bit of energy from the depths of my body and ancestry to fight, and win that fight."'

Another option was to take the more traditional path of going into the oil and pipe business, following his father's footsteps; after all, he was raised in a family that do nine to five jobs. You earn your pay and work your way up the ladder. Matthew had a change of mind after reading Og Mandino's philosophical book, *The Greatest Salesman in the World*, which he saw on a coffee table at a friend's house. Years later as a successful Hollywood actor, Matthew would keep numerous copies of the book around his house to give to friends, associates and journalists. 'My first reaction was, "That's a really aggressive, corporate-capitalistic title,"' Matthew later admitted to *Texas Monthly*'s Jason Cohen in 1996, 'but it was philosophy, it was self-improvement, and it was very, very practical.'

He told his dad during the sophomore final exams that he wanted to tell stories and was eager to go to film school. Pop told him not to be half-arsed and do it properly. 'I remember that call to Mum and Dad and, after about a twenty-second pause, they were very supportive,' Matthew confessed to the *Independent*'s Lesley O'Toole. 'They liked the hope, the individuality I took.'

So Matthew told his dad he was going to Austin to study film rather than to Dallas to study law. He fitted right in with the students in Austin and it's where he discovered his creative side, which enabled him to be artistic. He became the first member of his family to attempt to have a professional career in the arts, though his nearest and dearest had interests in literature and painting. He learned early on to do something you give a damn about. Matthew is big on family, though, and takes a photograph of his family with him wherever he goes to remind him where is from.

CHAPTER TWO

BECOMING AN ACTOR

'I think the core of innocence is healthy for anyone.'
Matthew McConaughey, *Scotsman* interview, 2012

M atthew McConaughey's first break came rather easily. He didn't set his mind on being a professional actor until he was twenty-one years old in 1991, though he'd been in a beer commercial for Miller Lite and a music video when he was nineteen while still at college learning about film. McConaughey played the male lead in that music video to Trisha Yearwood's song 'Walkway Joe', released in November 1992, and featuring Eagles singer Don Henley on background vocals.

Matthew spoke to Terry Gross of the NPR show *Fresh Air* about his first forays into acting: 'In film school I started [to act] – when I would be directing something or the photographer or even the AD [Assistant Director], I always found myself jumping on the other side of the camera and acting out what I meant, if I was trying to give direction or saying, "Well, let me do that."'

McConaughey was actually happier that he'd got his driver's license and saved up enough cash to buy his first truck than he was about the idea of being an actor. He had an Old Blue, a four-cylinder Dodge truck with a Ross Perot sticker on the bumper. McConaughey and his buddies, like many other college kids, would take her for a spin and pick up a pack of six beers and see what they could get up to. He had a thirst for exploration, which acting would help flourish.

'In high school – I'd always driven a truck – I got a brand-new red sports car,' he told *People* magazine some years later while talking about his most embarrassing pick-up line, or rather a bad move he made on a date. 'I started getting out of my car and leaning against it. So I was trying to let the car do the work for me! I noticed about four months later I'm doing horrible with the women. I was like, "I gotta get rid of this sports car." As soon as I got my truck back, I was back! I called it the curse of the red sports car.'

McConaughey simply fell into the profession. It wasn't something he dreamed of; he wasn't even sure if it was a practical way to earn a buck. He certainly didn't know what to expect from acting. '…I have looked back at my diaries from back then,' McConaughey admitted to Caitlin Martis of *The Film Stage*, 'I was more interested in acting than I was consciously saying to myself. It was not something that was even in the vernacular of my dreams, I didn't think that it was tangible enough.'

As luck, fortune and good timing would have it, Matthew McConaughey was soon cast as David Wooderson in *Dazed and Confused*, which was directed by fellow Texan Richard Linklater who was born in Houston and raised in Huntsville. The director would become a key person in McConaughey's career. Linklater's first film was the twelve minute long *Frisbee Golf: The Movie*, but his feature debut was *It's Impossible to Learn to Plow by Reading Books*, released in 1988 and shot on Super 8mm film. Linklater then managed to rake together $23,000 to make a film called *Slacker*, about a day in the life of a random collection of Austin bohemians. His next film was *Dazed and Confused*, a semi-autobiographical tale based on his Huntsville High School years and the people he met there.

McConaughey, a UT student between his junior and senior year, had met veteran casting director Don Phillips at the Hyatt Regency, a hotel bar, in Austin one Thursday night in the summer of 1992. It was McConaughey's Lana Turner moment. (Turner was spotted, aged sixteen, at a Hollywood pharmacy by *The Hollywood Reporter* journalist William R. Wilkerson who referred the stunning Turner to agent Zeppo Marx. Turner was quickly cast in the 1937 film, *They Won't Forget*, and the rest is Hollywood history.) Phillips had cast Sean Penn, Jennifer Jason Leigh and Forest Whitaker in *Fast Times at Ridgemont High* and was rounding up actors in Texas for *Dazed and Confused*.

'…My girlfriend talked me into going out to have some drinks,' McConaughey told *Texas Monthly*'s John Spong in 2003. 'There was this bartender I knew from film school who worked at the Hyatt and would give us a discount, so we went there. And when we walk in, he's there, and he goes, "Hey, man, the guy down at the end of the bar is in town producing a film." So I went down and introduced myself. That was Don.'

They had a long night in the bar – which even included getting kicked out because they got so drunk. McConaughey's girlfriend was long gone and the pair chatted for hours about girls, golf, movies and general life stuff. McConaughey asked about working as a production assistant on the project but was, instead, cast in the film. It was an unbelievable moment of good fortune. Fate, if you will.

The bouncer, a huge, muscular, red-shirted UT football player, escorted them out of the bar. McConaughey went back to Phillips' room to continue talking. Matthew was furious that they had been kicked out – and even called the manager to demand an apology. Phillips asked him if he'd ever acted before and McConaughey told him about the one beer commercial and music video. Phillips told McConaughey he was in town casting *Dazed and Confused* and mentioned a character from the film called Wooderson whose persona is all about four things: rock 'n' roll, weed, women and his car. It was too expensive to bring someone over from LA so McConaughey was invited to Phillips' office the next day to read the script. There was a handwritten note on the pages with the character's name, Dave Wooderson, and some of his lines written down.

'The one that sent me off – and I was just like, "Who is this guy?" – is when they're out front of the billiards joint and the ladies are walking by,' McConaughey confessed to Terry Gross of NPR's *Fresh Air*, 'Wooderson's checking them out, and Wooderson's like, "That's what I like about those high school girls, man; I get older, but they stay the same age." That was the piece for Wooderson that I was like, "That's not a line, that's his being. That's his philosophy. He has it figured out. He's not commentating."'

McConaughey got the job and received $300 a day. The director, however, didn't think McConaughey was the right man for the job when he first met him. 'I thought he was too good-looking,' Linklater confessed to *Texas Monthly*'s John Spong in

2003. 'Matthew looked like he'd do fine with college girls; but I needed Wooderson to be a little creepier. But Matthew just sunk into character. His eyes shut to little quarter slots, and he said, "Hey, man, you got a joint?" He just became that guy. I thought, "Okay, don't cut your hair. Can you grow a beard and a mustache?"'

A coming of age drama, *Dazed and Confused* features an ensemble cast that includes Renée Zellweger, Jason London, Ben Affleck, Milla Jovovich, Cole Hauser, Parker Posey, Adam Goldberg, Joey Lauren Adams, Nicky Katt and Rory Cochrane. Many of these actors would become well-known Hollywood names in the years to come. The story follows various social teenage cliques during the last day of summer on 28 May 1976. The title of the film was taken from the Led Zeppelin song of the same name. It features a fantastic soundtrack of seventies hard rock with such artists as Rick Derringer, Foghat, Alice Cooper, Black Oak Arkansas, ZZ Top, Nazareth, Ted Nugent, The Runaways, Sweet, War, Lynyrd Skynyrd, Deep Purple, KISS and Black Sabbath. Around a sixth of the film's $6.9 million budget was used on purchasing the rights for those bands' songs.

McConaughey, despite his short onscreen time, stole the show with some groovy lines. He was perfect for the role. 'Let's face it,' Phillips said in an interview on *Cinema.com*, 'Matthew has three things that make a star: you've got to be smart, you've got to have talent, and the girls have got to want to go to bed with you. He scores on all counts but at the same time he has a natural cool and humility about him.'

Dazed and Confused became the *American Graffiti* and *Fast Times at Ridgemont High* for its generation. Younger fans, who enjoy *That 70s Show*, would also appreciate it, while those who grew up watching *Happy Days* would dig its nostalgia. It's a wonderful and immensely entertaining film about a group of carefree kids who are naïve about the world and unsure of what adulthood will bring.

The chance encounter with Phillips ended up with a cameo in *Dazed and Confused*, which was shot late one night at the Top Notch, a drive-in burger joint in Austin. And it went more than all right!

'Actually, it's, "All right, all right, all right." It's three "all rights". Those were the first words I ever said on film, in *Dazed and Confused*,' he told Will Harris of *Bullz-Eye*, 'the very first time I was ever in front of the camera. Actually, I had heard lots of live tapes of Jim Morrison at a Doors concert, and there's…I don't remember what the album is or where the concert was, but between one of the songs, he goes, "all right, all right, all right, all right." He says it four times, right? And I was in *Dazed and Confused*, and it's my first scene, the first take, and my character was about to pull into the Top Notch to go try and pick up on the red-headed intellectual. And they said, "Action," and I was really nervous, and I just went, "All right, all right, all right!" And it sort of became a lead-in to get me to relax, and it turned out to be Wooderson-esque, and it's a line that's stuck. So that's pretty cool.'

Fans right up to the present day would repeat the line to him. He'd get it at ball games, in the shopping mall, anywhere he went. It's pretty cool and he likes it. They were the first words he ever said on film so there is poignancy to it.

Sadly, McConaughey's father died on 17 August 1992, during the making of the film, just five or six days into shooting. He died while having sex with his wife on a Monday morning. 'On

Monday mornings, he and I often said goodbye by making love,' Kay told *Us Weekly* in 2008. 'But one day, all of a sudden, it just happened… I knew that something was wrong, because I didn't hear anything from him. Just nothing. But it was just the best way to go!'

McConaughey was back on set just two days after the funeral. 'I remember walking around with Rick,' McConaughey told *Texas Monthly*'s John Spong, 'trying to figure out how to take the time to mourn but also get to the future quicker. I told him, "I can still have a relationship with my dad, but I've got to keep him alive. He's got to just keep livin."'

McConaughey wasn't just an actor on the film but also a hired hand, always offering assistance to director Linklater whenever he needed it. Linklater would refer to McConaughey as the cast's team captain, so whenever there were concerns, McConaughey was there to help and act as the intermediary between the cast and crew. A crisis happened regarding the script on the last night of shooting and McConaughey was there to offer immediate help. They had no money left to extend the shoot and the sun was coming up, which would disrupt filming. Shot in a typically indie fashion with improvised dialogue, the main arch of the story – whether quarterback Randall 'Pink' Floyd should sign an anti-drug petition – had not been resolved. It was an internal argument and the character's great source of angst. McConaughey suggested what advice his character Wooderson would give to Pink for the climax at an after-party with lots of pot at the fifty-yard line of the high school football pitch. McConaughey uttered that now famous line 'You just gotta keep livin', man, l-i-v-i-n.'

Everybody who knew McConaughey's dad called him Pop

whether they were family or not. He was a friendly and likeable man, and a beer-loving raconteur. He used to wear a pair of baby blue shorts every day. He loved to hang out with his buddies and watch sports on Sundays, drinking beer. Matthew owes his dad a lot for all the advice that was handed down from father to son. 'I remember my father telling us very early the birds and bees part,' McConaughey said to *Total Film*. 'He goes, "You're gonna kiss, and it's gonna go further. If you ever, ever sense the slightest bit of resistance, when you're approaching or trying to, you know, get under their shirt... if you feel the slightest sense of resistance, you stop." And he goes, "You will also have many times that girl, after you feel the resistance, telling you, 'No, no, no, – it's OK.' But do not go any further."'

McConaughey struggled to cope with his father's death and developed the personal mantra 'Just keep livin' – that now iconic line spoken by his character in the film. Sadly, his father never saw him as a screen actor, but he would have been very proud. 'I found all these old paintings and pottery he had done,' McConaughey said to the *Independent*'s Lesley O'Toole. 'I said: "Mum, when was he doing this?" So there was something artistic in the blood line that I didn't know about. It was neat to find out those things.'

Released in the US and UK in September 1993, *Dazed and Confused* was played in 183 cinemas across the States and grossed just $918,127 on its opening weekend. The film made less than $8 million at the US box office, barely breaking even, though it has since gained a huge cult following on video and DVD with total sales coming in at around $30 million. Sales of the soundtrack have since topped two million units, which was massively helpful to the filmmakers given how expensive the rights to purchase the songs were. The film was very popular in college towns where word of mouth spread like wildfire – here's a film about a bunch of college kids, driving around in cars, smoking pot and listening to Edgar Winter songs on the last day of summer back in the mid-1970s. What's not to like about it?

In a 2002 *Sight And Sound* poll, *Pulp Fiction* director Quentin Tarantino listed it as the tenth best film of all time and *Entertainment Weekly* magazine voted it third in their list of the '50 Best High School Movies'. *EW* also voted it tenth in their 'Funniest Movies Of The Past 25 Years' poll. *Newsweek* called it a 'crushingly funny and knowing ode to misspent youth.' It was the perfect film for McConaughey to kick-start his acting career.

Famed *Chicago Sun-Times* film critic Roger Ebert wrote: 'The film's real inspiration, I think, is to depict some high school kids from the 1970s with such unblinking attention that we will realise how romanticised most movie teenagers are. A lot of these kids are asking, with Peggy Lee, "Is that all there is?" Linklater's style is to introduce some characters, linger with them for a while, and then move on to different characters, eventually circling back so that all the stories get told simultaneously.'

San Francisco Chronicle's Michael Snyder said: 'The movie's episodic view of a collection of interesting friends, sweethearts and cliques often rings so true that it might be a documentary... It's so right, you might think Linklater has mastered time travel.'

Obviously McConaughey had not yet become a star so reviews of the original release barely, if at all, mentioned him, but retrospective reviews have since occasionally referred to his name, such as Simon Kinnear's piece on the 2011 DVD release in *Total Film*. He said: 'Team Austin's triumphs are more muted: Linklater's relationship with the mainstream continues to blow hot and cold, and even the film's biggest stars, Matthew McConaughey and Ben Affleck, have had careers that can be filed under "dazed" and "confused", respectively.'

Steven Beard wrote of the DVD release in *Empire* magazine: 'A commercial failure in the US, despite generally good notices, it hung around in limbo waiting for a UK release for more than a year. Characterised in some quarters as the *American Graffiti* for the slacker generation, this is in fact a very clever piece of retro seventies anti-nostalgia, which scrupulously avoids sentimentality. It just wants to tell us how genuinely strange the seventies were.'

McConaughey later reprised his role as Wooderson in Butch Walker and The Black Widows' 2003 music video for their song 'Synthesizers'. It seemed as if McConaughey's character took on a life of his own.

Dazed and Confused, along with Linklater's previous project *Slacker*, sparked a subgenre of similarly themed films throughout the 1990s generally referred to as 'slacker films.' New Jersey filmmaker Kevin Smith became a proponent of the genre with titles such as *Clerks* and *Mallrats*. These films are generally about aimless or disenfranchised high school or college kids and dropouts, who hang around shopping malls or liquor stores, smoking dope and listening to music. Many of these films were also influenced by the John Hughes classics of the 1980s such as *Ferris Bueller's Day Off*, *The Breakfast Club*, *Some Kind of Wonderful* and *Sixteen Candles*.

'For me personally, *Dazed* fans are my favourite fans,' McConaughey told *Texas Monthly*'s John Spong in 2003. 'They never want anything. They like to come by, say the first half of a line, and wait for me to finish it: "…It'd be a lot cooler if you did." Then they walk off giggling. Just giggling.'

McConaughey was far from a slacker, though; he set his mind on the entertainment industry. Sure, he originally wanted to be a filmmaker but once he'd dipped his toes into acting his mind was set and he dedicated himself to the craft. McConaughey is the sort of man who sets his heart and mind on something and pours everything he's got into achieving that goal. There was still a great deal of work to achieve but things were coming along nicely.

With his good looks and Texan charm, he appeared in TV commercials, including one for the *Austin-American Statesman*, a Texan daily newspaper based in Austin, which gave him one of his earliest speaking roles in front of the camera. He said: 'How else am I gonna keep up with my "Horns?"' – a reference to the Texas Longhorns, his beloved sports team.

Another one of his earliest parts was playing Larry Dickens in an episode of the NBC TV series *Unsolved Mysteries*, Episode #5.12, which originally aired in December 1992. But of course, this was filmed after his first film acting appearance on camera in *Dazed and Confused*, but because films take much longer to get released than TV episodes do to get broadcasted, he appeared on TV before he was on film. *Unsolved Mysteries* was hosted by Robert Stack and used a documentary-style format to profile real life mysteries often concerning the unexplained and paranormal such as ghosts, UFO, alien abductions as well as government conspiracies and missing persons.

McConaughey's next film role was as Guy #2 in the cheesy low-budget horror film *My Boyfriend's Back*, released in 1993, but even though it was filmed after *Dazed and Confused* it was released before it, so *My Boyfriend's Back* was his actual theatrical debut. Such is the nature of B-movies that they are quick to make and quicker to distribute. An actor can star in multiple films and one can have a release date sooner than another that was made before it, which can often create a rather confusing chronology.

Directed by Bob Balaban and produced by *Friday the 13th* creator Sean S. Cunningham, *My Boyfriend's Back* is about a teenage boy named Jonny Dingle who returns from the dead as a zombie to meet the girl he's in love with, Missy McCloud, for a date. Poorly received, *My Boyfriend's Back* grossed just $3,335,984 in box office receipts after its August 1993 US release and has faded into B-movie obscurity, though it also featured *Lost* actor's Matthew Fox's first film role. Renée Zellweger's only scene was cut from the film and the late Philip Seymour Hoffman also had a part as Chuck Bronski. Needless to say, reviews of *My Boyfriend's Back* were poor and, though some genre fans may have a soft spot for its cheesiness, it is a dreadful film.

*****

McConaughey had finally graduated college in the spring of 1993 with a Bachelor's degree in Radio-Television-Film originally thinking he would become a filmmaker, but not an actor. Before he left Texas for the bright lights of the City of Angels he read for a small part in the trashy *Return of the Texas Chainsaw Massacre*. He didn't get it. McConaughey was instead offered the lead role as the villain opposite fellow Texan, Renée Zellweger. After already appearing together in cult classic *Dazed and Confused* and that long forgotten B-movie *My Boyfriend's Back*, McConaughey and Zellweger both had similar experiences with bit parts, B-movies and cult indie films. It was good training and helped McConaughey gain notable contacts in the industry, both in Texas and out in LA.

McConaughey moved to LA in August 1993 and signed with the William Morris Agency, and took a job as a PA on a Coen Brothers film, which never happened because he met casting director Hank McCann and some parts came his way. One day, while crashing on the couch of casting director Don Phillips, he was sent scripts for *Angels in the Outfield* and *Boys on the Side*, his first Hollywood auditions. It all seemed to work out for him and it was easy money. However, he lost out on sturdy parts in *The Quick and The Dead*, *Assassins* and *The Great White Hype*.

Despite some minor setbacks, due to the critical success of *Dazed and Confused*, his good looks, Southern drawl and easy-going personality, McConaughey was quickly noticed in LA and soon picked up some small roles in low budget films. He dashed between California and his home state of Texas getting jobs in both cities. Some of the stuff he did was trashy but everything he did earned him a dollar. He needed cash to pay the rent. The irony is, although he never intended to be an actor when he'd made up his mind, the roles came easily enough. He was going to be the next James Dean or Marlon Brando. He hoped.

Now living in the City of Angels and focusing on films set or at least filmed in California, he was cast in *Angels in the Outfield*, a remake of the 1951 film of the same name, but while the original focused on the Pittsburgh Pirates the remake is about the California Angels, a team which had not been created at the time of the 1951 original. The remake stars Danny Glover, Tony Danza and Christopher Lloyd.

Matthew McConaughey plays the Angels outfielder, Ben Williams, and future stars Adrien Brody, Joseph Gordon-Levitt and Neal McDonough also appear in the film. Released in the US in July 1994 by The Walt Disney Company, which had a minority ownership of the California Angels at the time, the film received mixed reviews and grossed $50 million in box office ticket sales in the US. It wasn't released in the UK until May 1995. Two direct-to-video sequels were later released, *Angels in the Endzone* and *Angels in the Infield*.

With these bit parts McConaughey felt he was getting away with something he shouldn't be getting away with, and having a great time into the bargain. His projects could not have been further apart; he was appearing in a diverse range of films. There was no focus to his career other than getting whatever parts he could manage.

Reviewing the original release the late critic Roger Ebert wrote in the *Chicago Sun-Times*: 'The movie then reduces itself to a formula, alternating between baseball action (angels appear, work miracles, and announcer goes into ecstasy) and human redemption (the manager becomes more of a human being). The baseball action isn't very interesting because the angels (led by Christopher Lloyd) manipulate the outcomes. And the human interest stuff is canned and unconvincing. The only character who really rings true is the comeback pitcher played by Danza.'

McConaughey's next released film saw him return to his home state. *Texas Chainsaw Massacre: The Next Generation* is a loose remake and sort-of-sequel to the 1974 slasher classic, *The*

Texas Chainsaw Massacre, written and directed by horror movie master, Tobe Hooper. Directed by Kim Henkel, who co-wrote the original with Hooper, the film is about a group of teenagers who end up in a remote area of forest on their prom night and come across a family of murderers, one of whom is the chainsaw wielding bogeyman of horror cinema, Leatherface.

Texas Chainsaw Massacre: The Next Generation was filmed in Pflugerville, Texas in 1994 with a budget of just $600,000. It had a very convoluted history with various re-edits and reissues along with a long and laborious post-production which finally wrapped up in 1994, and was later screened under its original working title of *The Return of the Texas Chainsaw Massacre* at a few select cinemas in October 1995 and at the famed South By Southwest Film And Media Conference in 1995. Columbia agreed to distribute the film both theatrically and on VHS but the film had to be re-edited numerous times and the title was changed from its original production name *The Return of the Texas Chainsaw Massacre* to *Texas Chainsaw Massacre: The Next Generation*.

Producer Robert Kuhn said that Columbia rescheduled the film's release to await the forthcoming coming release of Renée Zellweger's new film, *Jerry Maguire*, starring Tom Cruise and directed by Cameron Crowe, which was slated for 1996. The filmmakers did not argue thinking it would add to the box office receipts.

In a 1997 interview with *The Austin Chronicle*, producer Kuhn stated: 'Well, we definitely feel that Columbia/TriStar has not done what they agreed to do in terms of trying to market this film in the best possible fashion. They have not tried to exploit this film to monetarily benefit as they should have. They've just low-keyed it. They don't want to be guilty of exploiting Matthew because of their relationship with CAA, which is the strongest single force in Hollywood these days. You get on the wrong side of them, you're in trouble. So I understand their problem, but at the same time, they should have either given the film back to us or they should have done the best release they could have done. And they haven't done that.'

It was shelved for three years, re-cut and released via Columbia Pictures and Cinepix Film Properties as *Texas Chainsaw Massacre: The Next Generation* in 1997, by which time both McConaughey and Zellweger had become huge Hollywood stars on the back of *A Time to Kill* and *Jerry Maguire*, respectively. The film was very poorly received by critics on its release and is generally considered to be the weakest film of the franchise.

In effect, the film was McConaughey's first major starring role and, while many critics had either not reviewed it or tried to immediately forget about it, as soon as McConaughey and his co-star Zellweger became huge stars they revisited the film and respective reviews were as equally bad as the original write-ups.

Entertainment Weekly's Owen Gleiberman said: 'Renée Zellweger and Matthew McConaughey try to out-bad-act each other in the luridly abysmal third sequel to *The Texas Chainsaw Massacre*.'

The New York Times' Luke Y. Thompson wrote: 'McConaughey's over-the-top performance is brilliant, but not a single person actually gets killed with a chainsaw.'

USA Today's Mike Clark on the film: 'The kind of cinematic endeavour where you suspect both cast and crew were obligated to bring their own beer.'

Nevertheless, it was a case of onwards and upwards, and both starring actors put the film behind them as new acting pursuits were already being lined up with gusto.

McConaughey was next cast as Abe Lincoln in the comedy drama *Boys on the Side*, released in February 1995. It was directed by Herbert Ross, his final film as director before his death in 2001, and stars Whoopi Goldberg, Drew Barrymore and Mary-Louise Parker as three very different women, each with their own problems, who travel cross country on a road trip to sunny California seeking different things in life. Averagely received by critics and a modest success at the box office, the film earned back its budget costs through box office receipts and video sales and rentals. It was entered into the nineteenth Moscow International Film Festival.

Peter Travers, *Rolling Stone*'s resident film critic, wrote a damning review of the film and said: 'The film itself loses all sense of shame with courtroom and deathbed histrionics that slide inexorably into camp. Who wouldn't want to see a rich, complex movie about women who keep friendship first and boys on the side? This isn't it.'

The New York Times' Janet Maslin was rather more positive. She wrote: '*Boys on the Side*, a three-woman road movie with a wonderful cast and an awful title, doesn't need courtroom drama, so it manages at such moments to seem clumsily contrived. What matters more is that Ms. Goldberg, along with her co-stars Mary-Louise Parker and Drew Barrymore, is so sharp, funny and wholehearted that this film creates an unexpected groundswell of real emotion.'

McConaughey was simply taking a chance on whatever parts came his way but not all of them were suited to his talents or even his blatant Hollywood good looks. Similar to any young, jobbing actors he didn't have much choice in what roles he could take. He had rent and bills to pay, and was eager to get noticed by the top producers and directors of the Hollywood film studios.

Released in the US in February 1995 and in the UK in May, McConaughey starred as an alcoholic rental truck representative in *Glory Daze*, an independent film directed by Rich Wilkes that also starred Ben Affleck, Sam Rockwell, French Stewart and Alyssa Milano, and Matt Damon in a very small cameo. It was called *Last Call* in some countries, notably Australia. Most of the film's actors would go onto to achieve great fame and success as Hollywood actors. The film is essentially about five buddies who share a house they dub 'El Rancho' while attending art school at UC Santa Cruz, and how they struggle after graduation to lead their own lives and move on.

Stephen Holden wrote of the film in *The New York Times*: 'This tiny nostalgic comedy, with its smart collegiate chatter, is a much better movie than slick fatuities like *The Jerky Boys*, *Airheads* and *Billy Madison*, for which Mr. Wilkes wrote the screenplays. Of course that isn't saying much. But *Glory Daze*, which opens today at the Quad Cinema, deftly sketches each member of its underachieving fivesome while sustaining a mood of humorously frazzled end-of-semester anxiety.'

Emanuel Levy wrote in *Variety*: 'Fear and anxiety about the real world of work and responsibility underline *Last Call*, an intermittently buoyant campus comedy revolving around five male buddies. Though poorly produced, [the] film's engaging premise, occasionally inspired writing and disarming acting will increase its prospects for limited theatrical distribution in college towns, with the late-teen and twenty-something crowd a strong potential audience.'

McConaughey subsequently had a minor role as Joe in the short film *Submission*, directed by Benicio Del Toro, and released in 1995. McConaughey cropped up in another short film in the same year called *Judgement.* He plays Deputy Sam Taylor in the thirty-minute film about a rookie cop in Judgement County, Texas, who faces a split-second decision when an APB for a child killer is the same man he stops for speeding. He faces a number of challenges when he is unable to contact his boss and check the suspect's ID, thus having to rely on his own judgement.

McConaughey had yet to gain the attention from critics and when he did, as with the *Texas Chainsaw* film on its initial limited release, it wasn't exactly the sort of attention he wanted, or needed. He was thirsty for a role that was going to loudly exclaim his talents and win him praise and awards and land him major Hollywood films.

Although he loved to travel and craved to visit places around the States and the rest of the world, he longed for the Texan fields, food and culture. Texans were his people. Texas was his home and in his mind he was never too far away from it, but his focus for now was on LA and whatever opportunities may come his way in the City of Angels.

CHAPTER THREE

BIG BREAK IN
A TIME TO KILL

'I'm looking at these offers and going, "Really?" I have more options, and options are power, which is good if you use it in the right way.'
Matthew McConaughey, *Texas Monthly*, 1996

After a few small roles and some less than appealing films, McConaughey's big break came when he was cast as Jake Brigance in *A Time to Kill*, a legal thriller based on the John Grisham novel of the same name. McConaughey was just twenty-six years old.

However, during the summer of 1996, McConaughey appeared in another film. *Lone Star* was not quite so high profile as *A Time to Kill*. It was not a lead vehicle and it was shot before his breakthrough role as Jake Brigance. Written and directed by the revered screenwriter John Sayles and set in a small Texan town, *Lone Star* features Kris Kristofferson, Chris Cooper and Elizabeth Pena. The central premise is of a sheriff's investigation into the murder of one of his predecessors. McConaughey was pleased to attract more work in his home state; *Lone Star* was filmed in Del Rio, Eagle Pass and Laredo.

Released in June, it won rave reviews from critics and was a modest box office success after its July release in the US and UK release in October. Reviewers of the film barely noticed McConaughey, focusing on the angle that it was a film by John Sayles instead, whose previous film debut *The Secret of Roan Inish* was released in 1994. *Lone Star* stands next to *Giant* and *The Last Picture Show* as great Texan movies. It's a cut above the dreaded *Texas Chainsaw* film McConaughey appeared in, that's for sure.

Kim Newman wrote in *Empire*: 'Even one-scene characters are unforgettable, but Sayles really gets under the skin of his struggling-to-be-heroic leads, Sam and Pilar. Long after this summer's crop of action flicks is gone, you'll watch this for the third or fourth time and see fresh material. Outstanding.'

A staff review in *Variety* enthused: '*Lone Star* is a richly textured and thoroughly engrossing drama that ranks with indie filmmaker John Sayles' finest work. Bountifully rich in incident and characterization, *Lone Star* recalls the vast canvas of Sayles' *City of Hope*. This time the maverick writer-director focuses on a small Texas border town where the sins of fathers continue to haunt sons.'

However, it was *A Time to Kill* that changed everything for McConaughey.

Directed by Joel Schumacher of *The Lost Boys* and *Flatliners* fame, and also starring Sandra Bullock – with whom McConaughey would later have a much-publicised romance in the mid-1990s – Samuel L. Jackson and Kevin Spacey, *A Time to Kill* also boasted Oliver Platt, Ashley Judd, Kiefer Sutherland, Donald Sutherland and Patrick McGoohan in supporting roles. The film was made by the same production company and distributor (Regency and Warner Bros.) as *Boys on the Side* and its director Schumacher was already aware of McConaughey's work.

As quoted on *Cinema.com*, the young Texan actor impressed Schumacher: 'At any rate he's a total original. I don't know anyone like him. There's an innate integrity and, yes, elegance about Matthew. Yet there's also a kind of shitkicking, dangerous side to him, too.'

McConaughey went to visit Schumacher on the set of the 1995 movie *Batman Forever* where he chatted to the director about a minor role in *A Time to Kill* (which ultimately went to Kiefer Sutherland). McConaughey then read Grisham's novel and convinced Schumacher that he was the best actor to play the lead role. McConaughey beat Brad Pitt, Val Kilmer and Woody Harrelson to the part. Schumacher even joked that he went through every actor alive from Macaulay Culkin to George Burns, but that he just couldn't see any of those actors as Jake Brigance. Schumacher, however, said McConaughey reminded him of a young Marlon Brando. The director had McConaughey in mind for over a year, and while Schumacher and Grisham preferred an unknown actor, the studio, Warner Bros., wanted a big name so they could sell the film to audiences whether they had read the best-selling novel or not. The director and author were initially dubious of how the studio would treat the casting of an unknown in the lead role, but Schumacher was convinced he'd found the right actor for the part of Jake Brigance. The overall say-so was down to John Grisham who still, at that point, considered his 1989 debut novel *A Time to Kill* to be his best work.

Grisham would not sell the movie rights until he was happy with both the director and lead actor. Schumacher had directed

1994's acclaimed Grisham adaptation *The Client* and the author was happy with Schumacher in the hot seat, but had yet to be convinced of a lead actor. Schumacher told Grisham he had a secret up his sleeve; a relatively unknown handsome Texan named Matthew McConaughey. McConaughey took time out from filming in Eagle Pass – in the aforementioned film, *Lone Star* – to undergo a screen test for Schumacher who would then send the tape to John Grisham in Virginia for his approval. A makeshift set was arranged for McConaughey on Mother's Day 1995 to deliver the climactic courtroom battle. Grisham and his wife watched it twice and were in awe of McConaughey's exhilarating performance. The actor went back to the set of *Lone Star* and received a call from Schumacher and Grisham in May 1995. He was ecstatic; he was glowing with the good news.

'I went out in the yard and yelled "(Bleep) yeah!" about twenty times,' said McConaughey to Billy Watkins of the *Clarion Ledger* in 1995. 'Then I went back into the house, got down on my knees and thanked God for the opportunity he had given me.' With Grisham's approval Warner Bros. were now happy to go ahead with the film despite McConaughey being an unknown actor; McConaughey's fee was $200,000.

Jake Brigance is an amiable white lawyer who is hired by the father of a black girl who had been raped in the Mississippi Delta. When the film was screened for test audiences – common practice by studios to determine if the film will connect with audiences – it was given 500 'excellents' out of 509 cards. Warner Bros. were thrilled with the feedback, as indeed was Schumacher.

The chemistry between the ensemble cast is palpable: Bullock could prove her diverse acting skills having starred in the action movie *Speed* and the screwball comedy *While You Were Sleeping*; Samuel L. Jackson was an actor of immeasurable talent as seen in *Pulp Fiction*; and Kevin Spacey, an actor of incredible skills, can do anything he puts his mind to. Donald and Kiefer Sutherland both excel in the film, too.

'The first day we started rehearsals, we went into Joel's office,' Sandra Bullock explained to Billy Watkins of the *Clarion Ledger*. 'I like to tell people how I work and let them know that no matter what they want to try, I'm game for everything. Some actors don't like to improvise or veer off what's there. But I do. I like to try different things, especially if it's not working. Matthew said, "I want you to know I'm dedicated to anything you want to try, too." And that's what it's all about in this business, working together.'

McConaughey filmed twelve consecutive weeks, five and six days a week. He had to learn hundreds of pages of dialogue, but he was dedicated to the role and poured as much energy and enthusiasm into it as he could muster. McConaughey didn't memorise his lines. He read over the script a couple of times before filming started and then went over his lines before a scene was shot; his reason being that if a co-star forgot their lines, all he had was what's in the script with no room for improvisation. He took some advice from veteran actor Robert Duvall who took out every comma and full stop and read it as though it was a general conversation, straight from the heart.

McConaughey knows how to create tension onscreen but you wouldn't think it by looking at him. Before filming the pivotal final scenes, he gave himself a night off and ate boiled shrimp and raw oysters and danced for four hours at the film's end of day shoot wrap party at Hal & Mal's in Jackson. McConaughey was staying at a Madison County lake house and turned down an invitation to dinner from his friends two days later so he could be in bed by half past nine as he had the final scenes to shoot the next day. Michael Singer, the revered film publicist, was on set the next day and was mesmerized by McConaughey's powerful performance.

'To be honest, the summation has very little to do with being a lawyer or knowing how lawyers talk,' McConaughey explained to Billy Watkins of the *Clarion Ledger* about the climactic sequence. 'In fact, I've tried to stay away from the way any of the lawyers talk that I've seen on TV, 'cause I don't really like any of them…This is more of a human thing. I want those people on the jury to see me as a person, hear me as a person. And anyone who would rather hear a lawyer talking up there…then I certainly hope they're not on the jury.'

John Grisham became one of the most popular authors of the 1990s. His readable and often exciting legal thrillers were perfect fodder for Hollywood. His books, like those of Maine author Stephen King, became almost a genre in itself. Lazy Hollywood producers looked to his books for material for upcoming movies. *The Firm*, still probably the best adaptation, began the trend in 1993, with *The Pelican Brief* released the same year. *The Client* followed in quick succession a year later, which then paved the way for *A Time to Kill* in 1996, the same year another adaption – *The Chamber* with Gene Hackman and Chris O'Donnell – was released, albeit to little fanfare (*The Chamber* is generally regarded as the poorest Grisham film). Hollywood quickly became bored of Grisham books and adaptations of his work slowed down by the 2000s, though Francis Ford Coppola did an excellent job with 1997's

The Rainmaker, starring Matt Damon and Danny DeVito. *A Time to Kill* was, in many respects, the perfect starring role for McConaughey's breakthrough role.

John Grisham said of the film to *EW*'s Tina Jordan: 'I had script approval, casting approval, location approval, so I got way too involved. When all was said and done I was happy with it, happy we were able to find a kid like Matthew McConaughey. It wasn't a great movie, but it was a good one.'

'That was sort of "Hello. Welcome." And then there was funny stuff like "McConaughey Saves The Movies" on the cover of magazines,' as quoted in an article in the *LA Times* by Glenn Whipp. 'Hell, I wasn't trying to save anything. After *Texas Chainsaw*, I just wanted to keep working, man.'

Released in the US in July 1996 and the UK in September, *A Time to Kill* was positively received and grossed $110 million at the box office with a modest budget of $40 million. It also helped raise the author's profile. John Grisham became one of the most talked about writers of the decade and is now one of the highest grossing authors in the world.

Rolling Stone's Peter Travers wrote: 'Grisham rejected the usual star suspects (Brad Pitt, Val Kilmer, Woody Harrelson) but sparked when director Joel Schumacher brought him Matthew McConaughey, a Texas greenhorn best known as Drew Barrymore's cop loverman in *Boys on the Side*. Grisham was right to hold out. McConaughey, twenty-six, is dynamite in a performance of smarts, sexiness, scrappy humour and unmistakable star sizzle.'

Ian Nathan wrote in *Empire*: 'Once it is assured McConaughey can do the business, whipping up sex appeal and camera hoggage like a thoroughbred, it is hard for Schumacher to mess up. An actual niggle is, ironically, talent overload: there are hints of too many cooks with scant opportunity to savour the likes of Sutherland, Platt and Spacey, even top billed Bullock is only a support player. With all the acting bases covered – jail-bound Jackson, as taut as a piano string, is fantastic – and the stormy southern location squirming with sweaty confrontations, lynchings and racial tension, there comes the reliable bluster of the movie courtroom complete with stir-'em-up staples – rent-a-mob riots, objections, last ditch evidence, wholesale implausibilities and Patrick McGoohan's sneery judge.'

Writing in the *San Francisco Chronicle*, Edward Guthmann was enthused by the acting: 'Untrained as an actor, with only three minor roles to his credit, McConaughey holds the screen against Samuel L. Jackson, Sandra Bullock and Kevin Spacey, and completely justifies the buzz surrounding his role...'

The film caused controversy in Europe, however, particularly with socialists who claim the film makes an excuse for the death penalty and the right of self-defence. Some even went so far as to call it a fascist film.

McConaughey's success was a saviour to Creative Artists Agency (CAA) after they had parted ways with Kevin Costner and Sylvester Stallone, then at the peak of their careers. McConaughey had switched over from William Morris and brought in his onetime Delta Tau Delta fraternity brother and childhood buddy, Gus Gustawes, to help run his business affairs through his production company, j.k. livin productions, which he had just founded. McConaughey's publicist was the much-respected Pat Kingsley. The company name of course comes from the line, 'just keep livin' from *Dazed And Confused*. It has since become a brand and even iconic turn of phrase. 'It's a verb, man. No "g" at the end. No period. Sometimes you wait life out; sometimes you drive right through it,' the actor said to *Details'* Bart Blasengame.

At this time the company only consisted of McConaughey and Gustawes, working out of a living room and arranging two or three meetings a day, but with plans to expand and hire staff, produce movies and venture into other avenues of work. Acting is hard work, taking up six or even seven days a week with more than ten laborious hours of work a day, so it was important for McConaughey to have something on the side hence the creation of his company. But for now, it was focused on McConaughey's acting.

*****

In the mid-1990s McConaughey was living in a modest house in LA with a Pacific view; he had not yet made the millions that are awarded to household names, one of which he would become soon enough. He kept Texas close to his heart, however: he had a Longhorn hung up on the deck; a UT clock in his living room; and on the stairwell, there was a highway map of Texas-New Mexico with marks on it from a recent road trip he had undertaken.

The awards and acclaim from critics and film buffs were coming in thick and fast in a whirlwind of activity. McConaughey could hardly catch his breath as everything was happening at such a frantic pace. McConaughey won an MTV Movie Award for 'Best Breakthrough Performance.' He was on the cover of *Vanity Fair*'s annual Hollywood issue in April 1996 and dubbed the new Paul Newman. Even John Grisham thought he was a cross between a young Brando and Newman.

The New York Times also mentioned comparisons to a young Gregory Peck.

Make no mistake, Matthew McConaughey was no longer an unknown struggling actor. He had become an overnight success. He got used to the meetings, handshakes and interviews that are an obligatory part of LA life. He had gone from being told 'no' a hundred times a day to being given scripts for any film he wanted to star in. The calls from Hollywood producers were coming in all the time; the phone just did not stop ringing. It was overwhelming but he journeyed through the media onslaught by concentrating on work. His life was turned upside down. However, whereas some actors struggle with the fame by turning to a hedonistic lifestyle of drugs and drink, McConaughey threw himself into more roles, albeit with varying degrees of success.

To celebrate his success, Matthew bought a one-way ticket to Peru where he hiked to Machu Picchu and canoed the Amazon. He was away for fifteen days. The first few days were tough as he had to face his demons and had to deal with his fears, but once he gained a decent level of confidence, he enjoyed the trip.

'I had a lot to think about,' he admitted to Tom Chiarella of *Esquire* in 2011. 'Just grabbed a bag and left. And I went up and further in, until I was about as uncomfortable and unfamiliar with things as I could be. You know why I don't go to Europe for these trips? Because in Europe everything pretty much works, or it almost works. I mean, it's almost what I'm used to. But Peru, Mali, Morocco? Nothing works. Nothing. So you have to give up on what you know. At least I do. And for a while it's very uncomfortable. Extremely. I mean you're faking the language as best you can, nodding at things you probably shouldn't be, and you start to miss the things you know. And you need to eat.'

It would be one of many open road trips he'd partake in throughout the decade and thereafter. 'My favourite thing to do alone is jam in my truck and drive,' McConaughey told *People* magazine. 'There are very few people I could take a road trip with. It's where I have my best thoughts.'

Thankfully McConaughey was able to overcome the disastrous Bill Murray comedy *Larger Than Life*, released in November 1996 in the US and March 1997 in the UK. A critical failure, *Larger Than Life* is about a motivational speaker (played by Murray) who discovers that his father's inheritance is an elephant. McConaughey plays Tip Tucker, a fast-talking, slightly paranoid trucker who is on a trip to LA when he meets Jack and his elephant Vera. Extra scenes were added to the film after the success of *A Time to Kill* – McConaughey had turned into a major celebrity and the filmmakers wanted to cash in on his success so they delayed the film's release until *A Time to Kill* had become a box office juggernaut. 'I went and got this ugly green stretch-material jersey, stuffed it, pulled my American flag cap on all bowed over, put a big ol' dip in, and just had fun,' McConaughey told *Texas Monthly*'s Jason Cohen at the time of the film's release.

Rob Nelson wrote in the *Boston Phoenix*: 'Originally slated for release in May, *Larger Than Life* has tried to piggyback on Matthew McConaughey's stardom by adding recently filmed scenes in which his character, a psychotic trucker, torments Murray's motivational-speaker-turned-elephant-tamer.'

After *Larger Than Life*, McConaughey needed a hit film. Despite *Lone Star* being a very good film, superlative actually, it didn't make a big enough splash at the box office as was expected for an actor who was touted as Hollywood's next big thing, even though it was filmed before his breakthrough role when he was just another unknown aspiring actor.

'When I go see a movie that I've made,' McConaughey later explained to *Terra.com*, 'you gotta remember that usually it was filmed like a year ago. Nine months to a year is about how long ago you finish making a movie. And to come back and watch it – I don't know, for me it's always been somewhat of an overwhelming experience because you're looking at three months of work, twelve hours a day, six days a week, compressed into two hours of film.'

Nineteen ninety-six also saw the release of the little-talked-about, straight-to-video film *Scorpion Spring,* directed and written by Brian Cox (not to be confused with the noted Scottish actor). Made in 1995 before *A Time to Kill* but not released until the following year, the film is about a desperate drug runner named Astor (Esai Morales) who, with his prisoner, is on the run from the law and struggling with the intense heat. The pair hook up with two naïve travellers after being offered a ride. Astor and his prisoner claim to be illegal aliens looking for a better life in the US but soon draw the two travellers into a dangerous world of drugs ruled by drug lord El Rojo, played by McConaughey. Inevitably, as with *Larger Than Life*, the film tried to cash in on McConaughey's recent burst of success.

Michael Sauter of *Entertainment Weekly* wrote that McConaughey 'only shows up a few minutes before the final, bloody showdown. It's hardly worth the wait: Saturated desert colours are the only thing worth seeing in this listless, witless, pointless exercise in south-of-the-border noir.'

Emanuel Levy was just a little more forgiving in his *Variety* review: 'Unfortunately, midway through, the director loses grip on his tale and the plot gets progressively silly and convoluted. Indeed, along the way, the quartet encounters a nasty Mexican drug lord (Matthew McConaughey), a bigoted white sheriff (Kevin Tighe) and a decent border patrolman ([Rubén] Blades), each motivated by his own personal agenda. Cox's strategy is to pile up more bizarre characters and more outlandish incidents as the picture goes along – until it falls apart.'

With a couple of dodgy films to his name post-*A Time to Kill*, McConaughey received a 'special thanks' on the 1997 documentary *Hands on a Hard Body*, directed by S.R. Bindler about an endurance competition. McConaughey spoke to *Bullz-Eye*'s Will Harris about the film: 'Yeah, that was shot in our hometown, where Rob, the director, and I met when we were fourteen years old. It was shot in Longview, Texas, and he went down and shot it, and then he needed some extra financing to go and finish it up, so I invested in it. But, yeah, I was a fan and knew of it, and it's a great documentary, too.'

The film follows the 1995 annual competition that lasted for seventy-seven hours, and focuses on twenty-four contestants competing to keep their hands on a pickup truck for the longest amount of time. The winner gets the truck. The contestants are given five-minute breaks every hour, and fifteen-minute breaks every six hours. The film won the 'Best Documentary' award at the 1997 Los Angeles Film Festival. Texas has always been close to his heart; no matter where he is in the world he takes Texas with him and to be involved in such a revered film about the culture of his home state was a major coup for him.

McConaughey had a two-film option deal with Warner Bros. as part of his contract for *A Time to Kill*; he had to pass on a remake of *The Day of the Jackal* as well as the sequel to

1994's Jan De Bont directed action flick, *Speed*. He had to be careful that his career would not veer off track, becoming the next Chris O'Donnell or Burt Reynolds, when in actual fact he desperately wanted to become another Gary Oldman or Sean Penn. Deep down, though, being the first – and only – Matthew McConaughey was unquestionably his main priority. He wanted to take on character parts, move between genres and work as a leading man. McConaughey was adamant that he did not want to be pigeonholed. Hollywood, though, is not quite that simple.

CHAPTER FOUR

FAME AND FORTUNE

'I think if you rely on fate, it bites you in the butt. If you blow
in the wind, you're going to get dropped in the gutter.'
Matthew McConaughey, *Cinema.com*, 2001

Matthew McConaughey had ceased to be the next Paul Newman almost as quickly as the press had labelled him as such. He famously lost out to Leonardo DiCaprio for the lead male role in James Cameron's 1997 blockbuster, *Titanic*. A part in Curtis Hanson's 1997 adaptation of James Ellroy's novel *L.A. Confidential* also never materialised. McConaughey's next released film was a science-fiction tale with philosophical ponderings on alien beings. It wasn't the shrewdest of choices, career-wise.

Contact is based on the science-fiction novel of the same name by the much-respected author Carl Sagan. The original 100-page story outline for the film was written by the late author with his wife Ann Druyan in 1979, and pitched to Warner Bros. with producers Peter Guber and Lynda Obst, but it entered development hell. Sagan published it as a novel in 1985 and then attempted to kick-start the film treatment four years later. Various directors came and went such as Roland Joffé and George Miller, but Joffé quit the project in 1993 and Miller left in 1995. *Who Framed Roger Rabbit?* director Robert Zemeckis was then hired and filming took place in New Mexico, Arizona and Los Angeles between September 1996 and February 1997.

McConaughey dropped out of *The Jackal* after being hired by Zemeckis – who had not made a film since the enormous success of the Tom Hanks' movie *Forrest Gump* – to play Palmer Joss, a respected Christian philosopher who becomes romantically involved with Dr Eleanor 'Ellie' Arroway, the film's protagonist, played by Jodie Foster. Arroway is a SETI scientist who uncovers evidence of extra-terrestrial life and attempts to make first contact. *Contact* also stars James Woods, Tom Skerritt, William Fichtner, John Hurt, Angela Bassett, Jake Busey and David Morse. McConaughey's fee was a reported $4 million.

When it comes to picking roles, McConaughey tries to mix it up a little – as his more recent parts have shown – though his decisions tend to be based on what else is going on in his life. Many of his performances are unforced. When he takes on a role he looks to some close friends and associates for their opinion as he tries to define the character and see how the whole thing comes together. The most important bits happen during pre-production so on the first day of filming he establishes the character in front of the camera. Actors become married to the roles for several months as they live and breathe the parts on, and even off, camera, such is their dedication to the part. McConaughey completely immerses himself in the film.

Contact offered science-fiction fans a different kind of film than had been seen in the 1990s, with alien invasion films such as 1996's *Independence Day* and 1997's *Starship Troopers*. Zemeckis' film was perhaps too ponderous and whimsical for some fans, though it does offer interesting philosophical notions on extra-terrestrials.

Contact was released to positive reviews in the US on 11 July 1997 and in the UK on 27 September and made over $170 million at the worldwide box office. It also won the Hugo Award for 'Best Dramatic Presentation' and earned some Saturn Awards nominations.

The *Total Film* review said: 'Jodie Foster, in her first film for three years, hogs the screen with a powerful performance, her faith an unshakeable, almost fanatical belief in science. McConaughey flits in and out as funky priest Palmer Joss ('I've been called a man of the cloth without the cloth'), while Tom Skerritt plays the sceptical scientist, prepared to step over Foster's crusading stargazer in the pursuit of self-advancement.'

Variety's Todd McCarthy wrote of Matthew's performance: 'McConaughey's role of a presidential spiritual adviser whose attraction for Arroway persists over the years comes off like a middleweight part unnaturally pumped up to heavyweight status in a misguided attempt to create a male lead; the film's one ridiculous scene has him turning up on remote Hokkaido Island on the eve of Arroway's top-secret mission to state his feelings for her.'

David Ansen wrote in *Newsweek*: 'Just about every scene with the philosophical reverend is a clinker, and he keeps popping up in implausible places to continue his debate with Ellie about the existence of God. It's a role that could make any actor look bad, and McConaughey, too young and too pretty for it, cuts a ludicrous figure.'

Time Out in London said: 'Regrettably, these visual coups only point up the inadequacy of a screenplay (from Carl Sagan's novel) which marries profound philosophical questions with hokey melodramatics, shallow characters and infantile conclusions. It's not just that it resorts to an albino Adventist to inject spurious suspense, nor that it foists McConaughey on us as a randy Luddite priest who is, coincidentally, the love interest (the pillow talk is physics vs. metaphysics).'

McConaughey's next released film saw him jump back into the world of criminal law after already having played a lawyer in *A Time to Kill*, but this part was much different. He went back in time to play a young attorney named Roger Sherman Baldwin who specialises in property law in the film *Amistad*. Based on the 1987 book *Mutiny On The Amistad: The Saga Of A Slave Revolt And Its Impact On American Abolition, Law And Diplomacy* by historian Howard Jones and written by David Franzoni, the film, directed by Steven Speilberg, is about the 1830 mutiny by the recently captured Menda slaves who took control of the US-bound ship *La Amistad* on the coast of Cuba. The mutiny became a Supreme Court legal battle in 1841 after their capture by the US Revenue Cutter Service, a maritime law enforcement agency.

'I've always been fascinated with the system,' McConaughey told Australia's *New Idea* magazine on his interest in the American legal system, 'and how the system works and lawyers are great characters 'cause they get to be the tour guide between guilt and innocence. How the system works is very interesting and it's not as idealistic as I used to think it was. There is a lot of deal making that goes on…'

The film also stars Morgan Freeman, Anthony Hopkins,

Nigel Hawthorne and Djimon Hounsou. The script was brought to Spielberg's attention via the actress and director Debbie Allen who was having fundraising problems with the project. Spielberg was looking for a serious film after the second *Jurassic Park* venture, *The Lost World*. His studio DreamWorks was in the process of being launched, and his WWII film *Saving Private Ryan* was still in pre-production, but it didn't stop Spielberg from immersing himself in *Amistad,* even though he was initially dubious about the project after his previous film about black culture, *The Color Purple*, was so badly received by African Americans on its original 1985 release. Nevertheless it was another string to McConaughey's bow, and he was picking up some more serious roles. But was he really the right actor for the film?

Released in December 1997, *Amistad* was fairly well received by critics though many admittedly approached it with caution knowing how cynical successful white directors can be when tackling black culture. Despite Spielberg's name and a strong cast it was not a box office success. Spielberg was probably hoping for something similar to his 1994 masterpiece *Schindler's List*, but, alas, it never happened.

The New York Times' Janet Maslin wrote of the film: 'The Africans are baffled by the hymn singing of grim abolitionists, whom they mistake for bad entertainers. They are also horrified by Matthew McConaughey, as a lawyer whom they call Dung Scraper, and the audience may not react much more kindly. Amiable matinee idol that he is, Mr. McConaughey should cease and desist from affecting mannerisms from previous centuries or playing any more smart lawyers.'

Empire's Christopher Hemblade wrote of the film: 'Spielberg has mounted a courtroom drama to rival the finest Grisham, with a coruscating civil rights debate resonating both within the film and into the present as the audience knows it.'

'I had some success. Now I wanted to go for directors. [Robert] Zemeckis, *Contact*. [Steven] Spielberg, *Amistad*,' McConaughey said to *LA Times*' Glenn Whipp. 'But the movies didn't stick, and my stock as an actor went down. Things dried up a little bit more. Off of that, which way can you go?'

*****

After *Amistad* other projects came McConaughey's way but they were not high-profile ventures. In October 1998, McConaughey starred with Eric Roberts in a thirty-minute short film written and directed by Sandra Bullock called *Making Sandwiches*. It was shot in Ventura, California back in 1996 and debuted at the 1997 Sundance Film Festival, and also played at the Austin Film Festival in October 1998.

Somewhat downbeat after losing out in some major roles, he directed a twenty minute short film called *The Rebel*, a comedy about an oddball guy who thinks living life on the edge is taking eleven items through the checkout express at the supermarket. He felt a great sense of pride after finishing the film. It was the best thing he could have done at that point in his career and was released in 1998.

'…I kept getting really close to jobs but I wasn't getting them, it was like I was getting too conservative,' he admitted to Cynthia Fuchs of *Pop Matters* in the early 2000s. 'But then I hopped up and wrote and directed a short, and then I started getting acting jobs, because I had that thing on the side that

I had pride in. It allowed me to be free, to take more risks. I respected every audition.'

McConaughey then hooked up with *Dazed and Confused* director Richard Linklater for a second time, and Texas screenwriters Claude Stanush and Clark Lee Walker in 1998's *The Newton Boys*, a drama based on the story of a family of Texan bank robbers. It had been in the pipeline since the days of *A Time to Kill*.

'*The Newton Boys* we talked about more but that isn't an issue,' McConaughey told Bill Graham of *The Film Stage*. 'The process of getting to the day of shooting is really fun for Rick and I. It's a really fun process. There's nothing formal about it at all.'

McConaughey plays Willis Newton who leaves prison after a miscarriage of justice only to learn that a good life is possible only if you have money, and so he is persuaded by two criminals to rob a bank. The film also stars Skeet Ulrich, Ethan Hawke, Vincent D'Onofrio and Dwight Yoakam. Filming took place in various cities around Texas such as Austin, Bartlett, New Braunfels and San Antonio.

McConaughey's oldest brother Rooster has a small part in the film. Asked by *Empire* in 2006 if he had any plans of working with Rooster again, he responded: 'Not necessarily. He has a day job. But he was right for this part, and he got in there and he had a good time. But if the right thing came up, I could see me directing him. Yeah (laughs). He's a real character. It was fun, but kind of weird. I just had to sit there and make sure I could keep him relaxed, y'know? He's a very relaxed guy, and then he started like going on, and I was like, "Don't worry, man. Loosen up. Cheapest thing on set is film. Go ahead, loosen up, let it ride, let it ride…"'

The film was only moderately well received and hardly set the box office on fire after it was released at the end of March in the US. It didn't reach the UK until March 1999. It's one of those films that has seemingly disappeared without a trace though it does have worthwhile merits and deserves far more attention than it got at the time.

Emanuel Levy wrote in *Variety*: 'An extremely handsome production that meticulously evokes the 1920s, and a likable male-dominated cast, headed by Matthew McConaughey in his best screen performance to date, only partially compensate for a story that's too diffuse and lacks a discernible point of view that would make it dramatically engaging… After a couple of disappointing performances (*Contact*, *Amistad*), McConaughey finally gets a role that integrates his handsome looks, authentic Texan dialect and easygoing style.'

Peter Stack wrote in the *San Francisco Chronicle*: 'McConaughey's Willis is driven to crime to finance his dream of becoming an oil millionaire. Flashy and jaunty, McConaughey isn't very convincing as the big brother who drafts his younger kin as soldiers in his larcenous army. When he goes after cigar girl Louise ([Julianna] Margulies) at a fancy hotel, he comes across as dapper cardboard.'

Though McConaughey's performances in *A Time to Kill*, *Amistad* and *Contact* had brought him varying degrees of critical acclaim, it seemed that some of the projects he'd been cast in towards the end of the 1990s were not connecting with audiences and McConaughey was worried about losing his bankable appeal. The way Hollywood studios and producers market an actor to audiences is incredibly important in the commercial success of a film. *Lone Star*, *Larger Than Life* and *The Newton Boys* were not commercial hits.

1999's *EDtv* was also a box office disaster. They had high hopes for the film but 1998's *The Truman Show*, which carried a similar reality TV theme and predicated the obsession with reality TV of the 2000s, eclipsed it.

McConaughey was disappointed the film did not performed to expectations. 'There were some reviews at the time where people would say, "this is where I think McConaughey was true and good and funny," or "this is where he wasn't," and I would go back and compare. I would look at diaries and see what did I think I was doing, compared to what I actually did, compared to what got edited – there is always a gap between those things and the goal is to close those gaps,' McConaughey explained to *The Film Stage*'s Caitlin Martis. 'That's why actors go into producing, because they want complete control. I've got some constructive criticism along the way where I'm like, "he's right, good point."'

The film, directed by former *Happy Days* actor and renowned filmmaker Ron Howard, is an adaptation of the Quebecois film *Louis 19, le roi des ondes*. McConaughey plays Ed Pekurny, who along with his brother Ray (played by Woody Harrelson), is being filmed twenty-four hours a day, seven days a week. The film also stars Jenna Elfman, Ellen DeGeneres, Martin Landau, Rob Reiner, Sally Kirkland, Elizabeth Hurley, Clint Howard and Dennis Hopper.

'He had recently come out in *A Time to Kill* and was the next big thing,' Harrelson said to *Variety*'s Jenelle Riley about his first meeting with McConaughey at a CAA event. 'He was very nice. And funny. I asked if he wanted a shot of tequila. He declined, as it was noon and he had a lot to do that day.'

It was released in the US in March 1999 and grossed less than half of its $80 million budget. It reached the UK in November. Sadly, the film disappeared without a trace though it does have its fans. It is a decent film, but at the time it was overshadowed by a similar, bigger film with a bigger actor.

Janet Maslin wrote in *The New York Times*: 'In a perfect casting coup, the film presents Mr. McConaughey and Mr. Harrelson (who do share a resemblance) as brothers who don't easily adjust to Ed's growing fame. Mr. Harrelson is a particular treat as Ray, the show-off Pekurny, who like Ed is easily lured into airing private matters while a camera is in his face.'

David Edelstein wrote on *Slate*: 'The problem with *EDtv* is that Ed's life looks and sounds like a tedious sitcom before the TV cameras ever show up. McConaughey's manner is TV-talk-show bashful. (Is this supposed to be the point? That he's deformed by television before he's ever on television? I don't think so.)'

Even in the 2010s, McConaughey was still affected by the failure of *Amistad* and *EDtv* as he told *Details'* Bart Blasengame: 'That hurt, and it pissed me off. Because everybody's telling the truth in Hollywood, right? But then I went, "It's not personal – get the joke." And six years ago I didn't get the joke. But I learned you don't do your business in Hollywood's game. It's a great town for hustlers, so you can't get mad. You play your own game.'

Post *A Time to Kill* and Hollywood's newest kid in town was riding on a series of box office flops. They were not bad films but they didn't take enough box office receipts. It didn't worry McConaughey, though. He simply moved on to other projects. 'That movie [*EDtv*] was backed, marketed, had all kinds of money on it, and it just bombed. I thought we had a home run,' McConaughey admitted to *Cinema.com*. 'I had experienced that kind of overnight success which was not dissimilar to what Ed went through. So it was also an interesting role to play.'

In 1999, he also voiced the character Rad Thibodeaux in an episode of the quirky animated comedy series *King of the Hill* called 'The Wedding of Bobby Hill.' According to online movie bible IMDB, McConaughey cropped up in a cameo as the character Nathan in the French film *Bonne Nuit* in 1999, but almost nothing else is known about this film. That same year he was arrested after police knocked on his door to find him playing the bongo drums naked with a bong nearby. His neighbours had filed a noise complaint. He spent the night in jail with his friend who was also hauled off with him. McConaughey was arrested for resisting arrest and possession of marijuana. The charges were ultimately dropped but he was slapped with $50 fine for disturbing the peace. Not much for a man who could demand $4 million a film. He sang sing-alongs with his cellmates and even had T-shirts printed that read, 'What part of naked bongo playing don't you understand?' Hilarious.

The incident was a turnaround point in his life. He later told the *Daily Express*' Garth Pearce: 'It was something that never left me. It kept on being mentioned. I needed to make changes in my life, the way I was living and the movies I was doing.'

McConaughey has since confessed he loves to play the bongos naked. His mother didn't even put him and his brothers in a bathing suit at the country club until they were nine. The residents of Austin had a sense of humour about McConaughey's arrest – if he hadn't have been naked it wouldn't have been as funny or as widely publicised. He also had a house in LA which he shared with Miss Hud, his Chow / Labrador cross, but his true home was Austin, close to his roots. Texans respected his space and tended to leave him alone – he was just one of the locals rather than big shot celebrity who's 'gone all Hollywood.' He managed to maintain a fairly normal life, though there was a bit of a cowboy in him, opting to hit the road whenever he felt the itch to travel, much like a character in a Jack Kerouac novel.

'It is an effort,' McConaughey said to *Pop Matters'* Cynthia Fuchs when asked how he maintained his sense of distance and down-to-earth attitude during his early years of fame and fortune. 'It becomes something that you tenaciously seek out. It's going back to the ranch for twenty-five days, taking that drive to Texas. I have a nice car named Midnight. It's a midnight blue 740 IL BMW, the ultimate driving machine.'

When he's out with his friends, they do things together; watch sports, play sports or go to a nice bar or restaurant. He doesn't watch movies. Being famous means that everyone knows a little something about your life, which for McConaughey meant that conversation was imbalanced, especially if he met a stranger whom he didn't know anything about. He grew to like Hollywood and enjoy the lifestyle. The one thing he wanted to do was to live a story as well as tell one.

It was around this time, to keep up his Hollywood image, that he started to use hair products. 'Regenix,' he later explained to *Ellie*'s Holly Milea. 'Back in 1999, my hair was fallin' out, so I started this stuff. And son of a gun if I didn't bring my hair back so well that people think I went and got plugs.'

In the space of just a few years as the decade was coming to a close McConaughey had gone from bit parts and cameos in dreadful long-forgotten B-movies to working with Hollywood's elite such as Spielberg, Zemeckis, Howard and Schumacher. Those earlier films certainly helped to get him noticed, and while he wasn't one of the finest actors working in American cinema he had a certain humble charm, obvious good looks and an everyday Texan attitude about him that helped propel him into the lower ranks of the A-list of Hollywood stars. But to become a household name and to demand millions of dollars for consecutive films he had to make some changes to his choice of roles. He had to star in cheerier films that would attract the mainstream audience more than the likes of *Contact* and *Amistad,* which were great for critical reverence (to an extent) but not so great for his bank balance. Michael Caine once said that there are two films you do as an actor – films for the money (*The Muppet Christmas Carol* and *Jaws 4: The Revenge* et al) and films for the critical respect as an actor (*Little Voice* and *Harry Brown* et al). This is certainly a path McConaughey was going to follow. Doesn't every actor? Every actor has to make a buck somehow.

Despite some misfires McConaughey was cast in the tense and controversial American World War II submarine drama *U-571*, directed by Jonathan Mostow and produced by heavyweight Dino De Laurentiis. Set in 1942, McConaughey plays Lieutenant Andrew Tyler who, along with his comrades from a disguised United States Navy submarine, board a German submarine attempting to capture her Enigma cipher machine, which was used to send secret cryptic messages by the Germans during the war. The film caused considerable controversy in the UK because the fictitious storyline was based on the real life story of the British officers of the HMS *Bulldog* who captured the Enigma machine from U-100 in the North Atlantic in May 1941. This was before the Americans had even entered the war. Even the British Prime Minister Tony Blair said that the film was an 'affront' to British soldiers. The *U-571* in real life had never been involved in any such events and had been sunk by a Short Sunderland flying boat from the Royal Australian Air Force in January 1994 off the coast of Ireland. Filming of *U-571* took place in the Mediterranean Sea near Rome and Malta. It stars Bill Paxton, Harvey Keitel, Thomas Kretschmann, Jon Bon Jovi, Jack Noseworthy, Will Estes and Tom Guiry. It was released in April 2000 and was fairly well received by critics, though journalists in the UK were dubious when it was released in cinemas in June.

Michael Atkinson wrote in the *Village Voice*: 'The characters are familiar – hot young fearless leader Matthew McConaughey, second banana Jon Bon Jovi, seasoned sarge Harvey Keitel, Noo Yawk greaseball Erik Palladino, black cook T.C. Carson, greenhorned spy Jake Weber – but the work is the story, blessed with only a single sacrificial death (offscreen, even) and no speeches.'

George Perry wrote on the BBC website: 'If *U-571* had been good this would have been forgivable. Alas, it's a noisy, cliche-ridden, incomprehensible mess. Matthew McConaughey, shaven-headed and sunken cheeked, plays a young officer denied command until he proves himself. He is given a mission to capture a U-boat by pretending to be a German supply crew.'

Writing in *Variety*, veteran film critic Todd McCarthy said: 'The key quality is not noble, but necessary: It's the ability to send soldiers into deadly situations without hesitation or regret. Paxton leaves the audience in no doubt he can do that. McConaughey leaves the audience in no doubt that he can't – not yet. *U-571*, among other things, is the story of a good soldier who, under pressure, grows into a commander. To compare

U-571 to *Saving Private Ryan* is like comparing a miniature to a mural, but there is one point of similarity: The audience is made to feel the full weight and terror of combat.'

U-571 was perhaps the wrong film for McConaughey, but as an actor who strives to explore his talents and as someone who wants to challenge himself both professionally and personally it was a film he was pleased to be a part of. Ultimately, it was another one that didn't win him any critical favours. The shaven-headed look didn't work for him, either.

In 2000 he cropped up again on TV, playing himself in an episode of *Sex and the City* called 'Escape from New York'. It's not uncommon for Hollywood actors to play themselves or make character cameos in hit TV shows – Bruce Willis had cropped up in a few episodes of *Friends*.

Throughout the late 1990s McConaughey was cast as the lead role or key supporting character in several major productions, including Robert Zemeckis' *Contact* and Steven Spielberg's *Amistad*. Those roles were not necessarily the right fit for his Texan accent, looks and charm, and after the failure of *The Newton Boys* and *EDtv*, Hollywood was slow to respond to his calls. McConaughey took some road trips to clear his head and to live a little. For some reason, though, the magic just didn't stick and he became just another Hollywood gimmick. He was no longer the next Paul Newman or Marlon Brando, but nor was he George Hamilton.

It was around this time when McConaughey had a change of heart about which direction his career would move towards. The paychecks were calling. The lure of the great Yankee dollar was too much to resist. His shirt was coming off.

CHAPTER FIVE

HOLLYWOOD'S LEADING MAN

'I've read all my bad reviews, and got them all out a
few years ago. It's a big file and I read them all.'
Matthew McConaughey, *The Film Stage*, 2013

The early 2000s saw a drastic turnaround in the career of Matthew McConaughey. Though he continued to be cast as a leading man, he was frequently starring in romantic comedies rather than dramas. He needed a formula that was suitable for his persona. McConaughey took a complete career change after *U-571* by starring with pop star-actress Jennifer Lopez in *The Wedding Planner*.

'There was a lot of responsibility on [*U-571*] because it was based on real events and there are conflicts [sic] to overcome,' McConaughey, then aged thirty-one, told *Cinema.com*. '[*The Wedding Planner*] was looser and not so structured. I got to be the lover, the knight coming over the hill. Being a romantic comedy there was more room for improvisation. My character's a doctor but he's not someone who's defined by his occupation.

It's more about his affairs of the heart and how couples can stay friends after they break up.'

In *The Wedding Planner* McConaughey plays a local paediatrician named Steve Edison who falls in love with Mary Fore (played by Lopez) who is planning to marry Massimo Lenzetti (played by Justin Chambers), a childhood acquaintance she had been re-introduced to. *Party Of Five*'s Jennifer Love Hewitt and *California Man* star Brendan Fraser were originally cast to play the lead roles but were then replaced by real life couple Sarah Michelle Gellar and Freddie Prinze Jr. Lopez and McConaughey were subsequently cast after their predecessors left the project due to scheduling conflicts.

'There's a real optimism to this film,' McConaughey said to Cynthia Fuchs of *Pop Matters* on his first romantic comedy role. 'It's buoyant, a fairy tale that we've all heard one time or another, that you're going to meet someone and it's going to be true love and you'll know it. It's very innocent. And it's a comedy set-up, so the thing to do is to play it at an even keel and as straightforward as possible. The dialogue and situations are already comedic, so I was trying to ground it as much as possible. But when I saw it, there were things that were coming out of my mouth where I was wondering, "Did you just say that?"'

Filming took place mostly in Golden Gate Park. McConaughey learned how to tango during the making of the film. It's a complicated dance but he managed it in the end. He took some lessons, though he knew how to dance in general. He's got rhythm but he was a little unschooled and didn't know any steps.

The Wedding Planner, directed by Adam Shankman, was released in the US in January 2001 and was poorly received by critics, as it was in the UK when it was released in April. However, with a budget of just $35 million it went on to gross over $90 million at the worldwide box office. It was a lucky escape for McConaughey because although it wasn't a flop, and he received some negative reviews, his co-star Lopez was nominated for a Razzie Award for 'Worst Actress'. For McConaughey, though, it was easy money. It's one reason why so many talented actors star in romantic comedies: the money is good and such films, if the chemistry between the co-stars is spot on and if the story is engaging and funny, are usually always box office hits.

'You're not supposed to get, you know, Hamletian about it,' McConaughey explained to *NPR*'s Terry Gross of the *Fresh Air* show about the genre. 'You're not supposed to go deep. You go deep on those, you sink the ship. I had fun doing that and also trying to do those without emasculating the male, which can be done in those romantic comedies often.'

The rom-com has become a hugely successful genre much to the dread of most men who are forced to take their girlfriends or wives to the cinema.

Writing in *Entertainment Weekly*, Lisa Schwarzbaum compared *The Wedding Planner* to *My Best Friend's Wedding*, and said: 'Where Julia Roberts turned the world on with her huggability, Lopez's vibe is that of someone afraid to get mussed. And where Rupert Everett was divine as a sidekick, McConaughey is mortally ordinary as a main dish who spends most of his time smiling like a party guest.'

Michael Thomson of the BBC wrote on the website that: 'Unfortunately, after the two leads become less wired in each other's presence, and the sexual tension begins to droop, everyone seems to be reading an autocue.'

Jessica Winter said in *Village Voice*: 'McConaughey is insufferably smug as always, while the bewilderingly miscast Diva appears bored and impatient.'

Desson Howe wrote in the *Washington Post*: 'Matthew McConaughey's her squeeze-in-the-making, buffed up like most male actors these days and doing his adorable Texan thang. But *The Wedding Planner* is definitely Jennifer's parade.'

McConaughey's critical stature was saved by a long forgotten film called *Thirteen Conversations About One Thing*, which eventually opened in March 2002 to reasonably positive reviews. Directed by Jill Sprecher, and written by her and her sister Karen, the film is about five different individuals who are in search of happiness when their paths intersect in different ways and impact their lives. McConaughey plays Troy, a district attorney, who is bereft with guilt following a hit and run accident in which he injures a cleaning woman named Beatrice (Clea DuVall). This spirals into the story of Beatrice who reassesses her life during her recuperation and begins to think about her colleague Dorrie (Tia Texada). An insurance claims manager named Gene (Alan Arkin) struggles to cope with his son's drug addiction and fires a cheery staff member but realises he made an error and feels guilty. A college professor named Walker (John Turturro), who teaches physics, has a midlife crisis and becomes embroiled in a relationship with a colleague, while his wife Patricia (Amy Irving) finds incriminating evidence in Walker's wallet after it was stolen and mailed to their home.

Scripted over the course of two months by the Sprecher sisters, the film took three years to make because of funding problems. The film did not receive a commercial release until early 2002, though it premiered at the 2001 Venice Film Festival and was shown at the Toronto Film Festival and various other international festivals throughout the rest of the year and into early 2002. It had a limited US release and opened in just nine cinemas earning almost $90,000 on its first weekend of release.

A.O. Scott wrote in *The New York Times*: 'It seems intuitively identifiable but strangely resistant to precise definition. Synonyms multiply by the dozen: chance, fate, coincidence, serendipity, the order of the universe – or, to give some human dimension to these chilly mathematical conceits: happiness, good fortune, kismet, grace, the meaning of life.'

Later that year McConaughey starred in *Frailty*, a psychological thriller marking the directorial debut of *Apollo 13* actor Bill Paxton. He took on a major change in role reversals by appearing as a serial killer in the film. McConaughey plays a man named Fenton Meikis who enters an FBI office in Dallas one night and requests to speak to Agent Wesley Doyle, played by Powers Boothe. Meikis believes that his brother Adam (played by Levi Kreis) is the 'God's Hands' serial killer that the FBI are tracking down. Paxton plays the widower father who is fanatically religious. As children, the brothers had been told by their father that they had been chosen by God to track down demons and destroy those whose names were given to him by an angel.

Screenwriter Brent Hanley spoke to *DVD Talk*'s Phillip Duncan about his experience working with McConaughey, a fellow Texan: 'One of the things I learned most about actors and from actors, and McConaughey has been a huge mentor for the directing actors thing. The thing I've learned is how much can be said without saying anything. How a good screen actor can get across what you need them to get across without saying a fucking word. That to me is magical. I love that.'

The film opened in US cinemas in April 2002 and was a

modest box office success with a budget of just $11 million. Reviews of the film were mostly positive. It reached the UK in September. *Frailty* has since become a cult classic amongst aficionados of dark thrillers and horror films. It is certainly an overlooked gem from this period of McConaughey's career.

The Associated Press' Christy Lemire wrote: 'McConaughey gets top billing, but Paxton steals the show. And O'Leary more than holds his own again here. Too bad it's in a movie that fails to live up to its potential.'

Robert Koehler wrote in *Variety*: 'Pic is McConaughey's most fully developed performance in several seasons; for Paxton, it adds to his growing gallery of nuanced, conflicted men from the heartland, while demonstrating that, in his feature helming debut, he already possesses the chops of a front-rank director… McConaughey reveals only as much about Meiks as he needs to, and never a moment too soon. It's a poker-face performance supreme, both a portrait of a son's tragedy and of a son absorbing his father's legacy.'

The Guardian's Xan Brooks said of the film: 'Bill Paxton's directing debut stands alone in a horror genre currently infested with pert teens and knowing plot tics. What we have here is addictive old-school hokum, an American Gothic comic-strip with a whiff of *Wise Blood* to its lurid design.'

Venturing deeper into mainstream Hollywood movies, McConaughey was cast as Denton Van Zan in the post-apocalyptic action fantasy film *Reign of Fire* about a breed of dragons that emerge from the earth setting fire to anyone and everything. It was his first action movie and his first stab at fantasy. Most of his past films had been dramas with real life characters so *Reign of Fire* was an altogether different movie.

'Actually the idea came to me in a dream,' McConaughey said to *Phase9 TV*. 'Every other character I played in a movie had some sort of a biography to look at. But playing a dragon slayer in 2025 meant that there was no research I could do. It was all about imagination.'

Directed by Rob Bowman, and starring Christian Bale and Gerard Butler, the film is set in 2020 England though it was filmed in the Wicklow Mountains of Ireland with the cast and crew staying over in Dublin. It wasn't filmed in England because at the time there was an outbreak of foot and mouth disease.

'*Reign of Fire* was a whole other fun thing,' McConaughey told *The Film Experience*'s Nathaniel R., 'but that was all from the imaginary dragon slayer future. And if anyone disagreed with anything I was doing there, I could always just go, "You know any dragon slayers?" and no one answered yes so I was always safe with that one, right? [Laughter...] Here's the deal: it's really part of the fun. We get one day a year where we can dress up and be what we want to be. Halloween. It's a costume. Well, the next thing is when you get to go perform and play and be someone else.'

There are lots of action scenes in the film and some fantastic computer generated effects, but also some lousy dialogue. It was rather odd to see McConaughey with a shaven head, beard and tattoos like a character out of the *Mad Max* films. He certainly got a few interesting reactions from family and friends as well as members of the public when he went outside. He just didn't look like himself. He looked evil, like some sort of satanic cult member.

Having tattoos in the film tempted him to get them for real. 'The tattoos were an idea that I came up with and worked on with a guy in a Dublin tattoo parlour,' McConaughey admitted to *Phase9 TV*. 'The tattoos are actually two dragons that wrap round my shoulder and come down to my navel. It was something very tribal that I was going for. They were painted on every morning and it took about two hours.'

When he shaved his hair he got a suntan on it to make him look darker. It took him eight months to grow the beard, and to get into shape he worked out at his ranch in Texas. He worked out with weights, ran four miles a day and boxed – which he continued to do during filming in Dublin. He has seventy cows at his ranch in Texas and he'd wrestle with them by throwing his shoulder into them trying to boost his strength. They didn't bite too much. He even tried to get them into headlocks. It was fun and got him into the sort of shape he needed to be in for the film.

'It's easier at night when they're kind of asleep, standing asleep,' he elaborated to *Total Film*. 'I wrestled some of the calves, some of the mid-sized cows, and then there are some big boys that I just booted around with. I got hit in the hip – pretty much had a black and blue hip for three weeks. It put me on my ass, for sure.'

He got some bumps and bruises on set too but he didn't hurt himself too seriously. The scene where McConaughey head-butts Bale was real, though it was an accident and a heat of the moment move. It gave Bale a lump. Bale worked through and finished the scene. Both actors tried to make the fight look as real as possible. They got their fair share of bloodied knuckles and knees.

'It dropped me like a sack of potatoes,' Bale told Alec Cawthorne of the BBC, about the fight seen between his and

McConaughey's characters. 'In the movie you see me crawl around the ground for a couple of seconds to try to find my bearings – that is real! Then I thought I had to get up and finish the scene or it was going to be no use. I could see that the film crew were staring to see if I was all right. When we finished I asked Matthew if he was OK. He said, "Yeah, you mad bastard – I headbutted you!"'

McConaughey had a blast making the film and was eager to jump right back into another action film. He's not Arnold Schwarzenegger nor Sylvester Stallone and some could argue he looks a little bit out of sorts in an action film, but he gave it a good try.

McConaughey joked with *About.com: Hollywood Movies'* Rebecca Murray and Fred Topel that dragons were easier to deal with than women: 'Dragons you know. Dragons are simple. They're in the sky, bang, bring them down to the ground, simple. Women, man, we're never going to figure you all out. I think if we can enjoy trying to figure you all out, that's the ticket. Forget trying to figure you all out – it's impossible.'

McConaughey enjoyed his time in Dublin and devoured some of the local customs, including pints of Guinness. He had to be careful of his weight, though, because Guinness is heavy on the stomach. His favourite aspect of Ireland, however, was the people and the culture. He loved the local music and enjoyed sitting in pubs listening to bands and chatting with the locals. It's a testosterone-fuelled film dominated by a male cast but what was life like together behind the camera and off set? 'We went out in Dublin a few times,' Bale told Alec Cawthorne of the BBC about his relationship with his co-stars, 'and Matthew had parties at his place, but most of the time he was down at the boxing gym – sparring and just hitting somebody.'

It opened at number three at the box office in July 2002 behind the Tom Hanks led gangster drama *Road to Perdition* and the Will Smith and Tommy Lee Jones blockbuster sequel *Men in Black II*. *Reign of Fire* grossed over $80 million and had a budget of $60 million. Reviews of the film were modest at best. It reached UK cinemas in August.

Alec Cawthorne wrote on the BBC website: 'The grimness of the wiped-out world is offset by the campy posturing of a tattooed McConaughey, and while Bale is earnest as the guilt-stricken leader Quinn, he also gets the best *Star Wars* gag you'll see in years, distracting the ragamuffin kids from the misery of their predicament.'

The Guardian's Joe Queenan said: '*Reign of Fire* falls into the category of bad movies that are not nearly as bad as they could have been, and not nearly as bad as some of us would have liked them to be. This is a phenomenon often referred to as the Sandahl Bergman Conundrum or the Van Damme Anomaly. Shunning the camp qualities that usually permeate this genre of motion pictures, the film could have used a few more laughs.'

Elvis Mitchell wrote in *The New York Times*: 'The movie might have been a minor classic if it had maximized its own possibilities. But until the rush wears off, the picture is as much fun as a great run at a slot machine: even when your luck runs out, you're losing only pocket change.'

In 2003 McConaughey joined a cast of noted actors, including Tom Hanks and Stanley Tucci, to narrate an episode of the sixteen part series on the history of America, *Freedom: A History of Us*.

U-571, *The Wedding Planner* and *Reign of Fire* were reasonably successful box office films but they were certainly not enough to gain McConaughey critical praise after some of his highlights of the previous decade.

He's an actor who enjoys playing character roles as much as lead roles as he told *Crazed Fanboy's* Michael A. Smith: 'I mean for me it's not one or the other. In *Reign of Fire*, that was a real character role. My character in *Larger Than Life* was a character role. I love doing that kind of stuff. And I like playing a character where I say, "I know that dude."'

*****

Simply put, too many of his early 2000s films were throw-away productions that gave him next to no credence or respect, with the exception of *Frailty*, which is often thought of as a minor classic and one of the most underrated horror films of the decade. Still, for an actor whose career was looking so prosperous in the 1990s he was appearing in one too many bad films. He needed a hit. The studios came calling with another rom-com. The money was good and the lead female co-star was bound to be sexy. He said yes.

'We needed sexy, hot, charming, intelligent – really, how many guys are there out there like that?' *How to Lose a Guy in 10 Days* producer Christine Peters told *Variety's* Jenelle Riley. 'He's a true Southern gentleman.'

McConaughey knows how hard it is as an actor to take a role that is so well known in such a popular genre and make it work. If you fail as an actor to provide the laughs the whole film can sink. 'I take the comedy real seriously,' McConaughey admitted to *The Guardian*'s Andrew Pulver. 'There's a whole plan behind it. Even though those characters look like I'm just skating through, there's a design behind it. They look easy-breezy, but if you go digging too deep into character, you sink the ship.'

How to Lose a Guy in 10 Days opened in the US in February 2003 and the UK in April to mixed reviews from critics though it was a box office hit making over $100 million at the global box office. Directed by Donald Petrie it is based on a short cartoon novel by Michael Alexander and Jeannie Long, and stars McConaughey as Benjamin Barry, an advertising executive and ladies' man who, to win an advertising campaign, places a bet that he can make a woman fall in love with him in ten days. Kate Hudson, daughter of Goldie Hawn, plays Andie Anderson, a writer who covers the 'How To' beat for *Composure* magazine and is commissioned to pen a piece on 'How To Lose A Guy In 10 Days.' The pair met at a bar after the bet is placed.

Like his character Ben, McConaughey has always been comfortable around women. He loves and appreciates women. McConaughey has certainly had his fair share of Hollywood beauties. He grew up in a loving family that was open about sex. He was taught about the birds and the bees from an early age when he started to date around thirteen or fourteen years old. He was told that if a woman was uncomfortable around him she wouldn't say so, so he'd have to pick up on their mannerisms. He was taught never to push a woman into doing anything she didn't want to do. His love and respect for women was one reason why he was drawn to the rom-com genre. McConaughey knows how to treat women and how to charm them. He knows when not to come on too strong and when to offer them space if they need it.

In the film, his character cooks a delicious meal. McConaughey is himself a pretty good cook as he confessed to *People* magazine: 'I've got some culinary skills! I would consider myself a bit of a saucier. I make barbecue sauces, marinades, salad dressing. I like to eat healthy, and how do you make healthy food taste good? Because usually it's boring. That's why I got into the sauces.'

Dating for McConaughey can be an odd experience if the other person is not famous. It means they know things about him and he's not aware how much knowledge his date has of him. What McConaughey likes about dating is the courtship between two strangers. It starts off with general things like name, family and job before the conversation gets deeper. If he meets someone who knows about him, and they ask him about his Airstream collection or his dog, he gets a bit freaked out because they know his biography.

'I'm not much on the "direct" romantic,' McConaughey admitted to *About.com: Hollywood Movies'* Rebecca Murray and Fred Topel. 'I'm not much on moves or lines or things like that, but I love to cook. It's a great comfortable place that I find to get to know somebody, [to] have a date over to my house and cook. It's a great place for conversation. I love conversation in the kitchen. I love having that one thing that I get to do, cooking while you're there.'

McConaughey saw Kate Hudson in Cameron Crowe's semi-autobiographical film *Almost Famous*, and thought she was great in the role of rock groupie Penny Lane. After just five minutes of meeting her he knew they'd have great chemistry onscreen. She was in her early twenties at the time and very ambitious and comfortable with her sexuality. 'Kate is really talented and really natural,' McConaughey said to *The Tech*'s Allison C. Lewis. 'She does every take different...she has great timing. She's very relaxed and very playful. There's chemistry between us on screen...it's easy to be attracted to her.'

It's a simple story – how hadn't it been done before? 'The funniest thing about this movie is not the jokes,' McConaughey, then thirty-three years old, told *The GW Hatchet*'s Andy Metzger. 'It's got a great setup... The chemistry on screen is one of the undeniable things about this flick. It's a chick flick but it appeals to dudes.'

A.O. Scott wrote of the film in *The New York Times*: 'For his part, Mr. McConaughey steps into the role of comic foil with gentlemanly aplomb. You don't believe this scrubbed and gleaming pair are really the love-struck and ambitious young Manhattan professionals they are pretending to be, but for the most part the pretending is reasonably enjoyable to watch.'

Writing in *Empire*, Anna Smith said: 'Hudson and McConaughey are a likable pair in a light but efficient comedy that succeeds where *The Wedding Planner* failed.'

When McConaughey was promoting the film in Australia he spoke on a talk show about Eileen Crocker of the Crocker family with whom he stayed for five months as an exchange student in Australia in 1988. Sadly, she died later that year. It goes to show, though, just how family and friends are important to McConaughey in his life. He doesn't forget those who help him.

How to Lose a Guy in 10 Days was a successful enough film that Hollywood remembered Matthew McConaughey just as he was dangerously slipping off radar with a series of poor films, and it led to parts in other romantic comedies. He became the go-to-guy for romantic comedies and the cheques were good. The thing is, he was not known for his acting ability. It's rare for a good-looking guy to be given credit for his talent. It would still be a few years before critics properly began to take note of his acting prowess. He needed heavyweight roles: a *Rain Man* (Tom Cruise) or a *Philadelphia* (Tom Hanks), or even a *Pulp Fiction* (John Travolta) to get the attention of the Oscar voters. Playing a handsome, charming man whom a woman may fall in love with didn't exactly stretch his acting talents or gain him many positive notices from the pundits.

Such is the nature of the business that an actor could work on a film, move straight onto another set, and have the latter film released first, due to the fact that production and distribution times vary. Throughout this period McConaughey was working on a variety of projects, but few of them had serious credentials. It would be unfair to attack him for appearing on the cover of glossy magazines with his shirt off, or for his high-profile love life with female actors or good-looking industry types, because that is the lifestyle of a Hollywood star. McConaughey is someone different, though. He is part hippie, part Beat poet and part loner who plays the role of the lone travelling man rather well. He isn't your usual celebrity – when he is fed up of the LA glitz and Hollywood lifestyle he goes back home to Texas where is treated as one of the locals and where he lives an ordinary life.

McConaughey spoke to *IndieLondon* about his obsession with linguistics and communicating '…whether it's trying to get something across now or communicating with a director, or whether it's going and travelling in different countries where they don't speak a bit of the language and you end up using sign language. You end up finding out that you're all speaking the same language but with different vocabularies. I love getting through that. I get more frustrated if I cannot communicate.

That frustrates me more than anything. I'm obsessed with trying to understand what somebody is talking about and trying to get them to understand me.'

He continued to explore other projects by appearing as a fire fighter in the low-budget film *Tiptoes* (also known as *Tiny Tiptoes*) with Rene Russo, which went straight to DVD in August 2004 after it was shown at the Sundance Film Festival in January (though it actually premiered at the French Deauville Film Festival in September 2003).

Kate Beckinsale plays Carol, a painter and independent minded and confident woman who falls in love with Steven, played by McConaughey. She barely knows anything about him other than that he is her perfect man. She becomes pregnant and Steven finally tells her of his secret – he is the only averaged sized person in a family of dwarfs, which means that their unborn baby may be a dwarf. Steven's twin brother Rolfe (played by Gary Oldman) is a dwarf, and as Steven and Carol grow apart as they struggle to deal with things, she becomes closer to Rolfe who teachers her about life as a dwarf. The director Matthew Bright was reportedly fired from the production, and the film was recut and promoted as a rom-com, possibly on the back of McConaughey's success in *The Wedding Planner* and *How to Lose a Guy in 10 Days*. It's one of his films that is best left unremembered.

Lisa Nesselson wrote in *Variety*: 'Terrific make-up and visual effects help render the completely unrecognisable Oldman entirely convincing as a miniature man, whatever the camera angle. Evoking the matter-of-fact feel of brothers talking, he and McConaughey give their scenes together an emotional veracity lacking in too much of the pic.'

Writing on *Reel Film*, David Nusair said: 'Likewise, McConaughey and Beckinsale make a convincing couple, though some of Steven's decisions are a little hard to swallow (particularly as the film's conclusion approaches). Director Matthew Bright seems to be going for a spontaneous, improvised sort of vibe, using takes that aren't necessarily perfect – a choice that doesn't entirely work. Presumably intended to lend the film an off-the-cuff feel, the decision instead contributes to an aura of sloppiness.'

Around this time, McConaughey let slip in interviews that he was trying to get a children's movie off the ground, but nothing has since come into fruition. '…it's a fairy tale with magic reality,' he told *Phase9 TV*, 'and it is about a little boy who is a fisherman. It's about his dreams. There are a couple of really nice morals to the tale. I'm going to be writer/producer/director on that but right now I've got to get the thing written.'

The critics remained divided on their opinion of McConaughey: on the one hand he's a box office success, handsome and charming; yet on the other he seemed more interested in appearing in lightweight comedies and cashing cheques than aiming for an Oscar. He was hounded by gossip magazines, dated leading Hollywood ladies and enjoyed a seemingly carefree lifestyle. In the 1990s he was just a humble kid from Texas who got lucky and became a Hollywood leading man; but then he became an A-list actor with a mansion in the Hollywood Hills with a tremendous view of Los Angeles. Years later he would own luxury properties in Malibu and Texas.

In 2004 he bought an Airstream trailer, his first of three, and when he felt LA was getting too much for him, he'd hit the road and stay in crummy motels, or even follow the route of his favourite bluesman Ali Farka Touré to Africa and backpack up the Niger River. He also visited a music festival north of Timbuktu. Sometimes he just had to check out, he had to get away from everywhere because he couldn't stand the lifestyle anymore, but then he would return refreshed and with a clear mind.

'Most of the time on a road trip, I'm just driving,' he told the *Independent*'s Lesley O'Toole. 'That's my favourite place to think, or not think. I don't go away to think about something, but I like to put myself in a place where answers sort of show up. My favourite place for that is behind the wheel, heading somewhere.'

CHAPTER SIX

JUST KEEP LIVIN'

'I'm starting this brand [j.k. livin] because it accents a positive.
It spreads a good word, puts a smile on my face.'
Matthew McConaughey, *Texas Monthly*, 2008

Based on the novel of the same name by Clive Cussler, McConaughey plays Dirk Pitt in *Sahara*, an Indiana Jones-style adventurer who goes on an adventure to the deserts of West Africa to seek the lost Civil War battleship known as the 'Ship of Death'. En route he helps a World Health Organisation doctor Eva Rojas (played by Penélope Cruz) who is being hunted down by a ruthless dictator.

'As executive producer, it proved challenging,' McConaughey admitted to *Hollywood.com*. 'It was a 700-page book that you had to break down into a 120-page script. You're going to go from A to C and sometimes skip out B. You're going to pick out the scenes that capture the essence of what the author was trying to get across. Even before I knew of Clive Cussler's books and his character, Dirk Pitt, I was looking for a role like this.'

The film started for McConaughey several years before

when he went to Clive Cussler, lobbying to get the film made. He visited him at his home in Telluride, Colorado and two more times subsequently in Phoenix, Arizona. He finally got the author's approval when the script and financing came together and the film was green-lit. McConaughey's name wasn't listed as an executive producer just for the heck of it; he had put in a lot of time and legwork into getting the film made. He was involved in all aspects of production. He met with director Breck Eisner, saw his work and had a couple of sit-downs with him to see if he was the right man for the director's chair. They agreed on what angles they should take with the film in terms of how much comedy was necessary and whether they should pitch it as an action adventure or action comedy. The original idea was that *Sahara* was going to be a franchise film. They also had Cussler's approval for casting and they both agreed on Steve Zahn together. McConaughey wrote Zahn a letter telling him about the film before the script was sent to him. Zahn enjoyed what he read and jumped on-board. Suffice it to say McConaughey was hands-on.

Dirk Pitt's main aim in life is to search for treasures and go on adventures. He's from a privileged background – his dad was a Senator – but he has his own agenda in life. He's got the knowledge, stamina and energy, as well as the training and history to hunt for lost treasures. Pitt always has a plan but the fun part for the audience (or readers of the books) is that the plan doesn't always go smoothly and so he becomes an action hero. He manages to get himself out of trouble by winging it, even though he is trained and skilled. McConaughey loved the character and thought he was a great hero for the modern day. 'Sometimes he's a scientist, sometimes he's an inventor, sometimes he's an adventurer,' McConaughey told *Cinema.com* of Dirk Pitt. 'He's a guy who's got plans, but those plans are always changing; he's ready for the unexpected. He's a great adapter. He's been a Navy SEAL, but he's also part pirate. He's definitely a lover before a fighter, but if he's got to fight, he handles his own.'

The film provided McConaughey with a chance to travel. Africa was one of the most stunning places he'd ever been to and he loved filming there. He'd already been to Mali – where the story takes place – twice on his own so it was a fantastic opportunity to go there for a third time. He adored the country, culture and people. He was taken aback by the history of the people and how they respect their ancestors. They have a simple way of life, which McConaughey found interesting. They don't make plans for the future but live day by day and it's something McConaughey appreciated.

The cast and crew had to respect the local tribes, their culture and way of life. This prompted McConaughey to do some research prior to filming. Their languages and how they lived intrigued him. He learned what some of the hand gestures meant and what the protocols of the villages are. He saw how they don't waste anything and use chicken, rice and spices. As a result of the villagers' hospitality, he took over some western goods such as aspirin and fungus cream to repay them.

Sahara is very much a buddy movie between McConaughey and Zahn. Their chemistry is not as obvious and their relationship is not as entertaining as that of Mel Gibson and Danny Glover in the *Lethal Weapon* movies, but it works for this sort of film. On the one hand you've got McConaughey's smooth southern charm, and on the other you've got Zahn's screwball slapstick comedy which bounce off each other well in a film with so many gun-toting action scenes and foreign locations.

McConaughey and Zahn had to undergo great physical endurance for their respective roles. Much of McConaughey's training, for example, included mountain climbing and hiking on location in Africa, and aside from that, during pre-production in LA, he did a lot of boxing, rock climbing and weightlifting. He saw it not only as a physical but also spiritual transformation. Zahn learned how to throw some flashy moves with hand weapons, slinging guns as though he was in a western.

Production was hit by a couple of storms so they had to shut down filming temporarily. It was something the locals warned them about. They decided to shoot through the sand storms and the locust storms just to see what happened. It's a struggle against Mother Nature in the Sahara Desert and they felt they were at her mercy, but they soldiered on and completed filming. There was also the scorching heat and insect infestations to contend with.

McConaughey spoke to *Hollywood.com* about Penélope Cruz's experience riding a camel: 'She got to be very good on her camel but saved it all for the take. She was lagging behind Steve [Zahn] and I but when we starting rolling film, she flew by us. This kind of movie is not for everybody, man or woman, especially going in as a woman in a big action adventure with the guys. But she dove in, she wanted to do that and she did.'

Released in April 2005, the film's box office receipts barely accounted for half of its overall expenses. It grossed $160 million in production costs and a further $81.1 million in distribution expenses. The film grossed $122 million in box office sales but it lost around $105 million overall. It was expected to make $202.09 million with an overall expense of $281.2. Such was the perceived box office failure of the film, that proposed ideas for an *Indiana Jones* or *James Bond* style franchise based on further Dirk Pitt adventures were scrapped.

'I thought the movie was close to what we were shooting for,' he reflected to *Chud*'s Devin Faraci in 2006. 'I was overall happy with the film. I thought it was a lot of fun, I thought it knew what it was, I thought the film never tried to be what it wasn't. Our plan, our hopes, was to make a franchise of them – that's why I got involved, because I wanted to come back as Dirk Pitt. There are a bunch of books. We didn't quite make the money that we had hoped to greenlight another film. It's doing great on DVD, and that might give us a chance to do another one. It did wonderfully international and it's doing great on DVD. You know how much money you can make on DVD these days.'

Such a franchise would have potentially been great for McConaughey's career, especially after a series of so-so films. McConaughey's career was hardly going smoothly, not for a man of his talents. The roles were not challenging enough. It seems as though the critical acclaim that had greeted him in the 1990s was a thing of the past, and any notion of becoming the next Tom Cruise – a talented good-looking actor with massive global box office appeal – was not going to happen; certainly not with films such as *Sahara* and risible nonsense like *The Wedding Planner* – not forgetting such howlers as *Tiptoes*. He desperately needed to reinvent himself if he was going to be taken seriously or if he was going to remain a legitimate bankable A-list Hollywood movie star. He could have become a household name, but with too many failures and distinctly average films, at least as far as box office receipts were concerned, his commercial appeal was slipping. However, for every perceived failure like *Sahara*, there was a little gem of a film like *Frailty*, and it was those small productions that kept him on the favourable side of the critics when his commercial films were often so badly received, especially as the rom-com genre had become very stale and predictable. McConaughey was simply a better actor than many of the films he was starring in.

Sahara was used by the *Los Angeles Times* in a special report on 15 April 2007 as an example of how Hollywood films can cost so much yet recoup barely half of their expenses. The film was involved in a multi-million dollar legal wrangle between author Clive Cussler and producer Philip Anschutz and some of the documents pertaining to the film's finances were made public.

McConaughey promoted its upcoming release by repeating trips he took in the late 1990s, such as sailing down the Amazon River or trekking to Mali. He drove his own Airstream trailer, which had a huge *Sahara* film poster on each side, across America, where he stopped at five military bases and several colleges.

McConaughey came up with the idea of using his Airstream for promoting the film when his production company partner said they should maximise the film campaign by going out on the open road. McConaughey loved the idea. 'We talked about it for a few minutes and then that night I woke up at three in the morning with a vision of the Airstream being wrapped in a billboard,' he admitted to *Crazed Fanboy*'s Michael A. Smith. 'So the next morning I called Paramount and said, "Hey, I've got an idea." I told them about the Airstream and they laughed. So I called them back the next day and reminded them that I was serious. So we got that done and they started working with me on that.'

The first stop on the journey was Daytona 500 where he marshalled the race. He had just six weeks so Canada and

Mexico were out of the question. From Daytona he ventured to Orlando, and then on to Macon, Georgia, Atlanta, New Jersey, New York, Detroit, Chicago, Kansas City, Denver, and finally to LA for the film's premiere, where he got out of the camper and walked the red carpet in front of the glare of the world's paparazzi and entertainment journalists. He totalled 6,000 miles! It was not the first time he'd done a road trip in his Airstream. The year before he'd driven from LA to Florida and back through Kansas City and Colorado in a forty-day venture. It was just him and his dog, alone and on a solo road jaunt.

Matthew attended premieres of the film, signed autographs for fans and did interviews at each stop: 3,000 hats and more than 4,000 T-shirts were handed out to fans at truck stops and cafes. It was a huge, heavily hyped publicity blitz.

'It's a little more organic, you know?' he said to *Empire* about the whole experience. 'I'm seeing new places, new faces, new parts of the land. It's been fun. I've just got out of a theatre and the film went down real well. We talked to a lot of college students, to a lot of people in the services who've just got back from Iraq. A lot of the guys missing their arms, their legs, on crutches. It was a pretty eye-opening experience.'

There was an *E!* channel special on the film release, too, and while all this was going on, McConaughey kept a blog of his trip on MTV's entertainment website. Viacom owns both Paramount, the film's distributor, and MTV.

Despite the perceived failure of the film, McConaughey was nominated for two Teen Choice Awards: 'Choice Movie Actor: Action/Adventure/Thriller' and 'Choice Movie Liplock' (with his co-star Cruz). McConaughey also made the celebrity headlines that year. 'I like the "Alive" part,' said McConaughey, then thirty-six, to *People* on being crowned their '20th Sexiest Man Alive'. 'Now I've made it. Wait until you see the roles I could take after this. You're going to see my gut hanging over, plus 22 (lbs.). It'll be a whole new kind of sexy!'

Kay, his mother, joked that it was about damn time when he'd called to tell her the news. 'Not much has changed, man,' he also said to J.P. Mangalindan of *The Cinema Source* in reaction to the poll. 'It's been fun, to be fair; it's funny too. When they called me, I laughed, and when I called my mom, she said, "It's about damned time!"'

Sahara doesn't mess about – as soon as the characters are introduced it gets straight into the action, which makes it appealing to young people. McConaughey enjoyed playing Dirk Pitt and spoke about returning to the character, but it's unlikely that will ever happen. 'The film knows what it is,' he explained to *Hollywood.com*, 'has a real definite personality to it. Sets up the rules in the first act with a wink. And then never really breaks them, so in that way it remains a classy action adventure. Doesn't take itself too seriously, got some killer action sequences.'

Sahara opened in the US and UK in April 2005. It received mixed reviews from film journalists and, suffice it to say, fans of the novels were not too pleased with the end result. The film provided another opportunity for McConaughey to show off his body, for which he was mocked. But in his eyes, if you've got it, flaunt it.

Stephen Holden wrote in *The New York Times*: '*Sahara* may be the ultimate test of Matthew McConaughey's still-unrealised potential to enter Hollywood's magic circle. If this movie can't propel the 35-year-old Texan actor into Harrison Ford's $20 million trekking boots, nothing can, and the longstanding heir apparent will never be king. His character, Dirk Pitt, an unflappably game treasure hunter obsessed with finding a Confederate ironclad ship that disappeared at the end of the Civil War and may have landed in Africa, epitomises Rhett Butler Lite. Twinkling and sinewy, his rakish insolence accented by a moustache, Mr. McConaughey's Dirk is the Flower of Southern Manhood, Texan-style, a fearless all-American pirate with a keen sense of humour and a social conscience.'

Empire's Dan Jolin wrote: 'At the eye of this silly, swirling desert storm is the winning buddy act of McConaughey's Dirk and Steve Zahn's Al Giordino. Buff, browned, with a blinding ivory grin and twinkly baby-greens, McConaughey fills out Pitt's grubby khakis perfectly. Here's a guy you believe can have a solution to every life-threatening problem, who matches brawn with brains and who rarely breaks a sweat, even when the bullets are flying.'

Total Film said: 'If the new plan is to dim down the star dazzle and focus on the action, then it's worked. Matthew McConaughey has coasted for too long now, and, perma-tanned and pearly toothed, he wholeheartedly dives in to Dirk Pitt, swiping Indy's raffish swagger but also factoring in bits of Bond, Brucie and even, briefly, *The Life Aquatic's* Steve Zissou. Whether the character is universal enough to sustain a series remains to be seen, but McConaughey's work is certainly done.'

The documentary, *Magnificent Desolation: Walking on the Moon 3D,* opened in US cinemas in September 2005. McConaughey was one of the voiceover narrators along with an ensemble cast featuring Matt Damon, Paul Newman, John Travolta, Morgan Freeman and *Breaking Bad* star Bryan Cranston. Tom Hanks is the main narrator and co-wrote and produced the documentary, which includes NASA footage and re-enactments, plus CGI about the first people on the Moon as part of the Apollo program. Mark Cowen directed it, and though it is only forty minutes in length, it received positive reviews. Maggie McKee wrote in the *New Scientist*: 'Though some such scenes are overly sentimental, the movie leaves viewers with the sense that they have experienced the Moon first-hand – and raises questions about how difficult a return to the desolate landscape may be.'

McConaughey was then cast as a gambling protégé to Al Pacino's gambling mogul in *Two for the Money*, which opened in the US in October 2005 and in the UK in March 2006. Directed by D.J. Caruso and set in the world of sports gambling, McConaughey plays Brandon Lang, a former college football star who takes up handicapping football games after his career ends due to an injury. He is so successful at it that he comes to the attention of Walter Abrams, played by Pacino, who runs one of the biggest sports consulting operations in America, and the pair begin to make huge sums of cash.

McConaughey was asked by *MovieWeb*'s Evan 'Mushy' Jacobs if he saw parallels between his character's rise and fall and that of the Hollywood lifestyle. 'What I saw was a guy who was a winner and all of the sudden starts losing,' he responded. 'That's where the drama was for this character for me. What do you do if you're a winner? Not that you think you can win, you are a winner. And you all of the sudden are not winning. What do you do? You go back to the world where it all made sense when you were winning. And all of the sudden you find out that that world wasn't real. That was all an illusion. Uh-oh, you go to people that have kind of become your family, and you find out that that rug has kind of been pulled out from under you, too.

To top that off, you don't only need to win to get somebody's money back, you need to win to survive and help your family survive, because some of the people that lost the money took it real personal, and went to make threats on your family.'

McConaughey thought it was a terrific story about a winner who starts losing. If you're a winner or have a consistent streak of winning things and then start losing, how do you change that? How do you start winning again and return to good fortunes? McConaughey saw great potential in his role when he first read the script. His character, Lang, finds out that the gambling world is an illusion and that everything is not as it seems. When Lang discovers this, and finds out that his relationships are also not what they seem, he decides he wants out as he realises there's more than just money to lose. McConaughey saw it as a survival story. McConaughey was attracted to the dramatic side of the tale in that his character loved football and excelled at it, but lost the ability to play again, which happens every day in some form another, so his character looked to other things that he was good at, one of which was picking the winner. He gets offered money by people to gamble, but the world he enters is not what it seems and it tries to corrupt him. It's not the gambling that changes him, nor his winnings, but rather the people who enter his life. McConaughey was drawn into the realism of the film.

McConaughey appreciated that his character was the one person in the story who was not addicted to anything and that's where much of the film's drama comes from. He's sucked into a world filled with addicts; people who cannot control their gambling. It's a business where people get addicted, rich or poor, and Lang is drawn to it. McConaughey didn't think gambling corrupted Lang; he's a winner and was good at what he was doing until he had a losing streak. McConaughey wanted to root for his character; he wanted Lang to keep on winning. Lang is not cheating, lying or stealing and McConaughey admired that. Sure, Lang has slicked back hair and talks a little faster than most people but Lang is a winner and McConaughey saw Lang as someone more than black and white. Winners, and indeed losers, go through role reversals when their fortunes change but it doesn't make them corrupt.

With varying credits to his name, McConaughey hadn't been in a drama like this for a while, so when it came across his desk he jumped at the chance to switch from light-hearted comedies to a meaty drama. The other side of *Two for the Money* that appealed to McConaughey was that he too enjoys sports and competition. Romantic comedies are designed for escapism but dramas depict real life, and McConaughey wanted to try his hand at something serious.

'He was so dedicated,' Rene Russo enthused to Rebecca Murray of *About.com: Hollywood Movies* about working with McConaughey. 'It was unbelievable. He was so serious about this part. During rehearsals he would ask questions, he was just so into it. It's wild working with him. You get the feeling that he's like really in the film. The character has taken him over. That's how much he's in it. It was fascinating to watch. You always learn something from everybody, but he was just like "Whoa!"'

Part of McConaughey's responsibility for the role was getting in shape. The Texan was portraying a quarterback and the one thing he hates about sports movies is seeing actors play sports people who don't have the right physique for the part, so McConaughey was dedicated to making himself look like a quarterback. There is a leadership mentality to playing a sportsman. McConaughey enjoyed the physical and mental training that came with the role of Brandon Lang. In fact, McConaughey spent some time with the man who inspired the part; the real-life Brandon Lang. He listened to him and learned from his experiences. McConaughey tried to pick up on lines and listen to the way he spoke. He gained first-hand knowledge about the gambling industry and touting services and learned a few secrets. McConaughey saw his character not as a gambler but as a winner.

McConaughey, speaking to *MovieWeb*'s Evan 'Mushy' Jacobs, said: 'I also did a lot of my own homework. Whether it was the football stuff, the actual playing of it, or calling a lot of these services on my own. And hearing different sales pitches, and types and Brandon's... there's all different kinds of ways you do want to hear that certainty, in that uncertain world. And that's one of the lines in about the whole racket, yeah know [sic]? If the phone is ringing, that person on the other end of the line is looking for direction. So you're already there. There's some great stuff in the movie about, "the person's already calling, TELL them what to do." As for what Brandon's pitch would be? Don't be the sell, sell, sell guy. He just says, "Hey man, I'm gonna tell you the truth. Here's what I know because I've played the game. I love the game. Now also, as well, both are true, if you want to make some money call the number at the bottom of the screen, let's do it." He didn't see it as an act.'

In some respects McConaughey – as with any other actor – is a gambler. Every film he makes is a gamble. Will it be a success? Or will he lose and struggle to get another part? He bets on himself in that sense, so he is more in control of winning. When he plays a game of golf he bets with his brothers, but he'll bet on himself too, so if he misses the shot the only person he'll be bugged at is himself. By betting on himself it makes betting very simple which is the way he prefers it. He's always been in a position where he's had money that he can't afford to lose, so if he slips up he can't pay the rent or his bills. That's a type of lifestyle he has always been drawn to.

There's an emotional scene in the film where Pacino's character fakes a heart attack. It was at a time in the story when Lang cares about Abrams. McConaughey, much like his character, doesn't play games with people; especially with those you're supposed to care about. You don't play with God and you don't tempt fate. McConaughey has a strict personal philosophy on that. He has a moral compass that he abides by. His character also doesn't like playing around with life and death. It took McConaughey back to his childhood when his parents told him that lying will bite you in the ass one day.

McConaughey was in awe of Al Pacino, one of the greatest American actors alive, with a string of critically acclaimed movies to his name such as *The Godfather*, *Serpico*, *Scent of a Woman* and *Heat*. McConaughey told Evan 'Mushy' Jacobs of *MovieWeb*: 'It's like dancing, man. Dancing with a great partner. It's fun. It's free. It's unexpected at all times. He gets on waves and he rides them all the way, sometimes they land in a perfect spot. Sometimes they don't but he rides it. Every time. That's one of the things I loved watching from the side. And also working with him, you give him something and you catch a wave. You don't know where it's going but while you're doing it you're not trying to stay ahead. And if you hit it, then you kind of have that feeling afterwards like, "Okay, I don't know what that was but it worked."'

It was a forty-three-day shoot, which was ideal for

McConaughey. On some of the bigger films he's starred in there's been an awful lot of preparation time which can get very tiring, and there's a lot of sitting around in between scenes with little to do. A tighter shoot, on the other hand, means there is more focus and time is more precious. There's no time to hang around and think too deeply about a shot or sit back and talk about a scene. You show up, discuss the scene with the director and get in front of the camera and act. The actors showed up on set in the morning and worked for twelve-hour days throughout the shoot. It was hard work but it was a learning curve for all involved.

Two for the Money worked for McConaughey; from the pre-production to getting the cast grouped together to the shoot and into post-production. He also liked the director and the crew and thought there was a strong unity between all concerned. It had an independent feel to it where everyone got down to work and did their best to make a good film. The director gave his cast room to offer ideas and to see how the characters fitted in to the story before constructing the shots and setting up the cameras on set. There was vitality to the film, which McConaughey admired.

'I think in a lot of ways it can encourage more and even better creativity because time is precious but you can't be precious,' McConaughey explained to Beth Accomando of *KPBS* on how constraints enrich creativity. 'So sometimes the sun's going down you have to combine two shots. Sometimes you have a scene and you don't have time to shoot that scene. So how can we get across what we want in that next scene in this scene and get what we wanted in this scene, let's combine them. You are always forced to compress, maybe you're going from A to B to C to D, well how do you skip B – can you go from A to C? Or can we pick up B along the way and take it with us into C. You have to think about how to streamline it while still tell your story.'

The entertainment board Bodog sponsored the world premiere of the film, which was held in Beverly Hills on 26 September. The reviews and box office performance of the film were poor, however. McConaughey's career at the box office was not going so well.

Simon Braund wrote in *Empire*: 'Before you can say 'mentor-protégé-surrogate-dad-dynamic', Brandon (rechristened John Anthony by Walter because "Brandon lives at home with his mommy!") hits a losing streak as disastrous as it is predictable, and the film careens across the border between mere silliness and outright "what-the?" absurdity with a flash of its arse to the customs officer.'

The A.V. Club's Scott Tobias wrote: 'Inevitably, the personal complications that infect Pacino and McConaughey's relationship coincide with a losing streak that's every bit as profound as the 80-per-cent record that brought them to glory. McConaughey's side of the story brims with gambling-movie clichés about the vacancies that his short-term victories create as the moral decay sets in; he's even given two separate personas, one the drawling, unpretentious quarterback from the sticks, and the other a fatuous, Benz-rolling city slicker named "John Anthony."'

Although the reviews of *Two for the Money* were poor, the film picked up a cult fan base on DVD and fans occasionally chatted to McConaughey about it. The DVD is huge business with many fans getting introduced to movies via DVDs rather than the cinema, which is the more traditional route. For many people watching a DVD is far easier and more convenient than going to the cinema. A trip to the cinema is a social event – dating, family and friends socialising and so on, but some people just prefer to stay at home; plus it is cheaper. The idea of watching a film with two hundred other people just doesn't appeal to everyone, so the DVD and pay-per-view and online markets have become a huge source of revenue for film studios.

McConaughey is fond of the film despite its lukewarm reception. He was trying to stay loyal to the big Hollywood studios with films such as *Reign of Fire* but venturing towards smaller dramas that meant more to him on a personal level. There was no set pattern to his career. He picked projects that he found interesting; the story and the characters had to appeal to him. Even though it would take time for critics and audiences to fully recognise his talents as a character actor, McConaughey could plausibly jump from a romantic comedy to a period drama to a military film. He had learned how to deal with fame and not allow it to take over his life. Some actors let it swallow them up and as a consequence enter a world of drugs, drink and other substances. McConaughey was at peace with himself and his career. His celebrity status was not that of megastars such as Tom Cruise or Leonardo DiCaprio, but he attracted a fair share of entertainment and gossip journalists and photographers who were interested in his latest squeeze or what fashion labels he was wearing. As far as mainstream audiences went, his career was going through a tumultuous period, which lacked focus and confidence. He was about to star in one of the worst films of his career, yet another rom-com, with a top-named TV actress after having appeared in a film – albeit not a very good one – with one of cinema's greatest actors in Al Pacino.

McConaughey wasn't simply making one film such as *Two for*

the Money for his male fans and then a romantic comedy for his female followers. He's drawn to films because of the characters and the story rather than the genre, though a successful film like *How to Lose a Guy in 10 Days* allowed him to make smaller dramas. He spent much of the decade moving between the glossy Hollywood romances to the smaller almost independent-type dramas.

There is usually a formula to the romantic comedy: a couple gets together, breaks up and gets together again before the closing credits. Some films see the male protagonist begging on all fours to get back with the woman, but McConaughey never bought into that so in his rom-coms he tries to be a man's man. He's less interested in a film that's about the battle of the sexes and more interested in one where the sexes are balanced. McConaughey tried to make his character not an outright deadbeat; he has sympathetic and empathic traits. He realises he messed up and tries to make amends but not by begging; it's through choice, not desperation, that he chases after the woman. McConaughey's view is that balancing the roles between the man and the women opens up the film to a male audience because the men can relate to the male protagonist.

By their very nature, romantic comedies are films that make a lot of money for the studios because they are accessible. Guys take their girls on dates, mothers take their daughters, and girlfriends go together and so on. Also, compared to action movies they're a lot less expensive to make, yet the returns can be very high so they're not as risky as other genres.

In 2006 Matthew co-starred with Sarah Jessica Parker in the rom-com *Failure to Launch*, which opened in the UK and US in March. A romantic comedy, McConaughey plays a thirty-five-year-old man named Tripp who still lives with his parents Al (Terry Bradshaw) and Sue (Kathy Bates) in New Orleans. Even his best friends, Demo (Bradley Cooper) and Ace (Justin Bartha), live with their parents, so he's not too bothered. However, Tripp suspects his parents of setting him up with his dream girl Paula (Sarah Jessica Parker) so he'll finally have to leave home. Paula is actually an expert hired by his parents to find out why he won't leave home, and he ends up falling in love with her.

'It's a good romance and it's got a lot of heart to it,' McConaughey said to *Empire*. 'I think SJP has great comedic timing. I think she's got a real freshness and buoyancy. And she's extremely cute. Kind of great sense of effervescence that's nice about her.'

For the role of Tripp, McConaughey had lost some of the weight and muscle mass he'd gained for *Two for the Money* by doing lots of running and Frisbee throwing.

McConaughey thoroughly enjoyed the script when he first read it. It made him laugh out loud, not something he normally does. He felt there was more comedy in it than in other rom-coms. The film is not solely based on the male-female relationship; he liked the idea that his character has a problem but doesn't think he does. Because of the loss of his fiancée in the past, Tripp struggles to move forward in life. His mum cooks for him and folds his clothes; his life is generally that of a teenager's in many respects. There are still plenty of gimmicks and comedic scenes to keep the audience engaged in McConaughey's character though.

McConaughey liked that Tripp wasn't turned into a slacker and a bad son because he lives at home. Tripp is a good son, a good friend and a good employee. It plays into the recent phenomenon that is happening with adults who stay with their parents because of financial pressures or failed relationships. It happens with both men and women. In some cultures people don't leave their parents' house until they're married. It often boils down to economics: some adults can't afford to leave home and some are forced to move back because their general expenses and costs of living are too high.

'The main thing I could understand is that he's got a great relationship with his parents,' McConaughey explained to *Chud*'s Devin Faraci his opinion of his character: 'He had a great relationship with his friends. He's a good friend to them and a good son. He loves women. One of the things why that was important and cool to me is that it would have been very easy to make the story that his parents want him out of the house because he's a pain in the butt; but he's not. They like him there, and he likes being there.'

One of the elements of the story that McConaughey liked about the script was that Tripp had never gotten over his true love. He had a woman who left him yet he still has love for her in his heart. Tripp hadn't gone out and purposefully met a woman because he still had love for his ex. He's a dignified guy, but he's troubled. His parents want him to evolve and to open up his heart by sharing it with someone else. He needs to move on with his life and his parents allow that to happen. It's not a heavy drama, and although it does try to tackle weighty issues that are relevant to many adults, it does so with humour.

Tripp thinks he's got his situation under control but it turns out to be something that it isn't and that's where the comedy comes from. McConaughey understood that as soon as he'd read the script and knew how to handle his character. Also, like his character, McConaughey enjoys keeping his relationships in the fun zone. His view is that life is hard and you face many challenges on a daily basis and so a relationship with someone should be all about having fun together and, if it's with the right person, looking forward to building a future together. At this time he was dating Penélope Cruz. They'd been together for almost two years and were still enjoying being with each other. They knew each other's likes and dislikes and how to make each other laugh. They'd also learned how to deal with the physical distance if they were both working on separate projects in different parts of the country or the world at the same time.

One aspect of making a romantic comedy that McConaughey found challenging in some ways was keeping it buoyant. He wants to make it light. Acting as though you are in a heavy drama doesn't work in this sort of genre so McConaughey learned to skim across the surface. In some respects he felt it had a similar vibe to *How to Lose a Guy in 10 Days*, another film he enjoyed making.

'You know what surprised me is he writes a lot,' Parker said to Rebecca Murray of *About.com: Hollywood Movies* about McConaughey. 'I didn't know he was a writer. He writes a lot. He really works on the script a lot. He really thinks about it. He breaks it down. I guess what was surprising is that he was really into talking about it and working on it, and taking it apart and putting it back together. I probably would have – if you'd given me truth serum before the rehearsal process – probably thought it comes pretty easy to him, which it does at the same time. And he probably gets a script, you know, but no, he was much more interested in fixing and doing things to it that he felt were important for the story.'

The sailing scene in the film was fun to shoot. McConaughey went sailing before filming so he could get used to it. He's very active and energetic and loves the outdoors. He's not a great sailor, though, but his character thinks he is so that was fun to play. His co-star in the film found that he liked to be in charge, that he has sort of traditional ideas about that.

Parker had made a return to the big screen with the film, after becoming a household name with the hit TV series *Sex and the City*. McConaughey admitted he had a crush on her in the series and the cult film *Honeymoon in Vegas,* but sadly for him she's been with actor Matthew Broderick for years. 'He has a sort of easy, breezy quality about him,' she said of McConaughey to *The Cinema Source*'s J.P. Mangalindan. 'He's very engaging and very effective on camera. It's quite easy to flirt with him. Let's just put it like this: it doesn't take a lot of effort for him to do what he does.'

A trashy, throwaway film, *Failure to Launch* received poor reviews and grossed over $90 million worldwide with a $50 million budget. McConaughey's career wasn't going so well after the commercial failures of *Sahara* and *Two for the Money,* and now *Failure to Launch*. This once promising young good-looking actor with box office appeal was in dire need of a hit film.

The New York Times' Stephen Holden wrote: 'The director Tom Dey obviously cherishes 30s comedies, and he confidently guides a screenplay (by Tom J. Astle and Matt Ember) that has some of the sass and bite of those oldies through the screwball rapids. It's all about tone. And until the movie succumbs to sugar shock at the end, it remains brisk and tart. Mr. McConaughey and Ms. Parker (in a role not far removed from Carrie Bradshaw) make well-matched sparring partners.'

Entertainment Weekly's Lisa Schwarzbaum wrote: 'If, for example, you like McConaughey's affect of sexy, sleepy-eyed drawl – is he toasted, or just a sun-kissed Texan? – then you are meant to like Tripp, even though screenwriters Tom J. Astle and sitcom-savvy Matt Ember abandon all hope of squaring the childish, spoiled-by-Mom slacker that Tripp appears to be pre-Paula with the far more competent, complicated, and sensitive thirtysomething adult he proves himself to be later on. This character is a bundle of What-If-We-Made-Hims who dribbles away his leisure with similarly unattached goofball pals, yet also takes seriously his responsibilities to a jaunty African-American boy he calls his nephew. And little black kids don't appear for nothing in a white creampuff comedy like this.'

Total Film said: '*Failure to Launch* is a sometimes jarring mixture of Farrelly brothers-style slapstick, amusing musings on what it means to grow up and schmaltzy relationship patter. Parker aces in a role seemingly written for Jennifer Aniston, but McConaughey, alas, has the sexual charisma of a battered cod.'

How does McConaughey react to negative feedback?

'There are good bad reviews and there are bad bad reviews,' he explained to *The Tech's* Alison C. Lewis. 'The good ones are very critical, very constructive. The [writers of the] bad ones don't have critical right. They just like to hear themselves talk. They were just having a bad day.'

McConaughey was dating Penélope Cruz, the stunning Spanish actress and model he'd met when filming *Sahara*. 'There's a bit of a language barrier, but it's like poetry when it happens,' he admitted to *Details'* Bart Blasengame. 'What I really love about her is that she sees everything for the first time, every time. And she's one of the best listeners I've ever met. She's not a right-and-wronger.'

They'd gone to Mexico together after filming *Failure to Launch*. McConaughey relaxed there. He ran each day, took the dogs for walks, swam, sat on the beach and read, went out for dinner and had dances and massages and generally enjoyed himself with his on-off girlfriend. McConaughey spoke to *Metro* about Cruz's opinion of McConaughey's less than glamorous Airstream. 'She likes it. It's not very hi-tech but it has got running water – if I have a place to hook up – and a stove you can cook on or you just build a fire. It has everything you need. It's very relaxing and highly luxurious – if you want a new front yard every morning, or a new view over a river or over a new ocean, you can get it.'

Questions came up in the press as to how serious the relationship was. Would they live together? McConaughey has admitted he wouldn't be the easiest guy to live with. Travelling is his favourite thing to do and in many respects he is a very adaptable guy. He tries to stay in every place he visits long enough to absorb the culture and way of life of the residents. He loves Spain, Cruz's native country, and even mentioned living there.

Though he has dated many beautiful women, his life was very much that of a bachelor's. He lived alone, ran his own business and often worked out and travelled alone. The paparazzi usually snapped pictures of him running on a beach with his shirt off, or working out by Venice beach or somewhere equally beautiful in Southern California. His love of the great outdoors – either outdoor pursuits such as hiking or working out as opposed to exercising in the gym – and working out goes back to his childhood when Kay, his mother, wouldn't let him stay indoors during daylight hours. 'It's always been a lifestyle,' he said to *Men's Fitness* writer Joe Warner. 'Then it became something that was like, "Hey, it's also good for my job." I'm not a professional athlete, but I have a job where I prefer to look good and be as healthy as possible.'

In the 1990s he tried his hand at thrillers, action, science-fiction and dramas; mostly serious films that were cold, but when he did *The Wedding Planner*, which is something light and fluffy, he realised he could make a whole lot of money. He got famous over the weekend after *A Time to Kill* and then he starred in films that he wanted to do because the director and the story meant something to him. The rom-coms didn't mean anything to him as such; they just made him very rich and raised his profile. The studios offered him fewer dramas as a consequence, and films such as *The Newton Boys* and *Two for the Money* didn't make much in box office receipts or see the studios come to him, but they were fun to make.

McConaughey then went on to star as Marshall head football coach Jack Lengyel in the film *We Are Marshall*, which opened in US cinemas in December 2006 and went straight to DVD in most foreign countries. Directed by *Charlie's Angels* director McG, *We Are Marshall* sees former *Party of Five* actor Matthew Fox as assistant coach William 'Red' Dawson as the pair try to rebuild the Marshall University Thundering Herd football team after the 1970 plane crash that killed thirty-seven football players, five coaches, two athletic figures, the athletic director, twenty-five boosters and the five members of the airplane crew. There were no survivors aboard the McDonnell Douglas DC-9 that transported the team to Greenville, North Carolina, via Stallings Field in Kinston, North Carolina.

It is the story of the year after the accident when the town was divided between those who wanted to drop the program and go out gracefully and those who wanted to fight and carry it on. It wasn't about winning but about keeping the spirit alive in honour of those who lost their lives. McConaughey was more than pleased to be part of the drama given the nature of the story and his love of sports. It was an interesting role for him to play, being a coach rather than a player given his obvious athleticism. He was thirty-seven when he made the film and in fantastic shape.

It's an outsider's film and as such they wanted to do two things: make it as honourable as possible so as not to upset the relatives and local townsfolk and to bring the story to those who did not know about it. McConaughey plays the outsider who was able to be part of the healing process and manage a tough job at the same time. His agenda was never to heal the town but to do his job, which was coaching.

'A lot of it for me with Jack was the rhythm of his speech,' said McConaughey to Andrea Tuccillo of *The Cinema Source*. 'That's where it started for me as far as from the outside in. Also, people in general sort of have three walks. You've got the pelvis walk, the heart walk, or the head walk. And Lengyel was a head first guy, he always led with his chin. So I think that just worked into a sort of physicality that allowed a conduit for me to understand him and also give my portrayal of the guy.'

Filming began in Huntington, West Virginia on 3 April and was completed a few months later in Atlanta, Georgia. It's a tragic story and they wanted to tell it as truthfully as possible, which is why they chose to film it in the same West Virginian town where the actual events occurred. Naturally it brought a lot of scepticism from the locals. The tragedy happened thirty-five years before the film was made, but because it was such a major catastrophe it was still fresh in peoples' minds. A couple of weeks into filming and the locals started to visit the set and were shown script pages by the crew to see how scenes were being shot. The crew wanted the locals to see they were doing the story justice.

'I got knocked on my butt the first day of filming. We had the kids do a drill, and I went to give one a chuck and I landed flat on my keister,' McConaughey admitted to *People* magazine's Natasha Stoynoff.

The film premiered at the Keith Albee Theatre in Huntington on 12 December 2006 and special commemorative screenings were held at Pullman Square. The film caused controversy because aspects of the storyline were changed for dramatic purposes, which is typical of Hollywood when dealing with real life events as previously seen with *U-571*. The producers, Deborah Novak and John Witek, of the 2000 documentary *Marshall University: Ashes to Glory* filed a $40 million lawsuit against Warner Bros. and others associated with the film citing fraud, copyright infringement and breach of contract. The case was dismissed in October 2008.

'From my experience, in a true story there's obviously a blueprint,' McConaughey explained to Andrea Tuccillo of *The Cinema Source*. 'So you have a certain responsibility. Not necessarily to go out and imitate what happened but to emulate what happened and to recognize that you're bringing it down to two hours of celluloid.'

The film was not a box office hit (its budget was $65 million but it grossed little more than $40 million) but McConaughey's performance won acclaim from critics who marked it as the film's highlight. After the risible *Failure to Launch*, McConaughey had (sort of) saved his credentials with this excellent albeit sadly forgotten little drama.

Roger Moore from the *Orlando Sentinel* gave it four stars out of five and said in his review that '*We Are Marshall* (it's the rally cry of the team) doesn't always have a handle on the grief, but it does keep emotions close to the surface. That allows McConaughey to be the most refreshing, funny and believable he ever has been.'

Frank Lovece of *Film Journal International* said: 'Leaving aside Matthew McConaughey's quirky performance as replacement coach Jack Lengyel – which actually does grow on you – yes. Very much so. Despite what qualms one might have had about pretentiously named ex-music-video director McG (a.k.a. Joseph McGinty Nichol of Kalamazoo, Michigan), whose only previous features are the two blustery *Charlie's Angels* movies, the guy clearly has enough human empathy and experience that his film conveys real emotion and not schmaltz.'

Empire's Helen O'Hara said: 'It tries hard to tug the heartstrings, but between McConaughey's eccentric mugging, director McG's uninspired helming and endless scenes of people coping with unbearable tragedy, it doesn't succeed.'

Still, despite the poor box office performance McConaughey was proud to be part of the film. 'I'd do movies like *Marshall* and *Two for the Money* that might look more like meter readers, and, as far as my stock in Hollywood, someone would go, "He's got a [price] quote for a romantic-comedy, but he don't get that quote for [dramas]. You want to do that movie, you've got to take a pay cut for us to take a chance."'

That same year he provided voiceover work in an ad campaign for the Peace Corps and on 21 January 2008 McConaughey became the new spokesman for the national radio campaign 'Beef: It's What's For Dinner' replacing actor Sam Elliot. The biggest piece of news came in January when he announced via his blog, 'My girlfriend Camila [Alves] and I made a baby together...its 3 months growin in her womb and all looks healthy...we are stoked and wowed.'

As if *The Wedding Planner*, *How to Lose a Guy in 10 Days* and *Failure to Launch* were not embarrassing enough, McConaughey was cast as Benjamin 'Finn' Finnegan in *Fool's Gold*. He is a treasure hunter on a quest to find treasure from a Spanish galleon called the Aurelia that was lost at sea with the 1715 Treasure Fleet. His wife Tess (played by Kate Hudson, his *How to Lose a Guy in 10 Days* co-star) divorces him and finds a job as a steward on board an expensive yacht owned by multi-millionaire Nigel Honeycutt, played by Donald Sutherland. Finn's coordinates take him to the yacht, *The Precious Gem*, and he convinces Honeycutt, his daughter, Gemma, and Tess, to help him find the treasure which ultimately helps Tess and Finn rekindle their estranged relationship. Along the way they meet gangsters Bigg Bunny (Kevin Hart) and Moe Fitch (Ray Winstone) who are also after the treasure.

McConaughey and Hudson had a fantastic rapport on set, often joking with each other and having fun on the Australian beaches. They had wanted to work together again and a few opportunities had come up, but *Fool's Gold* felt like the perfect project for a second collaboration between the two big screen actors. McConaughey knew there'd be people out there who wanted to see them pair up on screen for a second time and *Fool's Gold* was not only perfect for the script but also the exotic locations. The pair felt it was an extension of *How to Lose a Guy in 10 Days*, yet at the same time it was a different story with two different characters.

McConaughey spoke to *IndieLondon* about his friendship with Hudson. The pair are more like sibling rivals than anything else, often winding each other up. 'We're a pain in each other's ass,' he admitted, 'but that's a part of what works, I think, seeing us on screen in our relationship in real life. She said before: "We love each other but we don't like each other the whole time." And it's still true. We fight well, and we flirt well.'

'I think it's just a personal thing, our relationship. We can drive each other crazy,' explained Hudson at an LA press junket. 'It's also one of those things where it is like when you start knowing someone so well that you love them, like my brothers or even in relationships, the things that drive you crazy, you love even the things that drive you crazy about them.'

It was easy for the pair to reconnect. Working together again felt right. They love each other but also hate each other. There's certainly a lot of respect for each other's talents.

The film was scheduled to be shot in the Caribbean but Warner Bros. and director Andy Tennant decided to shoot in Queensland, Australia to avoid the hurricane season , which was likely to disrupt shooting. Scenes were filmed in Port Douglas, Brisbane, the Gold Coast, Hamilton Island, Lizard Island, Airlie Beach and Hervey Bay, as well as Batt Reef, which is where Australia's real life *Crocodile Dundee* Steve Irwin died from a stingray barb in 2006. Indoor scenes were filmed on the Warner Bros. studio lot.

While staying at a luxury home in Port Douglas, McConaughey had a python in his backyard. Some days he went out diving and even swimming with a dugong, a large marine mammal. Two crew members, in fact, were stung by Irukandji jellyfish which prompted some scenes to be filmed in the Caribbean because the actors were so frightened of the venomous creatures in the water.

McConaughey spoke at the world premiere of the movie about the indigenous wildlife. 'I had two pythons in my tree where I was living,' he said to journalist Rebecca Murray of *About.com: Hollywood Movies*. 'Two pythons – eight and half-foot amethystine pythons living in a coconut tree right out in front of my spot. Everything's cool when I see he's in the tree everyday, but then I come home after a month and he's gone. Now you don't sleep so well. Checking under the bed, under the mattress, in every single closet and I couldn't find that SOB. So, it was a wild shoot. We had sharks. I'm diving and I see bull sharks coming by. Thankfully we weren't on the menu.'

Sahara and *We Are Marshall* both faced lawsuits and *Fool's Gold* was no different. Warner Bros. were sued in 2011 by Canadian writer Lou Boudreau who alleged copyright infringement by the director and two others over the authorship of the script. Comment was not made by Warner Bros.

'Rom-coms are hard in a lot of ways: they're built to be buoyant,' McConaughey told *The Guardian*'s Andrew Pulver in a 2012 interview. 'It's easy to demean them. I did a few romantic comedies. I enjoyed them. They paid well; they were fun. I didn't know if I wanted to do any more. I decided to sit out, and I had to endure for a while. Another one comes with a big old paycheck; I had to say no. I was looking for something to be turned on by.'

'They're a staple of American cinema,' said director-cowriter Andy Tennant, the man behind *Ever After* and *Hitch*, to Rich Cline of *Shadows on the Wall* about the often derided rom-com genre. 'They're about people, and I like that. This particular one is about marriage – they want to kill each other, and then in the final moments they get to a point where they have to decide what's really important. And if you can say something like that and make people laugh, that's great!'

'This isn't one of those films where I get to be the white knight in shining armour and win the fights,' McConaughey said to *IndieLondon*, 'I'm actually the screw up who gets my butt kicked a lot and happens to get the gold and the girl in the end. It was fun.'

There's a great deal of honesty and respect between McConaughey and Hudson which is sometimes hard to come by between two major Hollywood actors because it's often the case that egos get in the way. Brit actor Ray Winstone was a good laugh, too, with his screwball English sense of humour.

'It just felt like it was – the relationship felt right, because it was kind of an extension of what worked with *How to Lose a Guy* but at the same time it was completely different – two totally different characters,' Hudson explained to Sheila Roberts of *Movies Online*.

The underwater scenes in the ocean proved difficult for cast and crew. They were taken through several emergency procedures, which lasted throughout the final month of filming. The entourage of cast and crew underwater was almost as large as that on land. They had to be sharp working underwater; there couldn't be any laziness or fooling around involved. It was too dangerous. The film made it look as though the underwater scene wasn't one take, but it was. It was hard to see (let alone breathe) in the ocean so filming was tough. The hardest part for Hudson was wrapping herself around the cannon. There was a mechanism close by which created the wave but it was scary for her as she struggled to see. She was a little nervous about it, though there were people on hand underwater to help her. There was a hand signal that was used if ever Hudson or McConaughey wanted to breathe; with that someone would go down with a tank of oxygen and share it with them.

For McConaughey, the underwater acting scenes were difficult to do: he learned that you had to choreograph the scenes thoroughly before filming because you might only get one chance to film them. He knew that you just had to go down, trust your gear, trust the people around you and concentrate on the job.

One reason why he chose dramas like *Two for the Money* and *We Are Marshall* was so that he could avoid being pigeonholed. 'Some of my most successful films have been romantic comedies,' he admitted to *Chud*'s Devin Faraci, 'and they have, absolutely, offered me more opportunities to develop more things that are personal. It makes it a whole lot easier if this film does well for me to get something like *The Loop* made for ten million dollars. It's not something people read and go, "Oh I can't wait to throw money at that." It's a very peculiar, weird mystery. I really want to do it, but there's no way I would be able to do it if I didn't have successful box office.'

Fool's Gold was released February 2008 in the US and in the UK in April. The film's budget was $70 million and it made over $110 in box office receipts, but reviews were bad with critics lambasting Hudson's performance and saying McConaughey used the story as an excuse to expose his chest. McConaughey, however, was enthusiastic about the film's simple premise and knew his fans and admirers would enjoy the flick, even if the critics took every opportunity to shred it to pieces.

Brian Lowry of *Variety* said 'The lure of Matthew McConaughey shirtless for extended stretches doubtless has some marketing value, but after that, *Fool's Gold* offers small compensation.'

The New York Times' A.O. Scott wrote: 'If only this hodgepodge offered more fun and less of the kind of frantic creative desperation that tries to pass itself off as giddy comic exuberance. Mr. McConaughey and Ms. Hudson, who were less than electrifying in *How to Lose a Guy in 10 Days*, appear to be suffering through a class in remedial chemistry, which they barely pass.'

Simon Braund of *Empire* magazine wrote: 'Absolute tosh. A ridiculous, unerringly tedious plot is weighed down by listless performances from a cast who clearly wished they were somewhere else, despite the sumptuous location.'

Derek Adams of *Time Out* in London was equally dismissive: 'We've all seen this kind of scenario in umpteen treasure trovers, yet what makes *Fool's Gold* at least vaguely watchable is the presence of Hudson, who shares many of her mother Goldie Hawn's more likeable comedic skills. It's the badly timed pratfalls that bother most: aside from one laugh-out-loud moment involving Hudson thwacking McConaughey across the head with a borrowed walking stick, they are almost universally insipid.'

Though the reviews were bad, the box office was good and it was obvious people wanted to see McConaughey and Hudson onscreen together again. They have a lot of respect for each other off screen, too. 'I think if it works,' McConaughey explained to *Movies Online*'s Sheila Roberts, 'as it did in *How to Lose a Guy*, I mean, in the same way we were looking for, anticipating finding the right thing, because we wanted to get together again. I think there are definitely people out there that want to see us get back together again. I don't know how they are going to do it, but [they] want to see them together again in the same way as we wanted to. It was just finding the right thing. How many years was it between?'

*****

McConaughey knew that his good looks and body got him jobs, and if having his shirt off would help make/sell the film, then he'd do it. McConaughey is his own creation; he follows his own path. Part commercial cop-out, part beat poet, part hippie, he's an enigma, yet one that seems so familiar.

Throughout the years McConaughey has learned how to live a relatively private life. He knows all too well that Hollywood is a fantasy land and that people there live in a different world than the rest of us, so when he feels like he's had enough he hits the road for another trip or he goes back to Texas. How he handles the paparazzi entirely depends on who he is with – like many celebrities he doesn't like to be bothered when he's with his family but if he's with his buddies he knows how to humour the paps. If he didn't like the fame, he wouldn't go out – he'd rent a palace and hire three bodyguards and end up like Phil Spector or Michael Jackson – but he's more humble and less paranoid. McConaughey has a rational, realistic approach to fame.

'...people see Matthew out always doing something,' Kate Hudson explained to Rebecca Murray of *About.com: Hollywood Movies*, 'whether it be out dancing at a bar or beaching around or taking a hike with some crazy bandana on – that was a good one. I think that, like anything, people take their image and what they want someone else to be and people just run with it. And when you really know the person and really love the person, you recognize that that person is like nothing that people really want them [to be].'

To keep up with the challenging nature of his job and balancing his home life with his career, working out and staying in shape was paramount. His trainer Peter Park, whom he met through his Texan buddy Lance Armstrong, helps him with weights (80–84 kg), press-ups, squats, hand walks, tree branch pull-ups and traffic-light lunges. McConaughey's fitness is incredible, sometimes he even worked out with Armstrong and while he may not be as fit as the now-disgraced cyclist McConaughey can certainly hold his own. His workouts often depend on the nature of the film he's making at the time. He likes the challenging exercises and sometimes takes his bike out for a ride. He hates the gym and much prefers being outdoors. If he finds a weak spot on his body, he wants to strengthen it. For a film such as *Fool's Gold,* it was important to the role to be in good shape.

'One of the things is that I try to do it outdoors as much as possible,' he said to *People* magazine. 'I try to change up my route, and if I'm going down a road and I come across a new road or a new trail, I'll always say, "We'll take that one. Let's see where we end up." Sometimes it can get into a lot longer run than I wanted. I'll be like, "Damn! I've got to find my way home."'

Since he first began his acting career, McConaughey has mixed it up by taking roles that were always different from ones that he'd had before. He enjoys acting and the luxuries that come with it, but his main aim has always been to spice things up.

After Owen Wilson's attempted suicide in August 2007, McConaughey replaced him in Ben Stiller's action farce *Tropic*

Thunder, which opened in US cinemas in August 2008 and later in the UK in September. *Tropic Thunder* isn't a McConaughey film but he was pleased to be part of the ensemble cast nonetheless. The film stars Stiller, Jack Black and Robert Downey Jr with co-stars Steve Coogan, Jay Baruchel, Brandon T. Jackson, Bill Hader and Nick Nolte.

'*Tropic Thunder* was a different kind of comedic role,' McConaughey told Caitlin Martis of *The Film Stage*. 'It was fun to play a character and not characterise it, but it's a little of that. There's a character there, it's not me being funny. It's a character and hopefully being funny and I really like comedy. I am really turned on by comedy. I think it's really fun and I like the timing of comedy. And that was sort of a fictitious guy they said it was based on, but it was fun playing with the imagination.'

Directed by and starring *Dodgeball* actor Stiller, it is a satire of Vietnam War films such as *Full Metal Jacket*, *Apocalypse Now* and *Platoon* that were popular in the late 1970s and 1980s. McConaughey plays Rick 'Pecker' Peck, Tugg Speedman's (Ben Stiller) agent and best buddy. Speedman is sort of a young Sylvester Stallone-type action movie star who was once the world's biggest action hero because of the *Scorcher* franchise, but his career stalled due to box office bombs. The film's premise is essentially that a group of pampered actors are making a fictional Vietnam War film; only when the director drops them in the middle of the jungle and then gets killed, they are forced to rely on their acting skills in order to survive. Filming took place on the Hawaiian island of Kauai over 13 weeks in 2007.

It received good reviews from critics and was a box office hit, making over $180 million from a $90 million budget. However, it was not marketed as a McConaughey film – his role is only small – so he was still in desperate need of a hit film of his own to rejuvenate his flagging career.

The Observer's Phillip French wrote: 'Stiller and Co toy with these resonant notions rather than examining them, but the rich confusion of themes and aims saves the film from being merely a series of spoofs and sketches like *Airplane* and *Naked Gun*. Yet with its Oscar-night coda, the film is ultimately an affectionate celebration of Hollywood values rather than something truly subversive like *Sunset Boulevard*.'

McConaughey's personal life was in bloom – as was his bank balance – from the success of *Fool's Gold*. His partner, Brazilian model Camila Alves McConaughey, whom he would shortly have children with and would later marry, was very supportive of his career. They had met at a bar on Sunset Boulevard in 2006 after his relationship with Penélope Cruz ended.

'I met her in a club on Sunset [Boulevard], of all places,' he admitted to *Vogue*'s John Powers. 'The first time I saw her walk across the room, I didn't say, "Who is that?" I said, "What is that?" The way she moved, I could see a person who knows who they are. There's a person who spends time with herself, and is not advertising for this world, and is not asking permission. From that night I haven't been on a date with anyone else.'

They became friends and didn't exclusively date until a year and a half later. Alves arrived in the US aged fifteen to visit her aunt and never left. She started modelling in her teens and worked as a TV presenter and designed handbags with her mother. Having a family changed everything for Matthew. 'One thing I always knew I wanted to be, since I was eight years old, I knew I wanted to be a father,' he said to the *The Scotsman* in 2012. 'I didn't know what I wanted to be. When I was twenty years old, I didn't know what I wanted for a career. But I knew I wanted to be a father. It has been the thing that, since I was very young, I looked up to. The men I looked up to the most were fathers – men who raised good kids.'

Their eldest Levi Alves McConaughey was born on 7 July 2008, weighing in at 7 lb, 4 oz. McConaughey spoke about his excitement for impending fatherhood in early 2008 to *IndieLondon*: 'We're six months into it, and everything's healthy so far. We don't know if it's going to be a boy or a girl, and we'll find out the day that he or she greets the day. But I'm excited. It's going to be a new chapter.'

OK! Magazine paid $3 million in mid-2008 for the first photos of McConaughey, then thirty-eight, with his wife and their newborn child, Levi, then just two weeks old. McConaughey bragged at the time of playing Brazilian music for fourteen hours straight during labour. The money from the *OK!* shoot went to j.k. livin, which is a non-profit company. There had been photographers outside the McConaughey family home for weeks desperately hoping to catch that first shot of the baby. The McConaughey's decided to beat them to it. As soon as the *OK!* pics made the Internet that was it for the paparazzi!

'Bringing a baby into the world is something I've always wanted,' he's quoted as saying in the *Daily Mail* in 2008, 'and now I'm completely ready for my life to start revolving around another human being. I carefully maintain relationships and friendships. I'm committed to my acting career. But to be the architect of a little creature's life is my next big adventure and I can't wait for it to begin.'

Becoming a father was a great new chapter in his life. He told *People*'s Brenda Rodriguez that as a mother Camila has a 'real strong sense of calm'. He added: 'We have a good flow, and neither one of us wants the other one to change. We've both said it, if we did change, that could be a problem! We love each other for who we are.'

When McConaughey was asked by *Movies Online*'s Sheila Roberts in 2008 if he anticipated a change of lifestyle after he became a dad, he responded: 'You know my instincts will take over when the young one greets the world. One thing I've heard that's consistent – and I've got a lot of great moms and dads around me from my own to elders to peers of mine – is that all the grand plans you want to make, you might as well throw them out buddy, because it doesn't happen like that.'

Five years before the birth of his first child McConaughey reckoned that if he were to have a wife and child then he wouldn't want to live in Hollywood, instead he'd rather pack up and move back to Texas and do something else, but he'd turned that around. Now he chose to continue to act while juggling family life and living in Southern California and Texas.

We are the architects of our lives; everyone has dreams, ambitions and desires. McConaughey had new projects on the go and ideas about what he wanted to do with his career but being a father changed everything for him. He knew that raising a child was going to be his greatest achievement over anything else. To raise a healthy child and bring him up the right way, and then let him venture into the world as an adult with the knowledge that he had gained from his father, was going to be McConaughey's finest goal in life. His days as the lone contemplative travelling man were over and so were his days as a bachelor and single Hollywood hunk. Being a father had changed everything for him. Raising a child would be his proudest achievement over anything he'd managed to succeed at in his film career.

'I think he will be an incredible dad,' McConaughey's co-star of two films, Kate Hudson, said to Sheila Roberts of *Movies Online* back in 2008. Their home life was simple: Camila wakes up first before McConaughey gets up and makes a breakfast shake. They'll feed Levi a shake, put some music on and play with Levi. He'll stand on his mum or dad's chest and start dancing. He started learning Portuguese words as soon as he could talk. Levi wasn't a big fan of baby speak; he tended to look at his parents as though he was wondering what on earth was going on. 'Levi is into everything. You don't go out and walk in the backyard and daydream for five seconds or they're on top of the house,' McConaughey said to late night US talk show host Jay Leno.

Aside from her obvious good looks and personality, what attracted McConaughey to Camila? What does McConaughey look for in a woman? 'A sense of humour,' he told the UK's *Metro* newspaper in 2006. 'Respect for themselves and respect for others and a certain amount of talent in whatever area they want to work in. Knowing what she does and doesn't want. You've gotta have soul to be sexy. It's more than a snapshot. When I see grace in a woman, that's very sexy. You can tell by how someone moves or their rhythm.'

How does he cope with being a celebrity and going out in public? Some celebrities are closely guarded by bodyguards and assistants and either avoid going out in public or cause a scene with their entourage; others prefer to remain low key. McConaughey has learned how to carry himself in public. He explained this to *Chud*'s Devin Faraci: '…sometimes someone will walk up to me and I'll say, "Not right now. I'm thinking." Honestly. I'll be working on something and someone will walk up to me and, not being rude, I'll say, "Not right now, I'm eating." Or, "I'm going to a movie." Sometimes you have to remind people why you're here. Like at the airport – I have to catch the flight. If they say you're being rude, you say, "Wait, what are you doing here? Don't you have to catch a flight too?" And then they laugh and you move on. But no, going out in public for me is something I've practiced and not ever will not do.'

His production company, j.k. livin, is based in Venice Beach, California with nine staff. His long time business partner Gus Gustawes was also on hand, as was John Chaney, his personal assistant of many years. McConaughey prefers to surround himself with trusted friends and associates rather than the usual 'hangers on' that are so prevalent in Hollywood. At this juncture, McConaughey was raking in around $8 million per film and his production company was making preparations for his next acting ventures, and for the forthcoming release of a small film called *Surfer, Dude*; the first film j.k. livin had made entirely in-house. In a profile of McConaughey in *Texas Monthly* in October 2008, journalist John Spong describes the offices in these terms: 'With dark hardwood floors and exposed brick, the glassed-in offices looked down on an open lobby. The walls held framed script pages and large posters from McConaughey's favourite movies – Dino De Laurentiis's *King Kong*, S.R. Bindler's *Hands on a Hard Body*, his own *Sahara*. A twenty-foot-tall screen on one side of the room showed a Cubs game.'

Surfer, Dude had a limited release in the US in September 2008 and went straight to DVD in most foreign countries. The film was co-produced by McConaughey who takes the title

126

role of Steve Addington, a surfer who's having a soul-searching existential crisis after he can't catch a wave for over a month.

McConaughey spoke to Beth Accomando of *KPBS* about his reasons for producing the project: 'As an actor I'm hired to show up, hit my mark, know my stuff; if it's a big movie I work three months and I'm gone. There are movies that I've seen and I go, "Aahhh, that was better than I thought it was going to be." But there are a lot of movies where, "Oh man there must be something on the cutting room floor that we're never going to see in there." So I was like I want to get into the pre-production of it, the production of it, and the post-production so at the end of the day I can look in the mirror and go, "Yup, now I got a big responsibility." Like it or not like it, I know that I had my hands in the clay the whole time and I was responsible for a lot of it. I learned so much in this thing. I learned that I definitely don't want to produce every movie that I'm a part of. It's hard and it's long. But it was stuff you can't be taught; you can't read it in a book.'

Directed by S.R. Bindler, who had made mostly music documentaries and commercials since making the 1996 documentary *Hands on a Hard Body*, the critically acclaimed Texan film, and co-starring Woody Harrelson, *Surfer, Dude* has long been forgotten about. Bindler and McConaughey have been friends since they sat next to each other in art class at high school in 1985. 'He [Bindler] was already doing a lot of writing and a big movie buff,' McConaughey said to Rebecca Murray of *About.com: Hollywood Movies*. 'I wasn't, and we became friends then and we started swapping out our weekends. On Friday night, he'd go out with me and we'd go party and on Saturday night I'd go to his place and we'd get some grub and then watch a movie. And so he started introducing me to films.'

The script was optioned in 1998, but then it had rewrites in 2004 and 2005 before McConaughey and Bindler came on board. They rewrote the script until they were both happy with it and then shopped it around LA. It was a tough film for the pair to finance. They had wanted to work together for a while but had to find a project that didn't cost $40 million. They managed to scrape together the $6 million for this film and only had twenty-eight days to shoot it. It's a low budget film as far as Hollywood is concerned. It's almost like guerrilla-style filmmaking or something from student film – McConaughey understands that on films with tight schedules you spend less time in your trailer because you do a scene, go back to your trailer so the cameras can quickly be set up for the next scene. Because of the weather and the ambitious nature of the script, and with several locations, it meant there were a lot of camera setups in and around the Malibu area. Jimmy Skotchdopole, the producer, and also the location producer, were vital in helping them stick to the limited budget.

Bindler spoke to *Collider*'s Charlie Mihelich about the central theme that brought the cast and crew together: 'Matthew and I grew up in the country and got to be around nature, and the central theme for me was what is the cost when nature goes away? Which is something we're all going through right now.'

Trailers become a home away from home for many actors on set. 'The unsaid rule for living in a trailer park is: If the door's shut, don't come a-knockin',' McConaughey explained to *Details*' Bart Blasengame. 'But if it's open and you're walkin' by, feel free to say hello.'

Surfer, Dude has got the j.k. livin stamp all over it. McConaughey spoke to Rebecca Murray of *About.com: Hollywood Movies* about the company and his family's part in the making of *Surfer, Dude*, which really was a family affair. 'My brother Rooster helped out, my nephew helped out, my mom was always kind of there helping out. We had a lot of thank-yous to all of our family members because … it wasn't a big studio project that we just had them bankrolling the thing. So this was more like door-to-door sales. We had to go run around town to try and get the money and then to get it made we had, get people to work for scale.'

McConaughey wanted the film to have a seventies feel it to. He wanted the joints that the characters smoke to be almost an extension of their hands, where nobody passed judgement. It was who they are. It's a situation where if they don't smoke they go a little crazy. It's the antithesis of what most comedies do today which tend to be gross-out films or tongue-in-cheek comedies.

McConaughey spends most of the film shirtless. Was it a parody of the media's seeming obsession with him having his shirt off all the time? 'It's sort of a wink, you know, to pop the bubble, and say "Guess what? Now I've had a whole movie to do it" and sort of get the joke,' he said to Charlie Mihelich of *Collider*. 'I found a character who I got to know for twenty-eight days, shooting wise, and surfing, and there was also reason behind it. It was not to paradise anything. I mean, the stuff about me being shirtless in the current culture came from working on this movie. It happened at this time. So we found a character who never wears a shirt and shoes. That's nothing but a black and white bathing suit, which is kind of like a jail because there are no waves. That's all part of the wink.'

Some people suggested that *Surfer, Dude* was McConaughey's

version of *Ocean's Eleven* in that he's just hanging out with his buddies such as Woody Harrelson or Texan country hero Willie Nelson. It was essentially a low budget film that McConaughey made with his friends and acquaintances, though in some respects it was more like Robert Altman's *Nashville* than anything else.

'Like, Woody (Harrelson) came in, and Willie (Nelson) came in, and all us lived…there's about sixteen trailers we had in a trailer park,' McConaughey told *Bullz-Eye*'s Will Harris, 'so it really felt like that old commune feeling that you got from the Altman films. We wanted that feeling where we woke up in the morning, and we drove just down the street, and we were on the set, which was the beach. And we came home after work, and everybody kinda congregated, laughed about the day, had a cocktail, ate some dinner, crashed, and got up and did it again. It was a real feeling of a traveling circus…so, yeah, that's a fair description.'

It's a very planet-friendly film and Harrelson and Nelson are proponents of environmentally friendly projects so they were keen to work on the project. They also liked the idea that *Surfer, Dude* is about a bunch of misfits. McConaughey and Bindler were not trying to preach any messages with the film, though. They liked the idea of an organic character who leads a very simple life in a complicated world. Their idea was to see what could happen to make his life complicated and this came in the form of taking away the wave. He's not angry because of a family illness or anything, but because he can't surf. It's almost a throwback to 1980s goofball films such as *Caddyshack* where the characters are authentic and sincere, but they're also misfits and somewhat naïve.

McConaughey hadn't surfed before but when he began practicing for the film he really enjoyed it and went surfing a few times after filming was completed. He liked the idea that to surf there's no membership card or club, you can just go and catch the waves. There's something very free and earthly about it.

There is a scene in the film where McConaughey plays the didgeridoo naked; surely a homage to the 1999 incident where he was caught playing the bongos *au naturel* by the police after neighbours filed a noise complaint. McConaughey had been in Australia so he picked up a didgeridoo and started playing it. He thought it would be funny to add it to the film. It's an odd instrument that is not very well-known in America, so he wanted to broaden its fan base.

The *Los Angeles Times'* Daniel Ordona wrote: 'The film is awash in doobies and breasts, clichéd cinematic language and clumsy exposition. It's reminiscent of the stoner-culture movies of the late '60s and early '70s but without the naïve fun.'

Austin Chronicles' Kimberley Jones was equally unenthused: 'From *Hands on a Hard Body* to an 89-minute ogling of another hard body: It boggles the mind that eleven years after his engrossing documentary about an endurance competition to win a truck in Longview, Texas, filmmaker Bindler has channelled his talents into this regrettable comedy.'

The money McConaughey was making from films allowed him to extend j.k. livin – which he founded in 2008 – into other avenues such as music and lifestyle. On 18 February 2009, Ron Spaulding, the Executive Vice President and General Manager of Fontana, the independent distribution division of Universal Music Group, announced an exclusive deal with McConaughey for his indie record label, j.k. livin. 'There is no question that Matthew McConaughey is one of today's most popular personalities and successful entrepreneurs,' Spaulding said. 'He's translated his simple, yet enthusiastic approach to life into his company j.k. livin and now his record label. We are thrilled to partner with him to bring j.k. livin's music to not only his loyal fans worldwide, but to music lovers everywhere.'

McConaughey's first signing was the reggae musician Mishka whom McConaughey first encountered randomly and then set about trying to track him down. He subsequently saw Mishka at the House of Blues on Sunset Blvd. His debut album *Above the Bones* was the first release from McConaughey's label. The label's biography read: 'In 1993, Matthew McConaughey was filming *Dazed and Confused*, struggling with the passing of his father when he was overtaken by a saying that would soon change his life. That saying was "just keep livin" or "j.k. livin" as it's now called. His father "Pop" is the man stencilled in the logo in remembrance of its origin. As life continued forward, he found that the j.k. livin approach to each day helped him navigate through the good times and bad, stay true to his ideals along the way and make the best out of this adventure we call life. j.k. livin is not a rulebook, it's a lifestyle.'

That image of his father was the only image McConaughey had in mind for the brand's logo. It is a silhouette of Pop, designed by one of McConaughey's artist friends, in the last picture taken of him at Navarre Beach in Florida wearing his famed baby-blue shorts and hat.

McConaughey spoke about the success if the album *Above the Bones* and j.k.livin to Rebecca Murray of *About.com: Hollywood Movies*: 'It held at number two on the reggae *Billboard* charts for seven weeks. We're about to surpass the sales of the very first album that he had put out in a much shorter time. Mishka's actually supposed to be here tonight. He played Surfrider

Foundation yesterday. The brands on www.jklivinstore.com are selling great. We're coming up with four new products this week. And the film production's doing well. We're just getting into TV. Sold two things to TV. We're going have a couple of TV series' that we're working on.'

However, ties between Mishka and McConaughey would be quickly severed, as is often the case in the entertainment industry. 'Initially, it was a big boost,' Mishka said to Mike Voorheis of *Star News* in 2012. 'I wasn't signed to any label, and it was quite a struggle at the time. Matthew lost enthusiasm and got busy with other projects. You go so far and then they didn't know what to do with me. That left me with my hands tied.'

McConaughey's own choice in music reflects his passion for telling stories and travelling, absorbing new cultures and ways of life. He dug into the local Texan tales of country outlaw Willie Nelson, the inspired blues of African player Ali Farka Touré and the wisdom of Bob Marley. Those guys followed their own agenda, free of shackles and society's conventions. They were akin to the intellectual Beatniks of 1950s and 1960s San Francisco, New York and Paris. McConaughey also likes the music of Americana-folk singer James McMurtry (son of author Larry McMurtry) and Dennis Brown.

'It's very similar to making movies. It's very similar to telling a story,' McConaughey said to MTV News about songs and the art of storytelling through different mediums whether it be music, movies or books. 'That's what's really neat about it. Maybe it's a different vocabulary, but each song's its own story. Each song kind of has their own three-act structure... We start with a tease, then intro everybody, take it high, climax, pull off, give it a rest and then leave them wanting a little bit more.'

There has also been a philanthropic side to McConaughey. McConaughey has immersed himself in charity work over the years, juggling it both with family and acting. In February 2008 he ran the Nike + Human Race in Austin. The 10-km run took place on the same day in 25 cities around the world raising money for the Lance Armstrong Foundation, the World Wildlife Fund and NineMillion.org.

There is a part of McConaughey that has always wanted to give back to society by helping those that have been less fortunate in life than he himself has been. McConaughey has had it fairly easy – after returning from Australia in 1988 as an exchange student he went to college, got into the movies, moved to LA and became rich and famous. Since *A Time to Kill* the decisions he has made have governed his choice of roles and the direction of his career. And now he is all about giving back to those who have been less fortunate.

The charity side of j.k. livin is 'dedicated to helping teenage kids lead active lives and make healthy choices to become great men and women.' It was reported that he had rescued various pets stranded after the flooding of New Orleans from Hurricane Katrina in 2006. He once rescued a cat from two youths who doused the animal in hairspray and were attempting to set fire to it in Sherman Oaks. He is a person who cares about humanity and animals.

j.k. livin is both a brand and a philosophy, and McConaughey is both something of a shaman and a salesman. 'We can talk about j.k. livin a lot of different ways,' McConaughey explained to *Texas Monthly*'s John Spong in 2008. 'It's a decision-making paradigm, not a rulebook. It has structure, but it doesn't put life in a box. It's not all aphorisms. You take your own counsel with yourself on what it is. It's a lyric, a philosophy, a bumper sticker. It's a rap, a rhythm, a bass line. It's not about treble, 'cause we got a lot of that out there. Let's keep to our bass line.'

Though he had endeavours outside of acting, he had already moved on to his next project – yet another rom-com. The paychecks were simply too good to turn down and he enjoyed making them.

'As you know, a script with a $100,000 offer isn't near as funny as the exact same script with a $10- or $15-million offer,' McConaughey admitted to John Powers of *Vogue*. 'The same words – they're just funnier.'

'The industry put him in a slot,' said director Richard Linklater, who'd cast McConaughey in *Dazed and Confused*, to Holly Milea of *Elle*. 'It's not like he was turning down great parts. The material wasn't coming his way. He was a character actor in a leading man's body. Then something changed.'

There had been rumours circulating in Hollywood that McConaughey was going to be cast in a big screen adaption of the cult 1980s detective series, *Magnum P.I.*, which starred Tom Selleck in the lead role as a private investigator living in Oahu, Hawaii. The show ran from 1980 to 1989 and was one of the most popular TV series of the decade. McConaughey reportedly turned down the $15 million pay cheque in order to reinvent himself after his final rom-com.

McConaughey spoke to *Pop Matters'* Cynthia Fuchs about how at ease he has become with himself in front of the camera: 'I can handle going to see dailies now, I can objectively see myself without being vain. I can see and tell the truth about the character and see what's working for me, and if what I've got is what I was trying to do. I can find something I like or dislike, and be constructively critical of my work now, and I couldn't before. I love the process, I love the making of them. But if I see a movie of mine on TV, I just keep flipping.'

*****

The phone rang. Time for another rom-com. *Ghosts of Girlfriends Past* was released in the UK and US in May 2009. McConaughey was still stuck in the role of rom-com actor after *The Wedding Planner*, *How to Lose a Guy in 10 Days*, *Failure to Launch* and *Fool's Gold* and now he was cast in the risible *Ghosts of Girlfriends Past*. 'I was good to them and they were good to me,' McConaughey told the *Scotsman* on his experience of making romantic comedies. 'Shoot, yeah. Some of those romantic comedies, they put food on my kids' table. Trust me. Absolutely. And they're quite fun to do. You've got to be in a whole different mind-frame for them.'

Loosely based on Charles Dickens' seminal supernatural tale, *A Christmas Carol*, *Ghosts of Girlfriends Past* is passable if only for it's interesting premise. While the Dickens novel features Christmas Eve and Christmas Day, the film is set the day before and during a wedding day. McConaughey plays a successful and famous photographer and womaniser named Connor Mead who is haunted by his ex-girlfriends at his younger brother's wedding. Directed by Mark Waters, the film also stars Jennifer Garner, Lacey Chabert and Michael Douglas. Filming took place between February and July of 2008 in Massachusetts.

McConaughey was asked by a fan in *People* magazine what he'd do if he was visited by his former girlfriends. He replied: 'I think I'd learn that the reason that they dug me when we

An unshaven Matthew McConaughey smiles at a press junket in 2005. ©WireImage

Matthew McConaughey, ever the adoring family man, often says that being a father is the proudest achievement of his life.

Above left: The famous bare chest that won him millions of adoring female fans.

©*Getty images*

Above right: A keen sportsman, McConaughey took part in the Bob Hope Chrysler Classic; an opportunity not just to show off his skills, but also to raise millions of dollars for charity.

©*Getty images*

Below: The LA Dodgers honoured McConaughey with the opportunity to throw the ceremonial first pitch in 2009.

©*Getty images*

Above: McConaughey poses for the cameras during some charity work for his foundation, Just Keep Livin'. ©*Wireimage*

Below: The famous Longview Lobo Yearbook photo citing McConaughey's good looks. He was awarded the 'Most Handsome' accolade in high school. ©*Filmmagic*

Above: Next to his pregnant wife, beautiful Brazilian model and television performer Camila Alves, McConaughey's dramatic weight loss for his role in *The Dallas Buyers Club* is very apparent.

©Wireimage

Below: Looking calm and collected with his *Magic Mike* co-star Channing Tatum.

©Gettyimages

Above: A classic shot of the elegant Hollywood actor.

©*ALBERTO PIZZOLI/AFP/ Getty images*

Left: At the premiere of *The Lincoln Lawyer* with his wife Camila and mother Kay, another movie in which McConaughey plays a defence attorney.

©*Filmmagic*

Right: With his *Mud* co-star Reese Witherspoon in Cannes, where the film was a favourite for the 2012 Palme D'Or.

©*Getty images*

Below: McConaughey is certainly no stranger to posing for cameras, as can be seen here by the wall of photographers behind him and his *Paperboy* co-stars Nicole Kidman and Zac Efron.

©*Getty images*

Below: A dream come true: Holding the Oscar with fellow winners Cate Blanchett, Lupita Nyong'o and Jared Leto in 2014.

©*Wireimage*

McConaughey with his Texan
buddy and long-time collaborator
Woody Harrelson. The duo missed
out on an Emmy in 2014 for *True
Detective*, but for many they were
the night's 'Best Couple'.

were dating was how excited I would get about details of little situations, like making pancakes in the morning. And I think the other thing would probably be my sense of humour. I'm actually happy to say I've been in some of my ex-girlfriends' weddings. I go, "Well, right on, man. That's good."'

McConaughey loved the script, especially the first twenty or thirty pages where he thought there was a lot of bite to the story. It was the clever dialogue that grabbed him and the strong male character was someone he saw himself portraying onscreen. 'It was just the best romantic comedy I've read in years,' McConaughey enthused to *People*'s Brenda Rodriguez. 'It had a big heart about having a second chance. And the ghosts in it levitated the comedy and allowed me to just be a fool.'

Michael Douglas's character Uncle Wayne was laugh-a-minute too; McConaughey thought the rich comedy dialogue was on par with *The Wedding Crashers*. Usually in romantic comedies the dialogue doesn't cut deep with the audience, but McConaughey felt differently about this film. The ghosts gave the script added humour. It's a fairy tale but with humour and warmth and it offered something different to the previous rom-coms McConaughey had been cast in.

Garner enjoyed working with her male co-star. She thought McConaughey was a sweet, gentle and funny guy who was very easy to get along with. Garner admired him as an actor and was more than elated to be working with him. Garner liked the film because it was a different variation on the clichéd romantic-comedy, not just because of the ghosts, but because of her character. She's never had a problem resisting someone in her life who has tried to break her heart and nor has she ever gone for 'the bad guy.' What she liked about her character was that her dialogue reminded her of the many conversations she'd had about romance with her girlfriends.

McConaughey wasn't about to change things in his life abruptly, the way his character does, as he told journalist Rebecca Murray at *About.com: Hollywood Movies* at the US premiere of the film: 'I'm not a big sort of signpost guy with things like that. I'm about to turn forty; I don't really see that as like a, "Oh my god, I've got to do this." No, I kind of roll with it a little bit more. We'll work hard at it. I've still got a lot of relationships and doing the same things that I have been working on for thirty-nine years, so that feels good – whether it's family or friends or job – to feel it all still connected from thirty-nine years ago, things that I started twenty years ago, friends that I met twenty-five years ago that are still here tonight. Things like that.'

To work with a revered acting icon as Michael Douglas was a major coup for McConaughey who had yet to enter the prime of his career (though no one knew it at the time). He learned a lot from Douglas just from sitting down chatting to him. Douglas spoke to him about the experiences he had on some of his own movies such as *One Flew Over the Cuckoo's Nest* and *Wall Street*. It was a dream for McConaughey to gain so much knowledge about the making of movies, the industry and what to do and what not to do in films.

Ghosts of Girlfriends Past debuted at the US box office at number two and though it was not a critical success it fared well.

The Guardian's Peter Bradshaw wrote: 'It's not a bad idea and Michael Douglas gives a game cameo as the spirit of a louche uncle who taught the teenage McConaughey all the moves. (If you want to see this idea done properly and funnily, incidentally, rent Dylan Kidd's *Roger Dodger* on DVD.) How crass and joyless the whole business is, culminating in a love-declaration scene prefigured by McConaughey knocking an elderly man unconscious, to get the boring, obstructive old dude out of the way. Yikes.'

Tim Robey wrote in *The Daily Telegraph*: 'Still, there's an undertone of satisfying bitterness before the gloop sets in: the recriminations are just an ounce more cutting and tart than you're ready for. McConaughey, who will be just as funny as Douglas in 20 years' time, looks suitably chastened. There's only one scene with his shirt off.'

Empire's Anna Smith wrote: 'The teen scenes have appeal, offset by Douglas' enjoyable rotter, but McConaughey, all charmless sleaze and corny chat-up lines, is neither funny nor ripe for redemption.'

Thankfully, that was it for McConaughey and rom-coms. He'd had enough and there's certainly an argument that film fans had had quite enough of seeing him in those types of films, too. 'What's tougher about a romantic comedy is that it's a whole different game,' McConaughey explained to *Vulture*'s Jennifer Vineyard. 'They're not supposed to have a super-clear definition. You have to float through those. [Makes a waving motion with his arms.] There's an amiability and a buoyancy, and you got to keep it afloat. And definition will go down, and if you go down in a rom-com, you sink the ship. It's dead. Over. Twelve minutes into the film, you're done.'

Matthew loves acting. He's one of few people who can actually say, 'I love my job.' He likes it more now than he used to and he knows how to handle the fame and the rigours that come with acting – being away from home, the travel, long hours, promotional work and such. But he was beginning to feel an itch that needed to be scratched. Change can be a good thing as he would soon learn more than ever before.

It was announced in June 2010 that McConaughey was teaming up with Marc Hyman to write a scripted comedy for FX, the popular TV channel, based on material by J.R. Reed. He also made an appearance in the critically acclaimed HBO Will Ferrell-produced comedy series *Eastbound & Down*. McConaughey plays Texan scout Roy McDaniel in three episodes in seasons two and three. Somewhere on the backburner was an idea for a biopic of Billy Carter, the brother of President Jimmy Carter, which he'd been discussing with *Dazed and Confused* director Richard Linklater.

The Guardian's Andrew Pulver noted: 'He could have been the new Brad Pitt, a stand-by of the Oscar nomination sheet; instead he became the young George Hamilton.'

McConaughey's career has evolved which has helped him as a person and as an actor as he explained to *Chud*'s Devin Faraci in 2006: 'The interesting thing about my career is that I went in reverse – I had a very successful film that made me famous right off the bat, *A Time to Kill*. And then later started to learn what the heck I was doing, started to work on my craft and take classes, which is what I'm doing now. I didn't have any of that experience before. Did I expect to be doing that? Sure. Did I expect this is how it would work out? No.'

Films that have been openly discussed but failed to find a backer are *Hammer Down* and *Dear Delilah* and *Tishomingo Blues* (based on the Elmore Leonard novel, with Don Cheadle initially attached as director). Such is the nature of Hollywood. McConaughey moved on to new projects and even expressed interest in directing a feature, but he knows what his first professional love is as he told *Empire*: 'I've gotta say to you, I'm really enjoying acting, I just feel like I'm learning so much, and kind of enjoying the wonderful mystery of acting and storytelling. I'm doing my work, learning my rules early then just throwing them out the back door when it's time to work and let it fly.'

However, despite his obvious passion and the commercial success of some of his mainstream films, McConaughey was dangerously close to becoming just another piece of disposable Hollywood fodder; a caricature of himself, taking whatever roles came his way just for the pay cheque. In a similar fashion to British actor Hugh Grant, who has carved out a career for himself as a bumbling upper middle class English gent, McConaughey was shifting between flimsy roles in romantic comedies to hardly taxing parts in mostly unmemorable dramas. Bar the odd exception such as *Frailty*, his films were memorable for all the wrong reasons.

Be that as it may, McConaughey soon surprised everyone.

CHAPTER SEVEN

NO MORE
ROM-COMS

'(I thought), "Oh man, this is what I'm doing. I'm growing
in my real life and I want to feel my growth in my career,
because that's my life too."'
Matthew McConaughey, *USA Today*, 2013

'I t's been different throughout my career,' McConaughey
explained to *Total Film* about what governs his choice of
roles. 'The one thing I ever said that I've kind of stuck to is: keep
changing it up. And then I've had spans where I've done many
of the same types in a row and then I've had spans where things
that I did like for instance action, adventure and romantic-
comedy are all things that are accessible to the public and will
do well and playing to a lot more people and pay a lot more as
well. Those are the only ones that have real security and I know
my kids are going to eat and we got a home, two homes: one
in California and one in Texas. I don't have to be concerned at
the gas station if I'm going to be able to put unleaded or super
unleaded in my tank, thankfully.'

There is such a thing as too much exposure. McConaughey
realised this after a flurry of activity and mostly mundane films

between 2001 and 2009. After a brief sabbatical of almost two years he went under a sort of spiritual cleanse and re-evaluated himself and fathered a second child. (His daughter, Vida Alves McConaughey, was born in 2010. 'It was the only name that we had for a girl even before we had Levi. We had many male names but we only had Vida. She came out and she gave us life so we named her Vida,' he admitted to late night talk show host Jay Leno.) McConaughey chose to side-step his stereotype as a rom-com actor in favour of small, independent films. Eventually, these more challenging roles would bring him critical favour that he never had in Hollywood romantic comedies. But first, he wanted a break. Family is important to him. He is a very loving and loyal man, and a responsible and fun dad.

McConaughey made a cheeky reference to the conception of his second child while presenting the 'Top Male Vocalist Of The Year' award at the 2010 County Music Awards; he told the audience: 'After the show last year, my lady and I, Camila, we even went back to the hotel and conceived the little lady who is now our daughter Vida Alves McConaughey.'

'That's a true story,' McConaughey added with a smile. 'Now I'm back, I'm having a great time again, but I promise you me and Camila are going to try not to get so lucky this year…two's enough! We are flush for a while.'

The CMTs (Country Music Television Awards) that year gave McConaughey a headline in the gossip rags after country singer Carrie Underwood apologised for a cheeky sexual remark she made to him. At the 2009 awards McConaughey told a story of how George Strait's cowboy boots once got him 'lucky' when he went to see Dwight Yoakum with his brother and they met a couple of girls. When asked what they did for a living, they lied and said they made George Strait's boots and had an exclusive contract with him. George was in the audience when McConaughey explained the story. Underwood joked to McConaughey when she collected her ('Entertainer Of The Year') award from him: 'I don't know what to say. I got nothin' ... I want to see those boots, Matthew.' The audience were in hysterics, though perhaps Camila wasn't so amused. At this year's awards show McConaughey handed her a pair of boots. She told the press backstage: 'I'm so embarrassed, I totally embarrassed myself. I just blanked. You want to say something eloquent in a moment like that and I embarrassed myself. I'm sorry Matthew, I'm sorry to my family. I'm totally embarrassed.'

During his self-imposed break that began in 2009, he'd get offered major roles with huge paychecks but turned them down knowing that work may dry up in the increasingly fickle film industry. After several months scripts stopped being sent altogether and the powers that be got the message. He'd gotten a bad rap for a while and wanted to go into the shadows to disappear from acting, although he has never been overly concerned about how he is perceived.

'I went to my wife and my agent and said, "I'm going to stop for a bit,"' he confessed to *Variety*'s Jenelle Riley. 'I'm going to sit back in the shadows. I'm getting into my forties, a great time for a man. I've started a family. I want to take time to laugh and love and enjoy these adventures.'

'I never said, "Oh, I want to go do darker or edgier stuff,"' McConaughey elaborated to *Details*' Adam Sachs. 'I just said, "I'm going to take some time off. I have to take care of my family right now. We've got the means in the bank account, we've got a roof over our head, we're gonna eat well, we're fine. So let's take some introspective time." It wasn't a mini-retirement. It was just that I wanted to listen to myself and be a bit more discerning.'

He was offered scripts with handsome paychecks, and indeed some of the scripts were very good, but he just wanted to sit back and get inspired. When he decided to return to work it had to be with the right project. Tom Cruise had spiced up his career with *Magnolia* and *Tropic Thunder* and McConaughey was looking to do the same thing. McConaughey's wife was firmly in support of her husband's decisions. 'You'll have people around you who want other things [for you],' director Richard Linklater, McConaughey's friend and colleague of over twenty years, told *People* magazine, 'but she (Camila) will approach it as, "What does Matthew want?" That's the direction she pushes him.'

In 2011 McConaughey starred in *The Lincoln Lawyer*, which opened in the UK and US in March. It was a complete turnaround for the actor who had been stuck in lame romantic comedies and average dramas. McConaughey was enthusiastic about the story. He was attracted to the whodunit, cat and mouse aspect of it; plus he hadn't made a film like it in quite a while. It brought a refreshing change.

'I read the script about four or five years ago and it needed a little bit of work,' McConaughey admitted to *New Idea* magazine in Australia, 'and I didn't really feel like I was in the time of my life where I was turned on by it. And then it came back around, the script had improved and it was just where I wanted to be as an actor.'

He was surprised by the rewritten script, which he found suspenseful and engaging. His character reminded him of a cowboy and he liked that about the film.

'I got put in touch with Matthew for his passion project called *Bone Game*,' Brad Furman, the director, explained to *Ain't it Cool News*' Mr. Beaks, 'which is this gritty rodeo movie – sort of like *The Wrestler*. I loved that script; I thought he was perfect to play it. I went to meet him and pitch him on why I thought I'd be the perfect director for *Bone Game*, and we really hit it off; he really thought I was right for *Bone Game*. But as with most of these situations, the reality is... you know, is the actor going to make it or not, and if so, when? So I was like, "If you're interested, when are you going to do it?" And he's like, "I don't know. I'll let you know." And then two weeks later, I got a call from my agent, and he said, "You're going in tomorrow to meet for *The Lincoln Lawyer*. Matthew put you up for it." I was so confused. I was like, "What happened to *Bone Game*?" And he said, "Matthew decided he wants to make *The Lincoln Lawyer* next." I was like, "Am I the only guy going in?" I was really confused. [Producer] Tom Rosenberg loves to tell me that there wasn't a chance in hell he was ever hiring me for this movie. Then I met him, and I guess I won him over. It was just one of those things.'

Furman felt like he knew how to make this script. He had heard of Michael Connelly's books but had never read them, though he grew up on John Grisham. His parents were attorneys and so was his grandfather so the script interested him. He'd been in a courtroom since he was a child and worked as a runner for his grandfather at a law firm so he knew the business.

The days of *A Time to Kill*, *Amistad* and *Contact* seemed like such a long time ago and McConaughey was desperate to win back critical favour as a serious actor. After a decade's worth of mostly below average films, although McConaughey's performances were not all that bad, he desperately needed to reinvent himself. He was struggling to compete with leading comedy actors such as Ryan Reynolds and Bradley Cooper and he didn't have the comedic flair of someone like Will Ferrell. It was time for him to move on to other projects that would win him back the critical acclaim his younger self once had. The film took just forty days to shoot a 130-page script that would usually have taken sixty.

'I was enjoying myself,' he said to *GQ*'s Jessica Pressler. 'My relationship with acting was fine. But like in any relationship, you need to shake things up. It didn't mean what we'd been doing was less than. I just wanted a charge. Like, "Let's throw a spark into this."'

The Lincoln Lawyer is based on the best-selling novel of the same name by top crime author Michael Connelly, and stars McConaughey in the lead role as criminal defense attorney Mickey Haller who operates his business around Los Angeles County out of his black Lincoln car.

'Matthew McConaughey is not like the character in the book who is half-Mexican and described as very dark but with a name that did not indicate his background,' Connelly told Nell Minow of *Beliefnet*. 'He had lots of contradictions to add up to his feeling more like an outsider. I heard McConaughey had signed on. When I saw him as the sleazy agent in *Tropic Thunder* I leaned over to my wife and said, 'He'd make a good Mickey Haller." And months later, maybe a year later, I heard he wanted to do it and wanted to meet me and talk about it. He spent a year studying and preparing. It was very impressive. So it doesn't matter how he's described in the book. He's that guy. He totally owns it.'

Haller represents a client who has a plan to beat the system. 'This guy plays the game very well and knows the system,' McConaughey said of his character to journalists at an LA press day for the film. 'He's on the side of defending the people that can't defend themselves, that underbelly of society, but he knows the game. He knows the system and his challenge is to make the system work...and make the system work for him while not letting the system know that they're working for him.'

Haller is hired by Louis Roulet (Ryan Phillippe) who is a Beverly Hills playboy and son of Mary Windsor (Frances Fisher), a rich real estate mogul. Roulet is accused of beating a prostitute and Haller thinks he is innocent; a case of wrong place, wrong time. Haller and his investigator Frank Levin (William H. Macy) analyse the crime scene photos and notice how similar it is to a previous client who is in prison for murder. The film involves lots of plot twists involving his client and his ex-wife, prosecutor Maggie McPherson (Marisa Tomei), as he uncovers more evidence of the crime leading him to question whether or not Roulet is actually innocent.

'We're both kind of playing each other throughout the thing,' explained McConaughey about Haller and Roulet to journalists at that LA press day. 'I didn't want to know or even have an idea of what his hand may be, and I sure as hell didn't want to share with him what mine was. So I was just like, "Look, I've got my guy down and you have your guy down. Let's meet when we're in this scene. Let's meet each other there and go on this two month fun journey getting to know each other through our characters."'

McConaughey has been in films that require heavy rehearsals but he's also been in those where there hasn't been any need to rehearse at all. Off screen, McConaughey and Phillippe barely spoke for the first two weeks besides doing their scenes together. They had no issues with one another; they respected each other's talents. They were both there to do a job. '…I didn't want to show him my hand,' McConaughey admitted to *New Idea*, 'and he didn't want to show me his hand and that's fun because you get to surprise each other each day. But I quite like the young man. He's a very self-reliant young man. You know, he comes prepared. He doesn't really meddle in yours or anyone else's business. He is there to do the work.'

Once they found a rapport off screen the pair chatted about sports – the American football season was about to start – and they also talked about kids, exercise and diet. As you get old the metabolism slows down so it's all about diet, as McConaughey explained to his co-star.

McConaughey's kids visited the set on some days, which made a welcome change when he sat down with them for lunch. On one occasion they dropped in when there was a scene involving a group of Hell Angels-type bikers, which was filmed next to a nearby small airport. There were helicopters and planes passing by which kept the kids entertained. His son was enthralled; he got on one of the motorbikes and rode around. It was like being at an adventure park.

In terms of research for the part McConaughey spent time with a few lawyers to get to grips with his role. He watched them work and saw the movement of their daily schedules but he didn't gain anything specific. In McConaughey's eyes they were like bookies with lots of wheeling and dealing and telling war stories. Some lawyers are born showmen. They're always on the move, always juggling a few cases at once. They just love to talk, too. There's less of a morality issue with some cases and McConaughey noticed that right away – it's more of a case of, 'here's the job, go and do it.' The job of a defence lawyer is to get his client off or to reduce their sentence. McConaughey noticed that some lawyers had articles of their own high profile cases mounted on their office walls.

Mickey Haller has a lot to contend with in the film: he has to take care of his family, he has try to avoid being arrested, he has to do his job and defend a guilty man and also get an innocent man out of jail (Haller was responsible for him being there) while running his business out of the backseat of a car. McConaughey had a lot to consider for the character of Mickey Haller. There are many consequences as a result of the challenges he faces. Haller has to figure out what he wants and what he believes to be right. He is a man of conviction. With so much going on, his life has become a nightmare as he struggles to defend a man he knows is guilty. How can he resolve that and do the right thing? Working with seasoned actors Marisa Tomei and William H. Macy prompted McConaughey to up his game, although not by too much, because working with talented actors meant that he could react easily enough to them, he could listen to them and they'd react similarly.

McConaughey is glad he never became a lawyer for a profession. He can play a lawyer in a film and retire after six months and move on to another project. He has far more options now. *The Lincoln Lawyer* was a good role for him. Haller is a pragmatic character who knows how the legal system works inside out. He defends the underclass of LA society; he's helping people who can't help themselves. Many defence lawyers try to work the system without letting the system work them. However, in the film Haller is defending a wealthy client whom he knows his guilty. 'The thing is that most of these defence attorneys are defending people who are guilty, and they know that,' McConaughey explained to *Cinema Blend's* Eric Eisenberg. 'It's just to what degree, and how much you can ameliorate the sentence and bring it down. The system is much more of a game. It's much more, "Let's make a deal, out here in the alley outside of court, so we can go in and get this off our desk," than I ever thought it was. This guy plays the game very well and knows the system.'

Music is a vital part of the film and is generally a creative tool for McConaughey so he can get a feel for the character. The soundtrack for *The Lincoln Lawyer* was markedly different to anything he'd done before, with urban and hip-hop/rap songs dominating many of the scenes. The director, Brad Furman, gave him around thirty or forty songs to work with, which McConaughey hadn't heard before, so they helped him with the movement of the character.

McConaughey loved how the script moved along, especially its pace. The way the Lincoln enters and exits scenes is also impressive and it's something that grabbed his attention when he first read the script. There are some great shots in the film of McConaughey getting out of the Lincoln. The car is a vital piece of the film.

McConaughey spoke to *Terra.com* about his own use of cars: 'I've always loved to customise my own cars and work out of them. I once had this 1996 Savana GMC van. I stripped out the back, put in a nice couch that unfolded into a bed, put in a big table with a bunch of AC hookups. I had a fax back there, a printer, everything. It was my mobile office, pretty much like

Mick Haller's in this film. And then I moved up to trailers, started customising trailers, which I still do to this day. Part of its [appeal] is getting two things done at once: You're moving, you're heading somewhere, but you're taking care of business on the way. And it's still sometimes one of my favourite places to work.'

McConaughey decided it was time to shake things up. He was looking for fringe characters, unconventional roles that were the polar opposite to what he was known for. With Mickey Haller, he found a character that was strong willed and determined, one who played by his own rules. McConaughey found traits in Haller that reminded him of himself.

With excellent source material, McConaughey had made his best film since *Frailty* and, while it did not set the box office alight, it was a success. It grossed over $85 million with a budget of $40 million. *The Lincoln Lawyer* is a thoroughly enjoyable film and a delight to watch after so many fluffy romantic comedies. If Connelly fans were dubious about the casting of McConaughey, they were quickly proven wrong after the film's release.

Author Connelly saw a rough cut of the film on 12 November 2010 and said on his website: 'The movie comes out March 18. A couple days ago I saw an unfinished cut of it and could not be happier. I thought it was very loyal to the story and the character of Mickey Haller. Matthew McConaughey nails him. Those who loved the book will love the movie, I think. Those who don't know the book will love it just the same. The casting and acting is really superb. Like I said, I could not be happier. I'm very excited and can't wait to see what fans of the book think.'

Reviews of *The Lincoln Lawyer* were mostly positive and while criticisms were aimed at the clichés of the courtroom drama setting, McConaughey's performance was the film's standout part. There is no question that he had made the right move choosing to star in the film.

Peter Bradshaw raved about the film in *The Guardian*: 'Here is the week's unexpected treat: a terrific LA noir thriller based on a novel by Michael Connelly. It stars Matthew McConaughey, who gives a career-best performance as Mick Haller, a fast-talking criminal lawyer who has just regained his licence after some unspecified peccadillo; unable to afford an office, he does business on the move, from the backseat of his chauffeured Lincoln car.'

The Daily Mirror said: 'McConaughey's new film might be the best legal thriller since *Jagged Edge* – and no, I can hardly believe it either.'

James Mottram wrote in *Total Film*: 'Looking increasingly haggard as the trial unfurls, as Haller gradually comes to the realisation that this is no open-and-shut case, McConaughey gives his best performance in years. It may not quite be on the level of Paul Newman's ambulance chaser in *The Verdict* but it's subtle, assured work.'

The Lincoln Lawyer was undoubtedly the turning point in his career. It changed, or at least helped to change the opinions levelled at him by critics and audiences. It was not a massively straining role in some respects but it did help rebrand him. It gave him the push that he needed to reinvent himself. It is an excellent film, slick, stylish and polished but with enough grit and realism to give the story and the characters from the novel justice. It's a contemporary noir story with intriguing characters and an intricate plot with an abundance of twists and turns. The film certainly surprised the critics, many of whom had already written off McConaughey. It was just the right type of film that he needed to make at this juncture of his career. He just got lucky, to paraphrase a line from the film.

NPR's Ella Taylor put it best in her review: 'Just when you thought Matthew McConaughey had settled into pre-retirement content to play the (dry-aged) beefcake in a string of dippy romantic comedies, the actor comes roaring back with some real acting.'

What did the best-selling author think of the finished film? 'The truth is I can't believe my good fortune. I sold the book six years ago to Tom Rosenberg at Lakeshore Entertainment,' Connelly wrote in a blog for the *Huffington Post*. 'In a previous stage of his life he was a lawyer. A trial attorney in Chicago. He told me back when he bought the book that he knew the world of Mickey Haller and promised me that when he made the movie that he would keep the novel's gritty realism intact. Six years later he has made good on the promise. Along with McConaughey, Furman, Romano and everyone else involved. And that makes me say, "I just got lucky."'

'I'm pretty happy with *Lincoln Lawyer*,' McConaughey expressed to *Terra.com*. 'It was a lot of things I wanted to get across, and I think what we're all trying to get across happened. I think it's good. I think it's a good, strong, legal thriller. I think it's surprising as hell. It's got a killer cast. An all-star cast. It's the kind of movie I want to go see in the theatre, you know?'

Connelly's previous film adaption was *Blood Work*, released in 2002 and directed by Clint Eastwood. It was a greeted with modest critical reviews but was a box office failure grossing $26.2 million on a budget of $50 million. It took a while for Hollywood to be interested in green-lighting another Connelly novel.

Since the publication of the novel in 2005, Mickey Haller has appeared in four other novels (the most recent being *The Gods of Guilt* in 2013) by Michael Connelly, and has become a popular character in the world of legal thrillers. Since the film's 2011 release nothing has been confirmed regarding any film sequels, which is a disappointment, since Connelly's novels have progressed in quality as he has become more comfortable writing legal thrillers – his usual territory is detective fiction with his main character LAPD Detective Hieronymus 'Harry' Bosch, who features in the second Haller novel, 2008's *The Brass Verdict*. Haller made a cameo in the 14th Bosch novel, *9 Dragons*, published in 2009. With praise from Connelly and nods of approval from his fans, and given that *The Lincoln Lawyer* made a profit, surely another film could be green-lit. Time will tell on that front. There's certainly more chance of another Mickey Haller film than there is a Dirk Pitt film.

'Well two things have got to happen for a sequel,' McConaughey said to *New Idea* magazine when asked about any future Mickey Haller films. 'You've got to make a good movie. I think we've done that. Second thing is that movie has to make a certain amount of money in the box office. We're looking pretty good right now. I would love to be in these shoes again if the script is good'

McConaughey later expressed his interest in a sequel in 2012 during an interview with *Total Film*. 'It's actually a mix of two. I won't reveal what those are, but it's a mix of two. I got good reviews on *The Lincoln Lawyer*. There's a lot of times that critics have written the review before they've seen the frickin' movie. They've written the review on me before they've seen it – maybe the critic doesn't like me.'

McConaughey had already been thinking about upcoming projects and what he wanted to do with his career. He knew he wanted to explore unconventional roles and that he was aiming to surprise people with daring characters but he also wanted to challenge himself as an actor and say to all those naysayers out there, 'Hey, look at what I can do.'

*****

In October 2011 Freedom Films announced Gerard Butler, Sam Worthington and Matthew McConaughey were to star in *Thunder Run*, an action thriller to be directed by Simon West (*When a Stranger Calls*, *The Mechanic*). A CG 3D film, Freedom Films said they would use proprietary facial-capture technology soon to be seen on West's upcoming *Night of the Living Dead: Origins 3-D* (eventually released in 2014; produced by West and directed by Zebediah De Soto), along with the motion capture technology used in *Avatar*, the massively popular James Cameron-directed science-fiction 3D venture.

Thunder Run is based on the book by David Zucchino, with Robert Port (*Numb3rs*) and Ken Nolan (*Black Hawk Down*) having penned the screenplay. The film's press release said: '*Thunder Run* is the untold story of the dangerous and bloody capture of Baghdad by American Forces at the onset of the Iraq War. In April 2003, three battalions and fewer than a thousand men launched a violent thrust of tanks and Bradley Fighting Vehicles into the heart of a city of five million, igniting a three-day blitzkrieg, which military professionals often refer to as a lightning strike, or 'thunder run'. In telling the story of the surprise assault on Baghdad – one of the most decisive battles in recent American combat history – this movie paints the harrowing picture of the soldiers on the front lines and the realities of modern warfare.' As of yet it remains unmade, even though IMDB are listing a 2015 release date but with no cast or director details.

Nostalgic for his east Texas roots and his fellow Texans, McConaughey collaborated with Richard Linklater for a third time on the film *Bernie*. Linklater had cast McConaughey in *Dazed and Confused* and *The Newton Boys* and had enjoyed those previous collaborations. They're good friends and have fun working with each other. Linklater is the only director where McConaughey can pitch something to him and say 'Hey, I've got something for you…let's talk.' They think very highly of each other and have much reverence for each other's work. For McConaughey, his work is so much better when he has fun. It's part of his 'just keep livin'' mantra.

The film is based on a 1998 article called 'Midnight In The Garden Of East Texas' by Skip Hollandsworth that was published in *Texas Monthly*. The article tells the story of the 1996 murder of the eighty-one-year-old millionaire Marjorie Nugent in Carthage by Bernhardt 'Bernie' Tiede who was her thirty-one-year-old companion. Bernie was very highly respected in the Carthage vicinity, so much so that despite having confessed to the police, the District Attorney had to request a change of venue in order to secure a fair trial, which is very rare in legal circles.

When fifty-year-old director Linklater spoke to McConaughey about the film and gave him the script to read, the actor thought he was being offered the title role, but was ecstatic to find out Linklater wanted him to show off his feminine side by playing the grande dame. Linklater laughed and said he wanted McConaughey to play a DA from East Texas. McConaughey had to wear a wig made of thin grey hair, oversized glasses, plumpers in his cheeks, and a weight belt that added an extra 20 pounds to his waistline. He was radically different from the handsome lawyer in *A Time to Kill*. McConaughey was on board for whichever part he was offered because he was so impressed. He thought it was hilarious. It's a dark comedy with murder, but it's not a cold film.

'There's something about him, either your charm or you give that kind of charm…' he said of his character, DA Danny Buck Davidson, to Donna White of *Austin Daze*. 'It's just moving. There was something innocent about it that attracted me in that way. I never read this and thought, no it's too dark. When I read it, I felt on pace with the tone. I thought it was much more funny than dark.'

Bernie is the story of small town funeral director Bernie Tiede, played remarkably well by Jack Black (he listened to audio tapes and spoke to Bernie in person to get the accent just right) who kills the grande dame played by veteran actress Shirley MacLaine. McConaughey enacts real life District Attorney Danny Buck Davidson who prosecuted the real Bernie Tiede in 1998. Linklater took around seven months to get a script together with the help of Hollandsworth who offered some plot points and dialogue. Linklater's producer Ginger Sledge, an ex-Austin teacher who had worked her way up in the movie business, was also on hand with suggestions.

Texas is almost like another country such is the way of life, culture, politics and general vibe of Texans. Linklater strove to portray a different side of the state of Texas, a more innocent version, to the one that is usually portrayed on screen with gun-toting cowboys, trigger-happy republicans, or rednecks and hillbillies. In the film Linklater breaks down the different areas of the state – and it's done terrifically and is very funny.

Making a film based on real life events can be difficult because there are many factors involved, so Linklater was careful to be true to the story and not offend anyone. He was concerned about the families involved and wanted to be as accurate as possible. He had no access to the key players (Mrs Nugent is gone and Bernie's in prison) so he came up with the idea of having the town's gossips tell the story. Gossip is very popular in small towns, often being the main source of entertainment.

Linklater spoke to Bill Graham of *The Film Stage* about the research that had to be undertaken prior to filming *Bernie*, his first film since 2008's *Me and Orson Welles*: 'I went to the trial over ten years ago, I was into it back then and felt I knew the guy. Just seeing him testify and seeing where he nails Bernie with the *Les Miserables* and all that. That's all word for word, that all really happened. So, Matthew did a bunch of cool stuff around that, but the gist of that it's tricky when you're doing something based on real events, real people. I was concerned [for] the Nugent family and the survivors, but you just dive in and be as accurate as you possibly can.'

McConaughey's mother Kay played one of the town gossips in the film named Tassie. Kay, who had raised McConaughey in Longview but had since moved to Sun City, a community for seniors near Georgetown, just north of Austin, was retired and spent her time doing Pilates and performing in amateur theatrical productions. For years she had begged her son to get her a small role in one of his movies but he always said he didn't have the power to do it and never acted on her requests 'One time when I was visiting him in Los Angeles,' Kay told *Texas Monthly*'s Skip Hollandsworth in 2012, 'I met Brian Grazer, the movie producer, and I said, "Hey, don't you think it would be a great idea if you did a remake of *The Graduate* with Matthew playing Dustin Hoffman and me playing Anne Bancroft?" He said, "Mrs McConaughey, do you realise you'd have to do a love scene with your own son?" And I said, "Oh, hell. It's no big deal. We'll fake it." Can you believe he still said no? Well, thank God for Richard Linklater, who's finally seen my real potential.'

Rooster, his brother, had a part in *The Newton Boys* and now his mother had a role in *Bernie*. Kay was ecstatic when Linklater gave her a part in the film, which she auditioned for. Linklater did not see anyone else in that role. 'And she goes, "Rick says I'm just right for it,"' McConaughey said to *Austin Daze*'s Donna White. 'So a couple weeks go by and I go, "So did he say you got the part?" And she says, "Well, I mean, Rick said I'm right for it." And I go, "No, no, no, a director can say anything like that. Did he say you got the part?" And she goes, "No." (Mimics her heavy sigh, laughs…) So I said, "You might be gettin' a callback. You better get after it some more." So I get her pumped up. I'm serious! I jacked with her.'

McConaughey worked with his mother for weeks with her lines making sure she got the pronunciation, the pace of the sentences and facial mannerisms correct. 'We get on well,' McConaughey said to *New Idea* magazine on his relationship with his mum. 'You know there is something I've noticed about I say [sic] elders, it's like when you are a kid and you're under twenty you're a revolutionary. Then in your 20s, 30s, 40s even 50s you get responsibility and then I think after sixty, you go back to being the revolutionary and you just don't give a damn. And I see that in my mother and her boyfriend and it's pretty funny and pretty inspiring to the zest for life they have.'

Principal photography commenced in September and was finished twenty-two days later in October 2010 and took place in various locations in Texas, including Smithville, Georgetown, Lockhart, Carthage and Austin. The budget was just $5 million. The film mixes documentary footage with fictional elements to create a film of authenticity yet uncertainty. The townspeople in the film play themselves and the talking heads are actors.

Bernie premiered at the 2011 Los Angeles Film Festival, seven months after filming, and was shown at selected international film festivals throughout the end of 2011. It opened in US cinemas for a limited run in April 2012. A special screening to benefit victims of the Bastrop County wildfires was held in Austin a few months after the premiere. The local gossips, extras and other Carthage residents were invited, including Danny Buck, to see the film. Bernie himself was in a special unit in New Boston where he was suffering from diabetes and fifteen years away from a chance at parole. Linklater contacted the prison to ask if a special screening could be arranged for Bernie but he was turned down months later.

The film received positive reviews from critics. Reviewers noted the strong performances of the three lead actors, notably Jack Black who is mostly known for goofball comedies. Linklater and Black had worked together on the successful goofy comedy *School of Rock*, released in 2003. Some critics pointed out that McConaughey is at his best when working with Linklater. *Bernie* was named by some critics as one of the best films of 2012.

The film won several nominations such as 'Best Feature' and

'Best Ensemble Performance' at the 2012 Gotham Awards, 'Best Feature' at the 2012 Independent Spirit Awards and 'Best Comedy' at the Broadcast Film Critics Association. Black was nominated for a Golden Globe and the Broadcast Film Critics Association nominated him for 'Best Actor' and MacLaine for 'Best Actress'. In the *Los Angeles Times*, a reader's survey named *Bernie* as the 'most under-appreciated' film of the year from a shortlist of seven films picked by the newspaper.

Caroline Frost wrote in the *Huffington Post*: 'Hilariously hammy and yet underplayed is Matthew McConaughey, once again proving that his professional life away from rom-com land is a rich fount, with a superb comic timing and his accent broad in its native glory, as he describes the corpse "frozen like a popsicle".'

The *London Evening Standard*'s Derek Malcolm wrote: 'MacLaine too is wonderful as the chopper-faced Marjorie, and Matthew McConaughey, as the one local who is suspicious of Bernie from the start, also does very well. But it is Black's film, and that of the townsfolk, about whom somebody says: "They've got more tattoos than brains."'

McConaughey summarised his thoughts on the film to Bill Graham of *The Film Stage*: 'There's something charming about this movie and there's something innocent about it that's attractive in that way, in that innocent charming way. So, I never read this and thought, "Oh boy." If I know it came from him as he actually pitched it to me for fifty minutes in his truck, and when I read it, I felt on page with the tone. I thought it was much more funny than I ever thought it was dark. I liked that it was dark comedy but I was just laughing.'

Ironically, the real life story of Bernie had a Hollywood

ending. Special Judge Diane DeVasto agreed to release Tiede early from prison – he would not serve his full life sentence on the grounds that he was sexually assaulted as a child and had been in an abusive relationship with his victim, the eighty-one-year-old Marjorie Nugent. It was agreed that Tiede would stay in an apartment above a garage in Austin owned by Linklater.

With *The Lincoln Lawyer* and *Bernie* under his belt, the 2010s had gotten off to a good start for McConaughey. The acclaim with which he had been greeted in the 1990s would be surpassed as he was slowly turning his career around to become one of Hollywood's most popular and revered actors. The industry was finally getting the message: McConaughey wasn't interested in romantic comedies anymore. He was looking for material that shocked him.

'I'm not much for seeing things as full stops, fresh starts. I think it's all part of the same evolution and career, you know?' McConaughey said to *Terra.com*. 'I think, probably, another stage is worth saying. Or maybe another chapter, same book – yeah, I'll go with that.'

CHAPTER EIGHT

FAMILY AND PHILANTHROPY

'I was an older bachelor than many of my friends. I enjoyed
the life I was leading but knew it could not go on like that.'
Matthew McConaughey, *Daily Express*, 2014

'I had a wonderful year last year. It was very colourful,'
Matthew told *The Daily Beast*'s Ramin Setoodeh about
working on films throughout 2011 and into the first half of
2012. 'I've never really had a year where for [so many] roles
back to back I was so genuinely excited. I was working with
directors who had a singular vision. But the hard part about
independent film is getting to day one of shooting. They're just
hard to get made.'

McConaughey married Brazilian model and TV performer
Camila Alves on 9 June 2012 in Austin, Texas where they resided
and decided to base themselves properly as from March of that
year. However, back in 2010 he told Rebecca Murray of *About.
com: Hollywood Movies*: 'Am I getting married in the future? Not
today. Honestly, not today. I don't have any plans for it. I was
asked this earlier. It's not an institution I'm against at all. I'm

actually for it, believe in it, and have seen it actually be very, very healthy for many relationships. Some people go through it some great ways. It's just not something I plan on doing right now and that I feel like I need to do right now, but I'm not against it at all.'

As a bachelor McConaughey had a house in the Hollywood Hills but it was his home – he'd poured his heart and soul into it. He detailed pretty much everything, both exteriors and interiors. But now he had found a woman he wanted to live with and with whom he wanted to have a home and family with so they bought a new property together. They also had a place together in Malibu, just outside of LA, which they built together. It has a fantastic view of the Pacific Ocean and the weather is wonderful. His production company offices continued to be based in Venice.

'Decorating and landscaping is my hobby,' McConaughey admitted to *The Tech*'s Alison C. Lewis on his homes and relationship with Texas. 'I can still talk to strangers there. It's a state that holds up and digs into its own identity. It holds onto traditions that work. It [also] progresses. [Living on the ranch] gets your body clock on the right time...you can do anything you want or nothing at all.'

Their Austin home is a Mediterranean-type mansion on nine acres of land. The 10,800-square-feet 'Old Oak Estate' has three stories and includes seven bedrooms and eight bathrooms. It's a beautiful home and Camila was more than willing to move permanently to Austin where McConaughey knows the people, the dialect and the culture. He likes the family values and common sense of fellow Texans, as well as the patriotism and humble way of life.

The couple were engaged on 25 December 2011. McConaughey had Camila's ring wrapped in several boxes as a gift and when she finally got down to the ring he dropped down on one knee in front of his family and proposed to her. It was a Christmas Day gift she didn't expect.

'The first word out of her mouth was not "Yes." I'm not gonna say what it was,' he recalled on *The Tonight Show with Jay Leno*. 'But I did say, "Look, I'm down on a knee. I'll stay here awhile. I will outlast you." And I did! She conceded.'

His fiancée's engagement ring was designed by Cathy Waterman. Their youngest child Livingston Alves McConaughey was born in 2012 joining his elder siblings Levi and Vida. They were a loving family and wanted to make it all official.

Camila expressed her views to *US Weekly*: 'A lot of people, sometimes they're so stuck on "I gotta get married, I gotta get married," that they forget that the really important thing is to have a healthy home, a healthy family, a healthy family for your kids and to have everything going in a good, peaceful way.'

Camila is the love of Matthew's life. She made him want things in life that no other woman had done. She encouraged him to see the future in a different way. He was happy and positive about every aspect in his life. Relationships by their very nature make people change want they want in life and it makes them view things differently because you're not only thinking about yourself in any given situation but your partner too. McConaughey had found the woman he was willing to do anything for. He was deeply in love and it felt wonderful.

The children were involved in their parents' ceremony – Levi, aged three, brought the rings on a necklace and Vida, two, was the flower girl. She didn't drop one petal along the twenty-five-yard aisle. It took around two minutes for her to diligently walk that distance, though she stopped to chat to people en route and her dad then crouched down at which point she went running to him.

'We have a family now, got two kids.' McConaughey told *MSN Entertainment*. 'One of the things that we've learned is that we've reminded [ourselves and] our kids to be thankful for all the things that we have, because a lot of these kids don't have the opportunity. One: a solid mother-father relationship in the house; Two: our kids don't have to worry about eating or college tuition.'

It was a union between themselves and God. It was a Catholic ceremony and was officiated by Benedictine Monk, Father Christian Leisy and the Reverend David Haney of Riverbend Church. Camila carried a beautiful bouquet of white cattleya orchids and artichoke flowers down the aisle. Their wedding bands were designed by Kathy Rose.

'We've been living a married life for over six years now. We have homes together, we have family together, we have kids, we've built a life together,' Camila told *ET Canada* 'So we've been living a married life this whole time.' She added: 'Levi actually understands what it means now that Mama's going to have the same last name as they have.'

Various reports were printed in the press about the typically extravagant and expensive Hollywood-style wedding. *US Weekly* reported that acclaimed singer-songwriter John Mellencamp 'sang a song for the bride and groom based on a bible verse'. Reports stated that McConaughey wore a three-piece black Dolce & Gabbana tuxedo at the evening ceremony and his bride wore white Stuart Weitzman heels and a wedding gown handmade by her favourite Brazilian designer. McConaughey wanted the wedding to be close to home so he had a makeshift campground set up for wedding guests to start the weekend on their Texas property. There were forty-seven air-conditioned tents, gourmet presents and plots of entrainment on offer. The tents reportedly had beds, cosy white fur rugs and outdoor seating with doormats at the front. Guests were made to feel warm and homely. Reese Witherspoon, Jim Toth, Meg Ryan, Richard Linklater and Woody Harrelson were said to be in attendance. They were close friends of McConaughey's whom he'd worked with or had supported him throughout his career.

A guest told *US Weekly*: 'There were about 100 of his close friends and family there. [The ceremony] was very emotional. There was a moment when . . . [Matthew] leaned down and whispered something in [Camila's] ear and you could see a tear coming down her face. Everyone let out a collective sigh.'

The evening ceremony included a live band playing American and Brazilian songs. The food catered for American and Brazilian guests with fine Brazilian meats and Southern delicacies and beer. The wedding cake at the reception was red-velvet decorated with flags of Texas and Brazil. It was a happy mixture of people and cultures all in celebration of two people who were in love.

'I had some wonderful women in my life,' McConaughey said to the *Daily Express*' Garth Pearce. 'But I was in no rush. When I married I intended to stay married. I did not want to make a mistake.'

When they met in 2006 he was very single and enjoying single life and working, and after a string of affairs with Sandra Bullock, Ashley Judd, Renée Zellweger, Patricia Arquette, US TV presenter Salli Richardson and Penelope Cruz, he wasn't looking to settle down. 'I don't dislike any of my exes,' he said to *Elle*'s Holly Milea. 'If I took time to form a relationship, it's gonna hurt when we move on, but are you puttin' Wite-Out over all that beautiful time together? That was real time in your life. It's connected to where you are today.'

Alves stole his heart and he fell for her like a lovesick teen. He wanted to go out with her every single night from when he first met her and he knew that was a good sign. He fell in love. He even learned Portuguese. 'Asking a woman to marry me – to want to do that, to find that woman and allow myself to love her that way and say, "I want to spend the rest of my life with you," that's a rite of passage,' the actor told the *Scotsman* in 2012.

McConaughey had to grow up for his children. He wanted to be a good father to his kids and so he put the partying lifestyle behind him and matured. His focus would be his home life and his career. 'The number one thing on my bucket list since I was eight years old [was to be] a father,' he admitted to *Stylist*'s Susan Riley. 'It's the reason as a kid I called men "sir" and ladies "ma'am". To have children is the most awesome position a man can be in – then and only then can you have any chance of going from a prince to a king. So I'm doing that. Steven Spielberg always said: "we do movies, but having children – that's your epic." It is.'

Levi wasn't even two years old and already his dad took him to a John Mellencamp show. 'We have a little bit more prep-time put into going places and doing things, getting him ready and everything,' McConaughey said to *People* magazine's Kelly Rondeau. 'But it's amazing.'

He learned a lot from his own parents but also learned from their mistakes. However, he is a bit softer on his own kids than his parents were on him and his elder brothers. He relishes being a family man; it suits his persona perfectly. Despite his success and fame he is a somewhat humble man and is close to his roots, but he also believes in giving something back to those who are not quite as fortunate as he has been, hence his charity commitments. With a steady family, a refreshed career and beautiful homes in Austin and Malibu, McConaughey was a happy man but he still kept that free spirit of his. 'Am I a fun-loving guy, man? Who likes running around in the summer with his shirt off, man? Am I a guy who likes to hang out with his friends, and party and go to concerts and football games with his friends?' he mused with Tom Chiarella of *Esquire*. 'Well, yeah! Yes, I am. Always have been. Always hopefully will be. You know?'

He wasn't done with big studio films, however – he wouldn't be that stupid. The money is too good. He wanted to let go of the leash and try new roles and he found one in a sadistic contract-killing cop.

*****

The Exorcist and *French Connection* director William Friedkin cast McConaughey as Police Detective 'Killer' Joe Cooper in the critically acclaimed *Killer Joe*. The film – which co-starred Emile Hirsch as Chris Smith (son), Juno Temple as Dottie Smith (daughter), Gina Gershon as Sharla Smith (stepmother), Thomas Haden Church as Ansel Smith (father) and Marc Macaulay as Digger Soames, a gang boss – is violent and full of dark humour.

Killer Joe is set in West Dallas (though shot mostly in New

Orleans which prompted criticism from Texans who felt it didn't quite look like their state) and sees twenty-two-year-old drug dealer Chris Smith struggling to pay off debts to loan sharks so he decides to murder his mother Adele to collect the $50,000 insurance money. Chris hires Joe Cooper – whose side job is that of a contract killer – to help him but the plan almost fails when he struggles to pay Cooper's fee. However, Cooper takes a shine to Dottie, who he takes as a retainer until the insurance money is cashed. The film follows the struggles between Chris and Cooper as it reaches a shocking finale.

'He was being interviewed on one of those Larry King-type television shows,' Friedkin explained to *Movieline*'s Jason Guerrasio, 'and I saw him as himself, not as a guy in a romantic comedy. I thought this guy is really interesting and smart and very self-knowledgeable. He's not this guy in the rom-coms. He's from East Texas and he had the right accent and all of those things went well. I was originally going to go to some grizzled old warhorse to play Joe. But after watching this interview I thought, "This would be interesting: A good-looking guy who could charm the mustard off a hot dog." I thought, "This is the way I want to go."'

When McConaughey first read the script he didn't get it; he wasn't sympathetic to the character at all. He made him feel sick; it almost repulsed him. He spoke to one of his colleagues about the script and they helped talk him around, and then he chatted to Friedkin who helped him look at the script in a different light. It was the film *Frailty* and McConaughey's knowledge of Texas, which, added to the DNA of *Killer Joe*, convinced Friedkin that Matthew was right for the part. McConaughey reread the script and then it clicked. He found the character of Joe Cooper to be hilarious, albeit in a dark way. He thought of it as an odd love story like *King Kong*, the 1976 version with Jessica Lange, which had made an impression on him as a child. The movie made him question what true love really is.

Friedkin had directed the likes of Gene Hackman in *The French Connection*, Willem Dafoe in *To Live and Die in LA* and David Caruso in *Jade* but he hadn't worked with such a good-looking and popular mainstream Hollywood actor as McConaughey. 'I know how little they value the acting of a great-looking guy in Hollywood,' Friedkin said to Dennis Lim of *The New York Times*. 'They don't want you to act, they just want you to show up and convincingly make love to the leading lady. A guy like Matthew has to take charge of his own career, because the studios will cast him in the same part every time out.'

Friedkin admired McConaughey for striving to progress his career. Hollywood studios didn't want him to act; they just wanted him to take his shirt off and show himself off in front of the camera. McConaughey was looking for roles that challenged him, even though the Hollywood studios didn't want him to as they didn't want to lose money, so going down the indie film route was his only option. 'McConaughey was making $10 million a picture just playing a kind of good-looking dude who gets the girl,' Friedkin said to *Den of Geek*'s James Peaty. 'A lot of actors are trying... I mean, DiCaprio is trying to stretch out and time will tell if he can. McConaughey obviously could and clearly has the chops. He could still go on and make those romantic-comedies looking the way he does, but that isn't really who he is or what he wants to do.'

Friedkin has, throughout his career, been attacked by critics for being a sensationalist and *Killer Joe* has some incredibly dark scenes. There is a lot of nudity and violence, with hints at incest and paedophilia. The scene where Killer Joe forces Sharla Smith to pretend to perform oral sex on him with a piece of fried chicken was not easy to shoot for either the cast or the crew. McConaughey didn't warm up for the scene; he just went in there and filmed it. It's the film's most sadistically memorable scene.

'When you get the schedule, that's the scene you look forward to – like, "What day is that?"' he said to the *Scotsman* about the scene. 'But I felt such ownership of the character by that point that I didn't think much about it, aside from saying, "I've got to do it." No easing into it either. This is one take, baby.'

McConaughey's character can be compared to Casey Affleck's Deputy Sheriff Lou Ford in the controversial Michael Winterbottom film from 2010, *The Killer Inside Me* based on the cult Jim Thompson noir novel. They're both sadistic men, tormented and corrupt but also a product of their upbringing and the morally questionable society around them. It was the sort of tough as nails role that would go to the likes of Josh Brolin or Tom Berenger.

He actually found shooting *Killer Joe* to be easier than some of the rom-coms he'd done. A rom-com is pitched at 'buoyant' rather than 'deep', whereas *Killer Joe* was evidently cold and distant with no trace of morale or humanity.

For the most part McConaughey prefers not to reshoot scenes over and over again. With *The Lincoln Lawyer* he averaged around three of four takes but Friedkin prefers a maximum of two and that's how McConaughey likes to work. He prefers it when there isn't a warm up to the scene; he just goes on set and gets it over with. Then again, there are times when he doesn't mind doing more takes (depending on the film) because he has a huge amount of energy and likes to try something a little different every now and again.

McConaughey spoke to *Cinema Blend*'s Eric Eisenberg about his method to acting: 'I can't go back to my trailer to wait, to then re-enter the next scene. Let's show up on set that day and everyone be prepared, and let's crank and shoot film all day. Let's rehearse it on film.'

The film struggled with censors who labelled it too violent for mass consumption and consequently it was cut down to 98 minutes from its original length of 102 minutes and given an NC-17 rating in the US and an 18 certificate by the BBFC in the UK. Generally, such a rating is considered to kill a film at the box office. The original cut was released on DVD in late 2012.

Killer Joe brought McConaughey great critical acclaim after it premiered at the Venice Film Festival in September 2011 and was shown at various international film festivals throughout the year but struggled to get an international release. LD Entertainment finally picked up the distribution rights to the film at the 2011 Toronto International Film festival. It made its UK premiere at the Opening Gala of the Edinburgh International Film Festival on 20 June 2012 and was introduced by Friedkin and actress Gina Gershon.

It was eventually given an official, albeit small, theatrical release in the UK on 29 June and finally opened in the States on 27 July 2012 in just three cinemas. It had only been released to seventy-five cinemas across the US and closed on 14 October 14. The film was not, by any stretch, a box office hit. It grossed just $1,987,762 at the US box office and only $1,677,307 worldwide, reaping almost $4 million in total. Its budget, though, was $10 million. On the plus side, McConaughey received an Independent Spirit Award nomination for 'Best Male Lead' and also received a nomination from the San Diego Film Critics Society for 'Best Supporting Actor'. He won 'Actor Of The Year' from the Central Ohio Film Critics Association, a 'Special Honorary Award' from the Austin Film Critics Association and 'Best Actor' at the Saturn Awards.

Some critics felt it pushed the Southern gothic into unnecessary boundaries of indecency while some praised its boldness. It certainly helped McConaughey ditch his Hollywood rom-com leading man persona even further. He was working overtime on a series of unconventional yet utterly mesmerising roles. Seen with a black cowboy hat and aviator shades, McConaughey gives the performance of his career – daring, witty and sadistically dark. His character is a monster. Friedkin had turned McConaughey's persona into something uncomfortably macabre, the way Hitchcock had done with James Stewart in *Vertigo* and *Rear Window*, or how Anthony Minghella used Matt Damon in *The Talented Mr. Ripley*.

The Guardian's Caroline Shoard wrote: 'Performances are across-the-board terrific, with Gershon and Haden Church blurring the lines of caricature, while McConaughey freezes blood as a man whose dogged adherence to a bent code of conduct fills the vacuum in a not entirely negative way.'

Ian Nathan wrote in *Empire*: 'McConaughey gives the film its Mephistophelean pull: his line-delivery lacquered with honeyed menace, he summons a dread-like gravity – a vilely hilarious stride along his quest to prove he is more than the jutting prow of Kate Hudson rom-coms.'

David Sexton in the *Evening Standard* wrote: 'It's a real actor's piece and the central roles have been brilliantly cast here. Matthew McConaughey, previously always the likeable rom-com hero who gets his shirt off, is a stone cold brute as Joe, intelligent and scary, stylishly dressed and speaking very slowly and formally, then suddenly exploding into violence.'

McConaughey was continuing to look for roles that would challenge him as an actor – and he found one about male strippers. So, is it irony that McConaughey was cast in a film about male strippers given his reputation for appearing bare-chested? 'I'm not a daily reader of page, whatever, Six,' he said to *The New York Times'* Dennis Lim. 'Hell, I didn't know until two years after it started that there was a phenomenon about me being shirtless.'

He was cast alongside Channing Tatum in the 2012 film *Magic Mike*, based on Tatum's early life. The film was directed by *Sex, Lies and Videotape* and *Ocean's 11* director Steven Soderbergh. McConaughey had been confirmed as a member of the cast on 16 August 2011 and was the first actor to be cast after Tatum. McConaughey spoke to director Steve Soderbergh over the phone pitching to him the character of Dallas. After ten minutes of banter and laughs, McConaughey accepted the part. It was only the second time he'd accepted a film role over the phone; the first time being for a Linklater film, either *The Newton Boys* or *Bernie*.

'Matthew understood the part so well,' Soderbergh informed Mary Kaye Schilling of *Vulture*, 'and had such good ideas that I had no desire to box him in. So I just said yes to everything, which turned out to be the right way to go. I think the only note I gave him, when I first pitched him the part on the phone, was that his character believed in UFOs.'

'When I first talked to Steven,' McConaughey explained at a press junket for the film, 'he called to offer the role of Dallas to me. He had pitched the story and told me who this guy was and I was laughing really hard on the phone and said yes. I said, "Can you give me one line just so I can hang up the phone and walk away here and imagination can go somewhere?" He said, "Well, this guy Dallas is pretty connected with UFOs, man." So, that was a great launch pad. It was a pretty roofless bit of direction on the phone in the beginning and so I knew that I was going to be able to fly. That was really fun to play someone so committed in many ways.'

The cast visited male strip clubs to get a feel for the role and visited strippers backstage; and McConaughey took a trip to an LA strip club to get used to regular waxing. Filming started in September and finished at the end of October 2011.

For research McConaughey visited a male revue in New Orleans with Tatum. They hit out in the back so they wouldn't get recognised. 'The one thing I got from that: this is not these guys' real jobs,' he said to *The Daily Beast*'s Ramin Setoodeh. 'One guy I met that night was back from Afghanistan. Another guy was a lawyer and had three kids. They all looked like accountants when they were in street clothes. The other thing I learned is the production value is horrible. I said to Steven, "Can I run this production?" I took off on that. I became P.T. Barnum. I was channelling Jim Morrison and Malcolm McDowell from *A Clockwork Orange*.'

Magic Mike tells the story of a nineteen-year-old man played by Alex Pettyfer who enters the world of male stripping helped by veteran stripper Michael 'Magic Mike' Lane (played by Channing Tatum). The film is loosely based on Tatum, who was once an eighteen-year-old stripper in Tampa, Florida.

McConaughey plays Dallas, a former stripper and

businessman who owns the strip club Xquisite and is Mike's boss. McConaughey had no stripping scenes in the original script but requested one, which became the closing dance number where he shouts 'Ladies of Tampa' and then strips. The song was written in three hours by music supervisor Frankie Pine, McConaughey and his guitar coach Martin Blasick. The rest of the cast includes Matt Bomer, Joe Manganiello and Cody Horn.

McConaughey had to work out for the role because he'd just finished filming *The Paperboy*, which hadn't been released at that point. He hadn't been to the gym in four months and had just eleven days to get ready. He had to be in great shape to make his character plausible because the one thing male strippers are in is fantastic physical condition. The better shape they're in, the more money they'll make from female punters. His character in the film is a capitalist and wouldn't have his strippers in poor shape; he'd knock them back. So he had to be in great shape himself. He had to learn some moves, too – stripers entertain for two hours and the music has to be on time, lighting, intros, exits and so on is all part of the show and it has to be perfectly arranged.

McConaughey was nervous shooting the strip scene (with 'Doctor Love' by KISS playing through the club's sound system) but reckoned that if he didn't film it, he'd regret it for the rest of his life. He likes the basic premise of guy in a very seedy world who is looking to get out of it and move on to the next stage of his life. His wife was very supportive of him and even turned up on set to his surprise. She was there on set the day he performed his strip and thought her husband was terrific. She knew how much work he'd put into it and how dedicated he was to the role. 'Before going out on the stage to dance,' McConaughey said at a press junket for the film, 'even if you're not taking your clothes off, for everyone live is kind of nerve racking, but then knowing you have to strip down – *very* nerve racking. Then after doing it once, God, I wanted to get up there and do it again. That was a lot of fun.'

Dressed in a thong, one side was ripped off by one of the extras in the audience and 'I remember that moment, it's really clear to me,' he told Ramin Setoodeh of *The Daily Beast*. 'I did feel the chill of the air hit me in some spots that it hadn't hit me before. As soon as I felt that, I stayed in rhythm, my hand went down, made sure I held the straps up, I cupped it between my legs and stood up and did a body roll out. I stayed on the beat and stayed right on tune, and then just kind of walked out of there, one hand up, one hand down, holding the thong on.'

When McConaughey first put on the thong he walked around trying to have normal conversations about football or what he ate the night before so he could get used to the thing, to feel normal and comfortable in it.

'It's a huge leap of faith to trust a thong,' McConaughey said at a press junket at the Four Seasons Hotel in LA as quoted in *The Hollywood Reporter*. 'It's your only protection up on stage. When I first tried it on, my body contorted. And I tried to get myself into every position to see what angles I was covered.'

McConaughey enjoys the creative process, especially on his recent films. There's no guarantee that the film will be a commercial or critical hit, or that it'll not go straight to rental, but McConaughey takes knowledge from each role and learns from the process, trying to better himself.

Magic Mike was a strong part for him. 'Something I've

learned in the last two years that's really been quite helpful,' he confessed to *The Film Experience*'s Nathaniel R. in 2014, 'and I'm enjoying it is I'm trying to seek out experiences, trying to seek out something I can do with the process. Not the result – we'll see. Man, if I'm thinking about that result I'm going to miss something right in front of me. So let's just make sure I do my best to look around me and go, "I think the director can be excellent, the people, we can make an excellent movie. The script is good enough and with all these pieces in place? Alright, check you later. Diving in!"'

McConaughey takes his characters very seriously, as if they are real people. He finds enjoyment in creating life outside of the script. He's interested in knowing what they would and wouldn't do off screen. 'And I was sharing all this stuff with Steven [Soderbergh],' McConaughey explained to *Vulture*'s Jennifer Vineyard, 'about Dallas breathing fire and whatnot, in these eight-, nine-, ten-page e-mails, and Steven did a cool, smart thing by only saying a little back: "Yep." "Sure." He put it on the actor's shoulders to go, "I own it." And if you can get to that spot, *then* you're on it. That's when you're like, "Yeah!" It's not always like that.'

Magic Mike premiered as the closing film at the Los Angeles Film Festival on 24 June 2012. There was a huge publicity blitz for the film, which involved McConaughey, Tatum, Manganiello and Bomer participating in a photo shoot for *Entertainment Weekly*, which was published on 25 May 2012. McConaughey, Tatum and Manganiello also attended the MTV Movie Awards where they presented the 'Best On-screen Transformation' Award. Manganiello attended the presentation as a fireman stripper.

'When I started showing the movie around,' Soderbergh said to *Film Comment*'s Amy Taubin, 'the first thing out of everyone's mouth was, "Matthew McConaughey, what a crazy-ass performance." He impressed the shit out of me. He showed up with a lot of ideas and they were all good. I described the part to him in one sentence and he said, "I know exactly who this guy is." And he did. How he dressed, how he talked. Really fine.'

Magic Mike opened in US cinemas on 29 June and in the UK on 11 July 2012. It was a box office success grossing more than $170 million with just a budget of $7 million. Reviews of the film were also very good. Such was the acclaim for McConaughey's performance that there was an Oscar buzz surrounding it and he won various nominations for best supporting actor from Broadcast Film Critics Association, Detroit Film Critics Society and Houston Film Critics Society. He won three awards for 'Best Supporting Actor' from Independent Spirit Awards, National Society Of Film Critics' Awards and New York Film Critics Circle Awards.

Since July 2012 there had been talk of a sequel but nothing had immediately come into fruition, however in April 2014 the Channing Tatum-penned *Magic Mike* sequel, *Magic Mike XXL*, received a release date of 3 July 2015. McConaughey would be interested in a sequel if the story was right. Would the story be a sort of 'where are they now?'-type situation. Sequels are often risky business, as punters usually want to see the first film remade; sequels rarely ever work as well as the original either, bar the odd exception such as *The Godfather II*.

McConaughey hopes that if the Broadway musical adaptation of *Magic Mike* goes ahead, they change his character's name from Dallas to something else. He looks forward to seeing it, though.

Critics noticed how the film has nods to the likes of *Shampoo*, *American Gigolo* and *Boogie Nights*. They also praised McConaughey for turning his career around and offering one of the most interesting parts since his minor but pivotal role in *Dazed and Confused* and his lead role in *A Time to Kill*.

The Observer's Philip French wrote: 'The film's most interesting and memorable character is Dallas, the club's flamboyant owner, whose aim is to move to Miami and get into the big time. As played by Matthew McConaughey in a Stetson, black waistcoat, leather chaps and little else, he's a warm-up artist who can bring the seated customers from zero to near orgasm in 10 seconds without leaving the stage... McConaughey's performance reminds one of two other great movie MCs, Gig Young's increasingly hysterical superintendent of the dance marathon in Sydney Pollack's *They Shoot Horses, Don't They?* and Joel Grey's sinister host of the Kit-Kat club in Bob Fosse's *Cabaret*, both winning Oscars for best supporting actor.'

Jenny McCartney wrote in *The Daily Telegraph*: 'I don't know what fundamentally audacious change has been wreaked in the career plan of Matthew McConaughey, once the lazily handsome love interest in so many a forgettable rom-com, but it's interesting to watch.'

The Daily Mail's Chris Tookey said: 'Another asset is Matthew McConaughey, dynamic on stage and off as Dallas, the egotistical owner of the club where Mike is the star dancer. McConaughey can look as if he's on auto-pilot in routine rom-coms and often seems most interested in finding excuses to take his shirt off... However, in the right movie, such as last year's *The Lincoln Lawyer* and now here, he is a powerful presence.'

McConaughey's career, once the subject of critical derision, had taken a massive turnaround with *The Lincoln Lawyer*, *Bernie*, *Killer Joe* and *Magic Mike*, and he had more films in the works that were to rejuvenate his career even further following that dip in the early 2000s.

Some reviewers were spot on in their praise for McConaughey in *Killer Joe* and *Magic Mike*, especially. McConaughey noticed how with *Killer Joe* he read the same four adjectives to describe his performance that he'd written in his diary and it was almost as if someone had stolen his internal thoughts. He'd never shared that passage before with anyone. The characters in those films had real identities.

Bizarrely, McConaughey joined British band The Cult on stage on Saturday 2012 and played the bongos. The band played a free gig at the Austin, Texas event as part of the Auditorium Shores Stage Concert Series and McConaughey jammed with lead singer Ian Astbury during 'Spirit Walker'. McConaughey is just full of surprises.

The actor spoke at a press gathering for *Magic Mike* about his recent success: 'I went back to back to back to back to back, and it was my most creative, constructive and fun working year I've ever had. I did not have one single day in all five films where I was not excited to get out of bed in the morning and go to work. I didn't have one hour of complacency in any of the work I did in five films, and I'm happy to be able to say that because that's not always been the case. It's fortunate to be able to say that, and I got to work with a lot of very interesting directors and some very interesting stories and all characters that didn't really pander or placate to any laws, government, parental guidance, what have you. When I say committed characters, that's really fun because it's boundless how far you can go, almost four dimensionally.'

*****

McConaughey was gearing up for more critical acclaim as his run of good luck was continuing. His wife and kids were healthy and his career was flourishing thanks to some bold decisions and creative manoeuvres. The film McConaughey released next was something altogether different.

The Paperboy had a limited theatrical release in the US in October 2012 but didn't reach the UK until the following March. The film competed for the Palme d'Or at the 2012 Cannes Film Festival and it also screened at the 39th edition of the Flanders International Film Festival Ghent, 2012 Ischia Film Festival, 2012 New Orleans Film Festival, 50th New York Film Festival, 2012 Toronto International Film Festival and finally, at the 2012 Stockholm International Film Festival.

The Paperboy also stars Nicole Kidman, Zac Efron and John Cusack and is directed by Lee Daniels; it's based on the 1995 novel *The Paperboy* by American author Pete Dexter. McConaughey plays Ward Jansen, a reporter who goes back to his hometown in Florida to investigate a death row inmate.

'I've always had an affection for the swamp, whatever it is, the murkiness, the humidity, the mystery,' McConaughey said to Helen Barlow of *SBS* on working in the swamps of Florida during the making of the film. 'I love the people there, I love the rhythm there, I love how time just seems to trickle along and gravity weighs more in the swamps. Mother Nature rules; that's the main thing. People live there but you have to say, "I am a guest". It's coming at you in four dimensions. It's not only coming from the ground up, it's coming from the top down, coming from front-to-back and the back-behind. I get very turned on by that and all over. Spiritually, all over. I really like it.'

Lee Daniels likes to cast actors against type so for *The Paperboy* he wanted to make McConaughey look physically unattractive. Even Daniels' mother, a fan of the actor, was shocked by the way he looked.

Critics were not overly keen on the film. Robbie Collin, writing in *The Daily Telegraph*, said: 'Readers of the film's Wikipedia page may spot the claim that it received "the longest sustained standing ovation of the festival at 16 minutes". As someone who was present at that screening, and the cacophonous quarter-hour of jeering, squawking and mooing that followed, I think Wikipedia may want to clarify its definition of "standing ovation".'

A majority of the reviews praised Kidman and yet barely mentioned McConaughey, but then again, her performance is show-stealing and she has the lead role. *Time Out*'s Dave Calhoun said: 'One minute *The Paperboy* grabs for crude comedy or racy vulgarity, the next it nods to swampy noir or issues of racial politics, sexual repression and generational divisions. The whole affair feels way off the mark.'

Rolling Stone's Peter Travers said: 'Boring it's not. This campy Southern trash-wallow is too jaw-dropping for that. Already infamous is the scene in which Nicole Kidman squats down and pees on Zac Efron. Hey, a jellyfish stung him; urine is the best cure. There's no cure for *The Paperboy*, the shamelessly lurid film version of Pete Dexter's 1995 novel.'

Much of the acclaim for the film went to Nicole Kidman

who plays Charlotte Bless, a woman who the inmate Hillary Van Wetter (John Cusack) has never met but has fallen in love with, and is adamant that he'll be released so they can marry and receives regular correspondence from her behind bars. McConaughey, nevertheless, won acclaim from critics too and won 'Special Award For The Best Body Of Work' at the 2012 Austin Film Critics Association Awards and 'Actor Of The Year' at the 2012 Central Ohio Film Critics Association Awards.

The Paperboy had a budget of just $12.5 million and barely grossed two and a half million at the box office, so much like *Killer Joe*, it was not a commercial hit at all, and although it did receive some criticism, it was another stepping stone in the right direction for McConaughey.

'…I just wanted to go do some [different films],' McConaughey expressed to Bill Graham of *The Film Stage* in 2012, 'and it actually ended up being five films. They've all been independents. The material was much more attractive, the budgets were much lower, but working on them, it's just so much fun.'

If McConaughey had any kind of conscious plan to rejuvenate himself as a serious actor and to reignite his seemingly flagging career then it was working. If it was an unconscious decision then whatever drove him to opt for these films completely revitalised him.

'I enjoyed what I was doing,' McConaughey said to Adam Sachs of *Details*, 'but I felt like I did it last time and I can do it again tomorrow. I just wanted to shake in my boots a little bit. I want to go deal with some real consequence in films. I remember writing this down: "I want to be able to hang my hat on the humanity of the character every day."'

McConaughey was a much better actor than he had been given

credit for, especially throughout the 2000s when he was picking projects that may have boosted his bank balance but had not won him much critical favour. Directors such as Soderbergh and Friedkin would not have even thought of, let alone considered, McConaughey as he was in the early 2000s. He was a different actor these days. 'Last year was arguably the best creative year of my career,' McConaughey said to John Powers of *Vogue* in 2013, 'and it was the first year I ever lost money. I wound up in the red – and had the best time doing it.'

Looking back at his career and the eclectic film roles, it is evident that he did not have any career path with regards to specific roles; he simply took whatever he fancied whether it was for the character, the story or even the money. He's gone from playing lawyers, to a crazed cop killer, an FBI Agent, a male stripper, a journalist, a photographer and many other varying parts. He's not a chameleon, an Alec Guinness or a Gary Oldman. McConaughey is recognisable in the parts. Maybe one day he will play a character that requires a complete makeover?

'So, for whatever reason, I attracted those things and then went after them,' he told Susan Wloszczyna of *Roger Ebert.com*. 'What I found – this is something I notice now as I explain it – is I really kind of said I really want to have an experience. I am going to go for something where I say, "I'm excited about this, I am scared about it for the right reasons, it's intriguing, I can't forget about it, it's on my mind, it's got its teeth in me." I want the experience.'

It's common for actors to move their career into different directions; sometimes it is for the money and fame, other times it is for longevity through acclaim and awards. Some actors manage to get the balance even, some don't. McConaughey's career path had been an interesting one with so many contrasting films. It was worrying in the early 2000s when he was almost becoming a lame Hollywood parody – a once notably talented actor, good looking and modest with a good career ahead of him and a small body of work in the late 1990s that had won him praise but whose films were now nothing but poor Hollywood comedies and sickly sweet dramas. It was as if throughout the 2000s, with a series of rom-coms to his name, that Matthew McConaughey had almost become a genre to himself. He'd usually play a professional of some sort, masculine but sensitive and indecisive. Those cheery smirks of his were usually part of his characters' appeal as cringe worthy as they are at times. McConaughey has a Lothario charm and a sneaky ability for self-parody with his Texan drawl and pitch-perfect timing. But then he got bored of those traits and has since begun to choose his roles much more carefully.

'I tell you one of the real joys, for me,' McConaughey confessed to *Total Film* on his motivations for acting. 'My favourite part is the making. I like the daily going to work. I love being on set, it's my favourite place to be. Daily making the construction of the character, making a movie with a bunch of people who've all come here to do this, that's my favourite part. Afterwards, what makes me feel the best? Well there's two things as an actor. One is if someone goes "I know that guy, I know him" that's a real compliment in the sense that you've created a character that is somewhat documentary for that person because it felt like a real life character.'

McConaughey gets a real kick out of members of the public who approach him to say they were affected by one of his characters and then quote some dialogue from the film. Usually he gets identified with Woody from *Dazed and Confused* but it's great when it's a different character from another film. And then McConaughey returns conversation by discussing the film from his point of view. It's not cool when he's hounded during important social functions or when he's with his family, but he does appreciate knowing how much people admire his work. His recent run of films saw McConaughey play characters that lived on the fringe, that didn't pander to society's conventions. They're almost like outcasts who live in their own world. McConaughey was intrigued by these roles and sought to solve the mysteries surrounding the characters.

'There's a science to it somehow, but I don't know the equation,' McConaughey explained to *Deadline*'s Christy Grosz on his recent choice of film roles. 'Honestly, I didn't have things that I was grabbing ahold of. Career was going fine. Enjoyed what I was doing. But I was like, "Let's spice things up a little."'

His track record showed that even his most successful films were not massively popular worldwide, while some of his critically acclaimed screen outings were box office failures. Nonetheless, films such as *A Time to Kill*, *The Lincoln Lawyer* and *Magic Mike* were successes both critically and commercially; McConaughey needed to land more of those types of acting roles if his career was to continue in the right direction. Lucky for him, it did. Directors had become more important, too, as he'd gotten older. He became much more interested in working with filmmakers who had fresh ideas and an original point of view.

'Somewhere in that endurance, after a year or two, other films started coming,' McConaughey admitted to *The Guardian*'s

Andrew Pulver on his more recent roles. 'I didn't go after *Killer Joe*, Billy Friedkin came to me for it. Soderbergh called me. Lee Daniels called me on *Paperboy*. I saw these as very determined, singular-willed fringe characters, arresting and kind of scary. I'm hanging my hat on reality and humanity, not morality. Not placating or pandering to any convention.'

CHAPTER NINE

OSCAR WINNER

'I'm surprising people. 'Jeez, You're really emerging
McConaughey. I'm seeing you differently.'
Matthew McConaughey, *The Daily Telegraph*, 2014

McConaughey with his wife and children rented a house in New Orleans where they would base themselves for the two movies that he was making back to back; first the already-released *Magic Mike*, followed by the soon-to-be-released *Mud*. Camila stuck with her decision to stand by her man wherever he went. When McConaughey goes to work he takes his family with him. They become part of the adventure.

Mud is written and directed by Jeff Nichols and co-stars Tye Sheridan, Sam Shepard and Reese Witherspoon. 'I remember seeing him in some of his romantic comedies. Actually, I saw him in *Dazed and Confused, Fool's Gold – Ghosts of Girlfriends Past*, that was probably the first one I saw,' Sheridan told *Red Eye Chicago*.

The film is about two fourteen-year-old boys, Ellis (Tye Sheridan) and Neckbone (Jacob Lofland), in De Witt

Arkansas who meet a fugitive named Mud (McConaughey) on an abandoned boat stuck high in a tree on a small island in the Mississippi River. They want to keep the boat and Mud promises it to them if they bring him food while he stays on the island. They learn that Mud is a fugitive and help him evade the vigilantes that are after him and also help to reunite Mud with his true love, Juniper (Reese Witherspoon).

McConaughey has known characters like Mud in real life. Coming from the South he has met people from provincial towns and rural areas who are fully committed to their own way of life. If someone like Mud were to go to a city or the mainland, he wouldn't know what to do, so in that respect he is institutionalised because he only knows one way of life. Mud gets his knowledge from the real areas – the rivers, the islands. His life is so ingrained in the ways of Mother Nature.

The premise for the film was hatched in Nichol's mind back in his student days when he read Mark Twain's *Tom Sawyer* in 1999. Nichols had McConaughey in mind for the lead role having seeing him in 1996's critically acclaimed film, *Lone Star*. Then Nichols watched *Dazed and Confused* and knew there was something about McConaughey that made him right for the part. 'I wrote it specifically for him,' said Nichols to *Elle's* Holly Milea. 'He's like Paul Newman. Put him in darker roles, and his innate likability still comes through. It makes for a compound statement.'

However, in May 2011 Captain Kirk actor Chris Pine was in talks for the lead role but McConaughey was finally cast in August, along with Witherspoon who had the same agency as Nichols. 'I finished the script in 2008, and I was telling people "Matthew McConaughey, Matthew McConaughey, Matthew

McConaughey…"', Nichols told Kevin P. Sullivan of *MTV*. 'I didn't know him at the time, so the first part [that] was cool was meeting him and thinking "Oh, awesome. This is the guy I hoped he'd be. This is the guy I've been thinking in my head for over a decade in this part."'

Nichols approached McConaughey in late 2008, early 2009 with the script. There is a likeability about McConaughey but also a smattering of danger, which intrigued Nichols.

'It's funny I had *Take Shelter* and *Mud* written at the same time before I made either,' Nichols admitted to *Starpulse's* Jason Coleman. 'And I'd worked with Michael [Shannon] on *Shotgun Stories* and I showed him both the scripts, not only because I wanted him involved in *Mud* but also because he's one of the smartest guys I know and I just wanted his opinion. So I asked him, "What do you think about *Mud*?" And he was like, "Well, I want to play Mud." And I said, "You can't play Mud – I wrote Mud for Matthew McConaughey. You're supposed to play Galen the uncle." He was like, "The uncle?! Okay Nichols."'

Nichols had to work against McConaughey's image to cast him as Mud. Much like the earlier performances of Paul Newman, McConaughey was struggling to gain the reverence he deserved because of his good looks, but Nichols knew he had something unique that made him perfect for the film. 'I bring up James Garner a lot, because they're innately likeable,' Nichols said to Jeff Labrecque of *Entertainment Weekly*. 'They're all guys you want to spend time with. And when you see them [play] darker, then you get a complex equation going on in front of your eyes and that's fun to watch.'

Filming took place in Arkansas from September to November 2011, which included using more than 400 locals as extras. 'I remember the second day of working,' Nichols said to *Starpulse*'s Jason Coleman about McConaughey, 'and he said the lines, and it was kind of like this decade-long relief that happened because I wrote it in his voice as best I could.'

McConaughey obsessed about Mud's unconditional love for Reese Witherspoon's character from frame one. Mud's love for the woman powers him through the story. It's what gives the film its humanity. It's the film's key hook. McConaughey felt that *Mud* was a sort of retrospective film like *Stand By Me*, the 1986 cult classic directed by Rob Reiner from a Stephen King story. *Mud* has a deliberate pace and tone that appealed to McConaughey. They shot what was on the script more than any other film he had worked on. McConaughey was fully immersed in the story and had come up with all sorts of musings and writings, which he would agree on with Nichols.

McConaughey didn't patronise the two child actors and he asked for their opinion, which they loved. 'It was very easy, I've always gotten along well with children, and long before I was a father,' he admitted to *Total Film* about the comfortable on-set rapport, 'I always kind of understood that when you talk to a kid you talk to them like this, you don't, you know even babies don't really like it when you're going [puts on baby-talking voice] "Coogicoo" you know? They're like, "What are you doing?".' They hear the tenor of your voice and they hear you talking to adults, the spacing between words, and they want you to talk to them like an adult, even if you're teaching them something.'

It was Nichols' first experience working with a bona fide movie star. McConaughey had come straight from shooting *Magic Mike* (which had a later release date) where he had shaped his physique to perfection. On the first night of filming he asked Nichols for a tent and a sleeping bag. He spent the night alone on the island in Mississippi where the story takes place. He sat up under a tree and read over the script and spent time contemplating his character. It made Nichols feel very secure that this A-list Hollywood actor was taking his role and the film very seriously. Nichols thought McConaughey was smart, funny, dedicated and easy to get along with. Nichols didn't have to explain the story to his leading man who got it straight away. But what pleased Nichols most of all was that he didn't have to put up with any Hollywood nonsense.

'He's a great guy, and he's very serious about what he does,' Nichols told MTV's Kevin P. Sullivan about working with McConaughey. 'There's this thinking that he's this dude, which he is. He's the guy you want to be with when you watch football, but we're both there to work. He took my lines very seriously. He was totally prepared and really got into it. I don't think he showered for a month. He stayed on an island for a couple of nights by himself. He just really got into it and took it seriously.'

Much of the film was made in Arkansas, which is where Nichols is from. It's a beautiful state. McConaughey was interested by the way people live down there in houseboats on the river. The houses are on floats so when it rains and the river rises, so do the houses. There are steps from the land to the boathouses for the residents to enter and exit their homes. McConaughey loved filming in the South.

For the rest of the duration McConaughey, with his family in tow, stayed in a trailer on the Mississippi for two months, despite having a rented house in New Orleans – no phones, toys, electricity were allowed in the trailer. It really was like something out of a Mark Twain novel. McConaughey wanted to get a feel for the place, the smell and taste of the South. 'Mud's an aristocrat of the heart. A poet,' McConaughey said to Holly Milea of *Elle* magazine of his character. 'If he grew up and let his heart come with him into reality, he'd die of heartache.'

The Deep South plays a major part in the film and as such it feels like a classic piece of Americana. Nichols' direction is excellent. 'He wants this to translate to humanity and not just be a small Southern picture about these people that happen to be in this small place with these few characters,' McConaughey said of Nichols to *Total Film*. 'It's not bound to that place in time, it's not even bound to a time.'

Nichols had specific designs about the character of Mud. The tattoo is his design and he'd had the lucky shirt in his mind already, as was the case with the chipped tooth. Mud has been in the sun for so long that he is sun-tarred and dry because he hasn't showered in weeks. Such characteristics all add to the superstitions of the character. Mud is a dreamer whose head is in the clouds, but as the story progresses it becomes symbolic, as the audience want Mud to survive. Lots of questions had to be asked and answered to make the film authentic. He's been living on a deserted island for weeks, so how did he get there? What had he been eating? One interesting aspect of the story is not only Mud's relationship with the boys but also his relationship with his mentor Ellis, the Sam Shepard character.

Mud is not a character of the modern world. He's not grounded, though he is practical. McConaughey was attracted to Mud's innocence and youthfulness, his naivety. There's a purity to the character, which appealed to McConaughey. Mud believes in fate and allows the powers that be to unfold events as though they are predestined. Things happen for a reason. The actor enjoyed working for four months in the South, getting into the heart and mind of his character.

Mud competed for the coveted Palme d'Or at the 2012 Cannes Film Festival where it received wide acclaim from critics. However, after its Cannes Premiere, it did not pick up a distributor straight away for a release in the US. Ultimately, in August 2012 Lionsgate and Roadside Attractions purchased the distribution rights to have the film shown theatrically in North America. It was shown at the Sundance Film Festival in January 2013 where it won applause from the 500 people in attendance.

'In a way, this film lives in the 1980s for me so it's a trip back to my youth, back to high school, when I had my first loves…' McConaughey said to the *Yorkshire Post* in 2013. 'Everything about the film feels like an eighties classic to me, with a full narrative, with entrances and exits and pacing and deliberation – like *Stand by Me*.'

Mud opened in April 2013 with a limited theatrical release before opening in more cinemas in May in both the US and UK. Roadside Attractions and Lionsgate had a very clever way of releasing the film in the US – first to 400 screens and then expanding to 900. The film became the highest grossing independent movie of the year with $21 million in box office receipts. Both Nichols and McConaughey were thrilled with the reception.

The film won rave reviews from critics. Noted British film critic Peter Bradshaw wrote in *The Guardian*: '*Mud* is an engaging and good-looking picture with two bright leading performances.'

The Observer's Philip French enthused: '*Mud* is a movie of striking performances and memorable images and of people who seem to belong in rather than being imposed upon their environment. After a rather fallow period of shallow movies, McConaughey has recently been doing fine work again, and he brings a raw, desperate masculinity to *Mud*, while Shepard invests the part of ex-soldier Tom with the authority and sense of understated probity at which he excels.'

Writing in *The Daily Telegraph*, Robbie Collin said: 'In his latest picture, Matthew McConaughey's name is Mud, and not for the usual reasons. For much of the last decade the handsomely weather-beaten Texan was a familiar presence in many agonisingly bad romantic comedies, but in the past two years, with juicy roles in all-American auteur pieces like *Magic Mike*, *The Paperboy* and *Killer Joe*, his career has undergone what he jokingly calls a 'McConaissance'.'

Empire's Dan Jolin said: 'And not only does it include a performance which further affirms the extraordinary on-screen rehabilitation of Matthew McConaughey – whose Mud exudes intense, sweat-sheened charisma – but also showcases a bedrock-solid supporting cast (including, in a small, against-type role, Nichols' mad-eyed muse, Michael Shannon), plus excellent turns from its two unknown leads: Tye Sheridan and Jacob Lofland, as Mississippi water-rats Ellis and Neckbone.'

Mud was named as one of the 'Top 10 Independent Films Of 2013' by the National Board Of Review and received the 'Robert Altman Award' at the 29th Independent Spirit Awards for its film director, casting director and ensemble cast. It also received the 'Grand Prix' from the Belgian Film Critics Association.

McConaughey has a keen sense of humour and knows enough about himself not to get depressed over bad reviews. They don't make him feel worthless or miscast. He appreciates funny reviews. 'I went through the negative reviews,' he said to *Vulture*'s Jennifer Vineyard. 'I pulled all the negatives. I said, "Pull all the negatives!" There were a lot of bad ones, but not as many as I thought. There was a lot of them where I was like, "Oh, this person just doesn't like me." But there was quite a few where I was like, "That's good constructive criticism! You know what? I would have written the same review."'

Continuing his run of good luck on a number of highly acclaimed films, McConaughey's next project would bring him the greatest praise of his career thus far.

Dallas Buyers Club is a biographical drama directed by Jean-Marc Vallée and written by Craig Borten and Melisa Wallack. The film tells the real life story of rodeo and electrician Rob Woodroof, who in 1985 was given thirty days to live. He smuggled non-government approved pharmaceutical drugs into Texas, which he used to combat his symptoms and distribute them to fellow AIDS victims, thereby establishing the 'Dallas Buyers Club.' The drugs that he sold did not cure AIDS but they helped victims live longer and lead healthier lives. He also faced opposition from the FDA, the Food and Drug Administration. Woodruff refuses to accept the diagnosis but remembers having unprotected sex with a drug-using prostitute. During one of his hospital visits he meets a drug addicted HIV positive trans-woman named Rayon, played in the film by Jared Leto. Woodroof is initially hostile towards Rayon but as the months go by he starts to show compassion towards gay, lesbian and trans-gender people. The duo have been compared to Joe Buck and Ratso Rizzo in *Midnight Cowboy*, the classic 1969 movie with Dustin Hoffman and Jon Voight.

'Certainly one of the reasons that I decided to do the film is because I knew he was doing interesting work in his career right now,' said Leto to *USA Today*'s Andrea Mandell. 'And I thought, if he had sussed this out, then there must be something really special there.'

'I only met "Jared" after the film had wrapped,' McConaughey admitted to *Rolling Stone*'s Charles Thorp. 'Our relationship was complex: He stayed in character the entire time we were shooting. It all sounds very weird, but it wasn't. We both showed up on set, put our heads down and did the scenes.'

Nobody knew where AIDS or HIV came from; they thought it was a homosexual disease, and though Woodroof was heterosexual, everyone immediately assumed he was gay. He originally thought he had the flu but couldn't get rid of it. 'He took his life into his own hands,' McConaughey told *The Daily Beast*'s Ramin Setoodeh, 'and really pioneered progressive research into unapproved vitamins and drugs that the FDA wasn't letting into America for people with HIV to take at the time. It's a wonderful story told from an original point of view. I haven't seen the subject matter told from the point of view of a heterosexual man.'

There were all sorts of conspiracy theories about where the disease came from and what it was. It was even more perplexing that heterosexuals could get AIDS, which is why Woodroof faced stigma. Even today, some people don't believe heterosexuals can contract either HIV or AIDS. When the basketball player Magic Johnson came out with HIV in 1991 and abruptly retired (only to play again sporadically) some players didn't want to play on the same court. They didn't want to shake hands with him either. Fear comes from ignorance. Both HIV and AIDS sparked taboos and superstitions in the 1980s and early 1990s when there was less research and knowledge about the viruses. People thought you could get it from saliva or sweat when we know now that it is from blood, and that shaking a victim's hand will not give you either HIV or AIDS.

Working on the film and researching his role, McConaughey was reminded about the time when he first understood what AIDS was when he was a senior at high school in 1988. 'I remember hearing about [HIV] in '86 but then realising in '88,' he admitted to Susan Riley of *Stylist* magazine, 'when I was becoming heterosexually sexually active, that I needed to talk to a doctor because everyone was looking for the pamphlet with the dos and don'ts and there wasn't one. So I said to three different doctors: "I'm a heterosexual male, I'm not having sex with hookers or things like this – talk to me about how careful I need to be."'

'I was the only one of my friends who did,' McConaughey added when told by Riley that it was a mature thing for a teenager to do. 'The doctors had three completely different [answers]. One said: "You're heterosexual? Nothing to worry about." Another said it's one in a million and the other said it's 1 in 110.'

The real Ron Woodroof died in September 1992 and had been the subject of a long, detailed feature in a 1992 edition of *The Dallas Morning News*. Screenwriter Craig Borten interviewed him before his death with the intention of writing a screenplay about the Dallas Buyers Club. Despite writing ten drafts based on hours of interviews and having Dennis Hopper direct and Woody Harrelson star as Woodroof, the film was never able to get financial backing in the 1990s. Towards the end of the decade Marc Foster was reported to have been asked to direct with Brad Pitt in the lead role. However, in 2008, director Craig Gillespie and Ryan Gosling were in talks to resurrect the screenplay. It wasn't until French-Canadian director Jean-Marc Vallée and Matthew McConaughey signed on that the project attracted financial backing.

The film had been declined 137 times before Vallée and McConaughey came on board. McConaughey had wanted to make the film for a while but the story was not popular enough for a studio to invest money in it. To the studio chiefs of Hollywood it was an AIDS drama with little commercial appeal. As soon as other people started to surround the project, the more interested Hollywood became and $5 million was raised to fund it as McConaughey explained to *Deadline*'s Christy Grosz: 'Jean-Marc (Vallée) and I were locked, and we're like, "Let's set a date and do this thing this year." We had Jared (Leto) and Jennifer (Garner) cast, and we budgeted for a lot less than Jean-Marc thought he could make it for. A week before the shoot, Jean-Marc calls me and says, "This is just not enough money to make this. We don't have it, and we shoot in a week. (But) I'll be there if you'll be there." I was like, "Yeah." I had been losing the weight, and then I kept hearing "This is not happening." And I was like, "This is happening." Then that last bit of money came like a wave.'

Dallas Buyers Club is a human rights story which one day may be spoken in the same breath as, say, *Guess Who's Coming to Dinner*, *Mississippi Burning* or even *Schindler's List*. 'No one in Hollywood wanted to touch the film,' said McConaughey to Garth Pearce of the *Daily Express*. 'Every time producers and financiers heard the words "AIDS drama" and "homophobic hero" they instantly turned off.'

The director Vallée didn't see McConaughey in the role at first, but producer Robbie Brenner got the pair to meet for a three-hour sit down at a New York hotel and he was instantly impressed. The way McConaughey spoke about the character and his vision for the film was inspiring. McConaughey wanted to go somewhere else with his career and was accepting new challenges. The role was a leap of faith. Vallée promptly changed his mind about McConaughey and the pair worked together to deliver a respectful film in Woodroof's honour.

Brenner spoke to *Variety*'s Jenelle Riley about the Texan actor: 'He's so great in *A Time to Kill*. Yes, he chose to take a lighter path after that, but I think there's something very deep behind the eyes, and he's incredibly charismatic and likable. And, of course, he's from Texas.'

McConaughey had read the script about three years before it was made. 'So after I would finish a film I would always ask, "Well, what about this one next?",' he admitted to Caitlin Martis of *The Film Stage*. 'But it never was really working out, but I would always keep it right there at the top of my desk. I thought it was an incredible original story. This guy and what he did: 7th grade education, big cowboy, bull-riding, electrician, hell-raising, womanizer, heterosexual gets HIV, 30 days to live and within 7 years becomes an absolute scientist of HIV.'

Woodroof's sister was reportedly keen on the casting of McConaughey from the get-go, though she had initially expressed concern when Pitt and Gosling were attached to the role during previous attempts to develop the film. It's McConaughey's swagger and personality, his Southern drawl, which made him the perfect fit for the lead part.

Asked in 2013 by *The Film Stage*'s Caitlin Martis what would he do if he was told he had just thirty days to live, McConaughey responded this way: 'I don't know right now, but I'm sure when you read that on the script that's the first thing that comes to mind. I thought what would Ron think of that? The first thing that Ron did and how he approached it was absolute denial. Number one [was] "No, I don't have it, I can't have it. You don't know what the F you are talking about," you know?'

McConaughey was totally dedicated to the part so much so that he lost 47 pounds going from 183 pounds down to 136, by eating small amounts of food; he didn't starve himself. Leto, on the other hand, appeared to stop eating altogether – which left co-star Jennifer Garner worried about his health.

'The surprise was how the energy that I lost from the neck down transferred to the neck up. I became clinically aware, almost hyper, I needed three hours less sleep a night,' McConaughey admitted to the BBC's Tim Masters. 'I had an amazing amount of energy from the head up. That was something I didn't know was going to happen.'

McConaughey had five ounces of fish twice a day, a cup of vegetables twice a day. He gave himself four months to lose weight during which time he met Woodroof's family and friends and studied Woodroof's diary, which he kept before he got HIV, and which was handed to him by Woodroof's sister and daughter. The diary was the real hook for McConaughey because it chronicled everything in Woodroof's life from the mundane to the deeply sensitive, such as jobs he'd won and lost, the women he was interested in, book ideas he had and personal secrets.

'The diary was: "I got nothing to do. I got up again this morning, six o'clock, I had my coffee. I tucked my shirt in, pressed my pants, waited for my pager to go off, to get a call, get a little job done and nobody called. So damn it – I got to get high",' McConaughey explained to Lesley O'Toole of the *Independent*. 'Seeing who he was before he got HIV really informed me because here is a guy who turned 30 days of life, as he was told, to seven more years. That was the first time when he had purpose in his life, ironically because he was having to fight for his life.'

McConaughey learned how to talk like Woodroof from listening to the tape transcripts; he also got a sense of who Woodroof was, or thought he was. He wanted to be like Al Pacino in *Scarface*. He was a smuggler and a dealer and became immersed in conspiracy theories, which he thought were aimed at him. Some of the cast and crew who hadn't seen McConaughey during those four months were shocked by his stark weight loss. It was frightening. He looked ill.

He explained his state of health to Ramin Setoodeh of *The Daily Beast*: 'My levels are fine. I'm as healthy as can be. My blood pressure, everything's fine. The real health challenge is when you put it back on. It's very easy to create a form of diabetes if you don't do it right. You can't just start eating cheeseburgers and ice cream. Your body will go into shock and it just won't work.'

The weight loss also affected his mood – he'd go from cranky to hyper and it affected the people around him. People online were suddenly very worried about his dramatic drop in weight. For McConaughey it was as much of a spiritual journey as a physical one. The days seem longer because most humans obsess about food – what's for dinner? Should I have a snack? He didn't give up red wine, though.

'The first time I ate a regular meal,' McConaughey confessed to Susan Wloszczyna of *Roger Ebert.com*, 'my body immediately remembered, "Oh, we live at 182." So it wants to sprint back. And you just have to pull the reins and go ease off and eat more healthy. But the first time I ate a meal the size I used to eat at 182, it immediately remembered. I could feel it. My diet has changed. It's not like it is before. On purpose.'

Other forms of method-type acting for the role included, allegedly, staying indoors at his Texas ranch for months, thus avoiding sunlight to look paler. He avoided socialising to find different ways to entertain himself and become smarter. When he dropped below 150 pounds his eyesight began to fail and he looked weak. He's body would seize up and his arms and legs were sore after doing just five push-ups. His legs locked after running only 30 feet. His co-star Leto also lost weight, 30 pounds in fact, and stopped eating altogether to lose weight quicker.

McConaughey also absorbed himself in AIDS and HIV medical journals, concentrating on the period 1981 to 1988. He read for an hour a day and hid from his kids so he could focus on learning. Woodroof had found an inner strength that he didn't know he had before he contracted the virus and McConaughey channelled that into his performance. Woodroof grew into a more understanding person even though he was not an educated man and enjoyed being a cowboy. He was educated to the equivalent of a Year 8 student and loved his Cadillac and gold watches. It was the simple things in life that he favoured, only for his life to be abruptly turned upside down.

Woodroof found loopholes in the law, which worked to help his cause. 'He was living paycheck to paycheck, week to week,' McConaughey said of Woodroof to *Deadline*'s Christy Grosz. 'I saw a guy who was lonely – this was before he had HIV – I saw a guy who wanted to get out. The ironic thing is when he got HIV, he found something to really fight for. His sister said this five times: "He never finishes anything." So he found the one thing he could finish (in) getting sick.'

The director and actor did discuss if they were going too far in turning Woodroof into such a nasty character. They worried that the audience wouldn't be able to emphasise with such a man. McConaughey, however, felt they were doing the right thing with the character. That's who Woodroof was. Everyone is different, everyone handles things differently. They had a human approach to the material.

'...I've got a nice relationship with his daughter and his sister, and they were wide open,' McConaughey said to *I Am Rogue*'s Jami Philbrick. 'They were so gracious in letting me into his life and their life. And they were very honest. They weren't trying to ever sugar-coat who this guy was, that never came out of their mouth. "But he was such a nice guy." They're like, "No, he was a son-of-a-bitch, but we loved him. You couldn't help but love him. He'd steal your car, but you couldn't help but just love him 'cause of it 'cause it's kind of just who he was." And that was a real approach with attacking this guy's blasphemic sort of P.O.V.'

The film also stars Denis O'Hare as Dr Sevard, Steve Zahn as Tucker, Michael O'Neill (Richard Barkley), Dallas Roberts (David Wayne), Griffin Dunne (Dr Vass) and Kevin Rankin (T.J.).

The film's production schedule was continuously delayed over concerns with the script from the producers and cast, but principal photography finally started in New Orleans in mid-2012. Jennifer Garner, who plays Dr Eve Saks, said that it took only twenty-five to thirty days to shoot the film. It was shot in natural light and the actors were allowed very few takes. McConaughey's performance and dedication to the part won him great praise from his co-stars. He'd moved out of his comfort zone and was on a mission to prove to people how well he could act. He'd started a new journey since *The Lincoln Lawyer* and he was on a roll, taking unconventional roles (at least for him) and surprising people with each performance.

Garner was keen to work with her *Ghosts of Girlfriends Past* co-star once again and that was part of the reason she wanted to do *Dallas Buyers Club*. She had been almost in awe of his dedication to acting, his charisma, drive and crazy work ethic when they'd worked together previously, and she was intrigued to know what he'd be like several years later. She likes him as a person and as an actor and respects him immensely. Garner was both proud and honoured to be part of the film.

McConaughey immersed himself totally in the project: he revised the script, offered scene changes and gave notes in the editing room. He was, at times, as arrogant and difficult as the character he was portraying, but it was all for the purposes of making a better film. 'To see Matthew talk,' Vallée told *The Daily Telegraph*'s Tom Shone, 'to see him act, it's a movement. But I must say that behind the acting it was Matthew's humanity that made the difference. This guy has something in the face, this energy, this way of talking that within ten minutes has you caring for him. The first audience we screened it for I could feel it, I was in the room, 250 people. I could feel the crowd behind him. The acting is something but the guy – the guy has such visceral humanity.'

'And he was all the things that I think we portrayed him to be. He was that bastard. He was selfish. He wanted to make money,'

McConaughey told *I Am Rogue*'s Jami Philbrick. 'He wasn't running around trying to crusade for the cause, he wanted to be Scarface, man. What he had always wanted before he had HIV. He wanted money. He wasn't making any, and he didn't really have a purpose before he got HIV, which is a sad truth. And he found something to fight for.'

The film originally premiered at the 2013 Toronto International Film Festival. 'We were a little bit concerned and scared at the seriousness of the subject matter and the dramatic content of the film. We went, we've got to make people laugh,' said director Vallée to *USA Today*'s Andrea Mandell on the film's reception.

McConaughey received a standing ovation at the ceremony and won high praise from the attendees. He learned a great deal from making the film, but primarily that if you want something doing right you have to do it yourself. He is a great fan of self-preservation and of learning from experience. Every day is a new venture that brings with it new experiences that sometimes require bold decisions to be taken. Sometimes you fail, but it's those failures that can often lead to bigger and better experiences. You learn from your failures to make yourself a better person.

Dallas Buyers Club gained wide critical acclaim after it was released in US cinemas in November 2013 and in the UK the following February. With a budget of just $5 million the film had grossed over $32 million at the box office by early 2014. The film communicated well with people and it translated marvellously to the big screen. There was a personal connection with audiences. Critics noted comparisons with the 1993 AIDS film *Philadelphia* where Denzel Washington was taught lessons in tolerance from Tom Hanks. That critically lauded film revitalised Tom Hanks' career; he'd been the star of mostly lightweight comedies and spoofs throughout the 1990s and, much like McConaughey, had barely caught the attention of critics. Hanks' portrayal of an AIDS victim won him an Oscar and set a new course for his career.

Mark Kermode wrote in *The Observer*: 'While McConaughey's dramatic weight loss may make attention-grabbing headlines, there's much more to his performance than the mere shedding of 30-odd pounds. Continuing the reinvention (dubbed the 'McConaissance') which has seen him lay the ghost of grizzly rom-coms such as *Failure to Launch* with harder-edged roles in *Magic Mike* and *Killer Joe*, McConaughey is utterly convincing as the ravaged rodeo redneck who is given thirty days to live after being diagnosed with AIDS, but who stubbornly refuses to lie down and die.'

The *Independent*'s Geoffrey MacNab wrote: 'Like other former juvenile leads who've appeared in too many romantic comedies, McConaughey has been consistently underestimated as an actor. Here, he gives an astonishing performance that combines sleaziness and venality with grace and pathos.'

Writing in *The Daily Telegraph*, Tim Robey enthused: 'McConaughey's recent run of acclaimed, full-throttle turns in left-field indies (*Mud*, *Killer Joe*, *Magic Mike*) has finally culminated here in a performance which Academy voters have been powerless to keep off their shortlist, and for which it's increasingly hard to imagine him not winning. The role feels at once crisply tailored to McConaughey's established gifts, and unlike anything we've seen him do before. His air of physical decrepitude is totally convincing, but it's the fear in his acting that counts – the film's most striking effect is watching this legendarily blasé star face up to mortality.'

'…I've got to tell you I've been witnessing the most spectacular, amazing, touching acting performance of my humble career so far,' raved Vallée to Adam Sachs of *Details*. 'He had to create a new way of walking and being and not having this confidence of being handsome and seductive. I think people will see something different here, really a new Matthew McConaughey. I think he wanted something new in his life, and you can see that in the choices he's made in the last two or three years.'

How did Woodroof's family react to the finished film and its overwhelming reception? 'We told them – this is not word for word what Ron did, but if I can capture his spirit and his rage and his will to survive…' McConaughey explained to *Stylist*'s Susan Riley. 'They understood that. It must have been superbly overwhelming [to watch] – this was their son, brother and father; his whole life put into two hours – but they reacted very favourably.'

There's a connection between some of the recent roles he's chosen – they're not only independent films but the characters he plays are also anti-heroes. The films have an identity, too. They're character-driven films which excel in directing, acting and writing. They're also the works of auteurs. Sure, not everyone liked *Magic Mike* and not everyone 'got' *The Paperboy* but each film has a distinct identity.

'What's the biggest compliment, is if I read a review,' McConaughey explained to *Vulture*'s Jennifer Vineyard, 'and it's exactly what I wrote down in my diary before ever filming it. That's really cool. That's the biggest signifier of closing the gaps. If I've written in a diary about a character, "This is who this guy is," and then I read a review two years later and they write almost word for word what I wrote about that character before I ever did it... Then I go [claps], "Now we're on to something! It translated!" Now the gap was tighter, the gap between who I am, what I'm doing, and how I'm perceived.'

*****

McConaughey was introduced to Skype during the making of *Dallas Buyers Club*. He began to have a better understanding of technology. He is less intimidated by it now but he has also refused to allow technology to control his life, as many of us have with social media and smartphones. McConaughey switched off voicemail on his phone – if he's not there, he's not there. Simple. McConaughey is more interested in being sociable in person. He's seen enough socially awkward people to know that technology doesn't always do you good as a person. He was impressed by the Spike Jonze film *Her* which tells the story of a man who develops a relationship with a computer operating system. There are too many people in the world, in the West especially, whose best relationships are with their phones or computers. McConaughey prefers real people. He rarely, if ever, goes online on his iPhone. He uses the device as a tool to write down ideas. He prefers to sit back and watch sports. College football is where he gets his kicks. It's real drama to him. He also enjoys a good round of golf. He likes baseball too, but football is his true sports passion.

Around this time McConaughey also recorded a public service announcement in Austin for LBJ Presidential Legacy. He launched his own clothesline in 2013 after partnering with the Canadian clothing maker Grand National Apparel for the launch of his sportswear collection, JKL, an extension of his company j.k. livin. The company had ventured into casual clothing – with sweatbands, hoodies, golf shirts and koozies – in September 2008, when it was originally sold online. McConaughey had been wearing the prototype clothes for a year before the online launch so the j.k. livin logo was often seen on such popular gossip websites as *Pink Is The New Blog* and *Perez Hilton*. Sadly, the tabloids were more interested in learning that he was just wearing a t-shirt rather than the fact that he was modelling his soon-to-be-launched clothesline. One line of T-shirts had the catch phrase 'Alright, alright, alright' from the 1993 cult film *Dazed and Confused* printed on them.

With ten per cent of all sales going to charity, the menswear line was launched in the US retail store Dillard's in March 2013. 'I want to be behind this, not in front of it. I'm the author, not the face or the definition,' he said to *Women's Wear Daily* (*WWD*). 'I personally don't like to wear clothing that is named for somebody or has someone's likeness all over it. Even if my name were on, I don't know that I'd want to wear it.'

Celebrity clothing reflects who the celebrity is and their interests, and McConaughey isn't the first high-profile name to venture into fashion. It's like a statement of intent. J-Lo, Bono and Justin Timberlake, as well as Britney Spears, P Diddy, and members of Mötley Crüe, Run-D.M.C., and blink-182 have their own clothesline. McConaughey's brand has an authenticity to it. He was inspired by his father, a man who wore casual clothes. He carries j.k. livin stickers with him wherever he goes.

McConaughey consulted fashion experts and designers before starting his line. It took him around sixty T-shirts before he found the right one. He was also heavily involved in the marketing of his brand. It was a gradual process and his clothes were sold solely online until they reached retail in 2013 with an extended collection of menswear. The line includes clothes for the casual man – khaki pants, shorts, jeans, T-shirts and swimwear. It links to his love of surfing, swimming, cycling (he's buddies with Lance Armstrong don't forget) and hiking. A portion of the proceeds for JLK goes to his charity, the j.k. livin Foundation, which involves itself with four schools in California and Texas, developing after-school exercise and nutrition programs for less well-off kids.

'In starting a family, you really start thinking about community,' McConaughey explained to Brenda Rodriguez of *People* magazine. 'We're teaching them about nutrition and about those choices that they make.'

McConaughey is known for his taste in casual clothes and has often been photographed wearing khakis and flip-flops. In fact, since an incident in June 2008, he was known as the flip-flop guy after he got drunk at a beachfront bar in Nicaragua and asked the locals to help him look for his lost flip-flop, which he'd had for eleven years. It made celebrity press headlines. A statement was issued to the press describing his love of flip-flops.

'I like to be able to wear something that is appropriate for wherever the day takes me: to work, on a hike and then out to dinner,' he explained to *WWD*. 'I like to take the formality out of the day's schedule and be ready for any off-road detour. One of the first things I had written down was "from the jungle to the opera". That's a bit of an exaggeration, but that's the idea.'

It's clear that McConaughey has vested interests outside of the world of film and acting. His company has stakes in music, fashion and charity work. He is a cultured man, someone who loves to travel – a man who is interested in the world, in absorbing new cultures.

'The best education I've had in my life has been to travel,' McConaughey admitted to *Shadows On The Wall*'s Rich Cline. 'And I get to do that with this job, so my kids will fill up their passport as soon as possible. They'll travel to every film set with me.

'I guess, if my children inherit anything from me, it would be loyalty,' he added. 'I'm a loyal guy. One thing we knew growing up was that mom and dad loved us even when we were getting our butts whooped. And we learned to respect our elders too. And to never say the words C-A-N-T or H-A-T-E.'

McConaughey is also interested in developing himself as a person; he is constantly striving to be a better individual. His enthusiasm for life, people and the world around him has surely impacted on his recent spate of superlative work. How could it not? He has a happy home life and a flourishing career. Having worked with such revered auteurs as Spielberg, Zemeckis and Soderbergh, it was then that a certain Italian-American director came a-calling.

*****

McConaughey's next role was Mark Hanna in *The Wolf of Wall Street*, a film directed by Martin Scorsese, about a New York stockbroker who manages a firm that involves itself in securities fraud and corruption on Wall Street in the 1990s. Hanna is Jordan Belfort's (Leonardo DiCaprio) boss and encourages him to adapt a hedonistic lifestyle of sex and drugs. The film was marketed as a DiCaprio film and McConaughey had a small but significant supporting role in the first third of the film.

McConaughey told *Rolling Stone*'s Charles Thorp that working with Scorsese was 'quite musical'. He explained further: 'In my mind, the perfect set is when everybody is free enough, creatively, to steal from one another. Even better, when you steal from someone and then you give it back to them in the scene. I stole some things from Leo – he told me a joke when we first met and I stole it. That whole "fugazi" bit. He told me about it, and I said, "I'm going to mispronounce that for the fun of it." Everybody is always talking about that scene, and I made that decision just seconds before we shot it.'

Martin Scorsese is one of the most admired directors in American cinema with a string of highly-praised films to his name, from his 1970s work such as *Mean Streets* and *Taxi Driver* to *Raging Bull* and *The Last Temptation of Christ* in the 1980s, *Goodfellas* and *Casino* in the 1990s and, more recently, *The Departed* and *Shutter Island*. If Scorsese comes calling, you pick up the phone.

McConaughey told MTV News: 'I studied Martin Scorsese in film school in 1992, at the University of Texas. All of the sudden, a year and a half ago or two years ago, I'm going to meet Martin Scorsese at this apartment in New York. I was just nervous to meet an icon like that. And the first thing I got from him was, "This guy loves funny." It occurred to me that most of the people who are great at what they do, they love funny.'

'Matthew has a musical rhythm,' Scorsese said to John Powers of *Vogue*. 'It's there in both his dialogue and his body language.'

His character has a scene where he beats his chest, which became one of the film's most memorable moments. McConaughey was interviewed by the *The Showbiz 411* about the origins of the chest beating. He said: 'It's something I do from time to time to relax myself before a scene, or to get my voice lower, and I'll do it to whatever the rhythm of the character is in the scene. I was doing it before takes, and Leonardo [DiCaprio] had the idea of "Why don't you put that in the scene?' so I did.'

The cast also includes Jonah Hill, Margot Robbie, Kyle Chandler, Rob Reiner, Jon Favreau and Jean Dujardin. During filming McConaughey was still losing weight because of *Dallas Buyers Club* and Scorsese told him he couldn't drop any more pounds. McConaughey looks very gaunt in the film, ill in fact, but cocaine and drugs were a major staple of eighties life on Wall Street so his weight loss was applicable to his character. The film is based on the best-selling book of the same name by disgraced investor Jordan Belfort.

'Well, it feels great. I'm excited about it. I'm proud of the films I've been able to be in – from *The Wolf of Wall Street* to *Mud* to *Dallas Buyers Club*,' McConaughey told the BBC's Tim Masters.

The Wolf of Wall Street opened in US cinemas in December 2013 and in the UK in January 2014. Reviews of the film were very positive although it caused uproar –Scorsese is no stranger to controversy – with some more conservative viewers attacking it for its regular use of vulgarity, drugs, animals, sex and overall moral ambiguity.

'There's a lot of disgusting behaviour,' McConaughey said to *The Hollywood Reporter* in reaction to the controversy surrounding the film. 'We wanted this to be a cautionary tale... It was a reaction to what happened in 2008. It was a giant Hieronymus Bosch painting... Martin Scorsese has never been a director who spoon-feeds the audience what the ramifications of these actions are. He purposely didn't cut away to the [victims].'

The film grossed more than $350 million at the box office and was nominated for five Academy Awards. It was acclaimed as Scorsese's best film since *Goodfellas*, released in 1990.

The Observer's Mark Kermode wrote: 'None of which is to say that *The Wolf of Wall Street* does not have its pleasures, notably Jonah Hill in versatile post-*Moneyball* form as Belfort's slimy sidekick Donnie Azoff, and a thin-faced, big-haired Matthew McConaughey teaching his protégé about the financial importance of masturbation.'

Writing in the *Independent*, Geoffrey MacNab said: 'They're in a sleek restaurant high above the city. Hanna (played with sly comic relish by McConaughey) is clearly intended as the devil-like figure, telling his young acolyte what rewards might be his if he follows the paths of corruption. The scene is echoed later on, when Belfort tries to bribe the FBI officer, contrasting the luxuries he enjoys on his yacht with the underpaid drudgery of the officer's life.'

McConaughey's co-star in *Dallas Buyers Club*, Jared Leto, praised McConaughey's performance in *The Wolf of Wall Street* during a London press conference for the UK premiere of *Dallas Buyers Club*. Leto said: 'By the way, I just saw it and holy shit I didn't see *Dallas Buyers Club* but you must be pretty good in this one. You were so good in that movie!'

He added: 'My first thought is that you were so damn good in that scene, he [Leo] saw you in that scene and thought shit I'm gonna step up, that's my motivation!'

McConaughey responded: 'When you go to work with people who are really good at what they do, you find out quickly that there's really no secret magic trick that they have that's different to anyone else but they do the simple things really really well and are confident enough to be free and open.'

The success and acclaim that greeted McConaughey in *Dallas Buyers Club* overshadowed his small but important role in *The Wolf of Wall Street*. Nevertheless, it was another string to his bow, and having worked with such masters as Spielberg, Howard, Friedkin, Soderbergh and Zemeckis, he can now tick Scorsese off the list of great living directors with whom he has performed. Actors don't turn down the chance to work with such heavyweight directors regardless of what the projects are.

'I've done a lot of work, over the last few years,' McConaughey told *Collider*'s Christina Radish. 'I was able to put some things out, and be in some things that I liked a lot, last year. We finished these things over a year ago, and now they're still vital. We're actually just now declaring them, and they're having a brand-new life. Other things that I've done had a quicker shelf life. These things are feeling really relevant, and they're piquing some people's interests, and they're resonating. I haven't really thought about them as a year, and I haven't thought, "Am I going to have another good year?" Part of it was that I haven't really been looking in the rearview mirror for a while. I hope I don't. It's nice to talk about, but I'm in no way in a retrospective mode.'

The Wolf of Wall Street is not McConaughey's sole enterprise with Martin Scorsese. The revered Italian-American filmmaker directed a much-publicised Dolce & Gabbana short film featuring Scarlett Johansson, titled *Street of Dreams*. The stylish black-and-white film is for the label's new scent 'The One'. The tale is about two ex-lovers who are reunited years later and, typically, Scorsese uses New York as a background. Stefano Gabbana expressed enthusiasm for McConaughey in a press statement: 'Matthew is the ultimate charmer. He is an outstanding actor, and a very handsome man whose good looks seem to be increasing with age. And he has also been blessed with style, not to mention a clever wit and boundless charisma. There could be no other face for "The One for Men."'

Some of McConaughey's recent films have been about addiction and how dangerous addiction can be. 'I know I can,' he replied when asked by *MovieWeb*'s Evan 'Mushy' Jacobs if he has an addictive personality. 'That just comes from me, if I'm doing something I do like to take it to the limit. I've got a high ceiling. A wide threshold for seeing what those boundaries are for myself. I'm very resilient inside. I find things that I like and do and boy, I do like to stick to them. I'm not necessarily a guy who gets addicted to more of certain things, but if I find something I like to do, I like to stick to it.'

McConaughey closed the year on an all-time high with two hugely popular films; both *Dallas Buyers Club* and *The Wolf of Wall Street* were making mega bucks and winning rave reviews from pundits. 'When I first saw *Wolf*, I just got a whole new buzz on life,' McConaughey enthused to *Rolling Stone*'s Charles Thorp. 'I'm a part of American filmmaking history with that one. With *Dallas Buyers Club*, I was attached to it for five years before it happened. And not only was it a movie that was good medicine for our community, it's also an entertaining movie. That doesn't happen very often.'

One could hardly believe that Matthew McConaughey, the star of *How to Lose a Guy in 10 Days*, *Fool's Gold* and *The Wedding Planner*, was now being mentioned in the same breath as Brad Pitt and Leonardo DiCaprio, two fine, high calibre actors whose talents live up to their good looks and celebrity appeal.

The years 2011 to 2013 were truly fantastic for the actor from Texas – both personally and professionally – but the success and good fortune did not end with release of *The Wolf of Wall Street*. Perhaps the greatest acclaim of his career was due in the New Year, and it was not on the big screen.

CHAPTER TEN

THE McCONAISSANCE

'I don't want to just revolve. I want to evolve.
As a man, as a human, as a father, as a lover.'
Matthew McConaughey, *Elle*, 2013

'My life outside my career is extremely enriching,' McConaughey enthused to *People* magazine. 'So I am letting that feed my work, and letting my work feed my life.'

Matthew McConaughey was now the comeback kid. His career was on a high and he loved every minute of it. In some respects it was similar to the path of actor Mickey Rourke, whose career had gone off the rails in the late 1990s. Rourke began to take smaller roles in the 2000s and then he got a starring role in the critically acclaimed film *The Wrestler*, directed by the much-respected Darren Aronofsky and released in 2008. Since the release of that film, Rourke has been cast in such major productions as *Iron Man 2* and *The Expendables*. Similarly, Julia Roberts kick-started her career, which had been stuck in stale rom-coms and modest dramas, with 2000's critically acclaimed, Oscar-winning *Erin Brockovich*, directed by Steven Soderbergh.

All of a sudden, Julia Roberts was on fire and one of the most successful and high-earning actors in Hollywood.

'His backstory is a lot like Sandra Bullock,' said Tom O'Neil, founder of awards tracking site *GoldDerby.com*, to *USA Today* on McConaughey's recent success. 'Somebody who was known for making cheesy commercial movies of dubious quality, who hung in there year after year and maintained a career until suddenly they got the good movie roles and critics' attention. Hollywood likes that. They like the survivor. And they like the happy ending.'

Acting in Hollywood has a very short shelf life. Ryan Reynolds faced a challenge after the action movie flop of *R.I.P.D.*, so he signed up for some independent films, just as Taylor Kitsch faced challenges after the failures of both *Battleship* and *John Carter*, so he signed up for *Lone Survivor* and HBO's adaptation of *The Normal Heart*. In a similar fashion to Matthew McConaughey, these actors knew that they needed to rebrand themselves in order to stay in the limelight and thus keep working. On the other hand Ben Affleck turned to directing after the failures of *Gigi* and *Daredevil* and came up trumps with *Gone Baby Gone*, *The Town* and *Argo*.

Talking about the change in his professional and personal life throughout the 2010s McConaughey explained to the *Independent*'s Lesley O'Toole: 'Part of it is just growing up and part of it is I'm very turned on and excited about all kind of things. Probably more things now than I used to be. I work hard to maintain the good things in my life that I've built – friendships, work, family, my own time. Sometimes you've got to go, "Ah man, I haven't seen my brother in three months." But it feels really great when you can think: "Boy, all my relationships are good, people that I love are good, and my relationship with them is good. My career, I'm dialled, it feels good. Health is good." But to maintain that, when things change, you've got to be nimble at times.'

'It was a lot of romantic comedies and action films,' McConaughey elaborated to *Entertainment Weekly*'s Jeff Labrecque. 'I just said I feel like I've done a version of that before. Or I feel like I can do that tomorrow morning. And I think I've done enough of that for now, and I want something that I don't think I can do tomorrow morning. I want something that scares me.'

*****

McConaughey was cast as Detective Rustin 'Rust' Cohle in the acclaimed HBO series *True Detective*. McConaughey had never played such an honest and bold character on screen as Cohle. His co-star Woody Harrelson was cast as his partner Detective Martin 'Marty' Hart. The rest of the main cast features Michelle Monaghan as Maggie Hart, Michael Potts as Detective Maynard Gilbough and Tory Kittles as Detective Thomas Papania.

True Detective was created by Nic Pizzolatto and directed by Cary Joji Fukunaga. Its central premise concerns two vastly different Louisiana State Police homicide detectives who hunt a serial killer in Louisiana across seventeen years; the series uses multiple timelines across eight episodes.

The series premiered in the US on 12 January 2014 and on 22 February in the UK. He was back on the map. *True Detective* woke up the world and made people aware of McConaughey's talents as a character actor. McConaughey did not watch the advance tapes but like the rest of the US he watched it on Sundays, week by week, as the story unfolded with nail-biting tension.

'Matthew is a divisive figure in Hollywood,' Harrelson said to *GQ*'s Jessica Pressler. 'I have found myself defending him to people who don't really know him, who for some reason feel very antagonistically toward him. He's a good guy, he's great-looking, has a perfect body, his career's through the roof.

'People resented that, and the way they justified it is, "He has never done a movie of substance,"' he continued. 'They can't say that anymore.'

Pizzolatto is the natural heir to *NYPD Blue* and *Deadwood* creator David Milch. Author of the excellent novel *Gavelston* and a former assistant professor of literature at DePauw University in Indiana, Pizzolatto has become one of the most respected writers in TV. Before *True Detective* his only produced scripts were a pair for the US remake of the hit Danish series *The Killing*. 'I wanted to look at the relationship between these men and how it changed,' declared Pizzolatto to *The Guardian*'s Sarah Hughes. 'I wasn't interested in doing what everyone else was doing. The point wasn't to write another serial-killer show.'

There are a lot of non-verbal scenes in the film, which says as much about the relationship between the two detectives as the dialogue. Theirs is a tough relationship as Hart tries to understand Cohle. They are on very different planes of thought. Cohle's reactions are often monk-like with little or no expression just dialogue, while Hart is easier to read but is still a troubled soul who betrays his wife with his extra-marital affairs and has anger management issues.

Both onscreen and off, the two lead stars clicked. They'd first met back on the set of *EDtv* in 1999 and subsequently hooked up on the long-forgotten movie *Surfer, Dude*. They try to meet as often as they can on a social level so it was great to collaborate again in front of the camera. There's a lot of brotherly love between them, as well as mutual respect and admiration for each other's talents.

'Part of why Woody and I are friends,' McConaughey reflected to *Collider*'s Christina Radish in 2014, 'is that we get on each other's frequency, and we affirm each other and one-up each other. It can turn into an improvisation, but it can go into the ether, and then some. I have a really big mag full of films [sic], but this is the first time we worked together where there's real opposition. This was not about us coming together. Early on, I remember that we said, "Boy, we gotta put some kind of fun in this. This thing can be a lead weight." We found a new sort of comedy, but it was not the comedy of the two-hander, where I pass it to him, and he passes it back. We were not playing catch, back and forth.'

'I love Matthew McConaughey, he's like a brother to me,' Harrelson enthused to the *Metro*. 'I honestly wouldn't have done it, except that Matthew was doing it. He jumped into it and said "yes" before any other actors were involved. He related to the writing and knew how good it was from just the two episodes he'd read.'

Woody Harrelson had already worked with HBO on *Game Change* and was impressed by how the network works.

'I can't imagine anyone playing that part better,' said Harrelson of McConaughey at the HBO panel of a Television Critics Association event in early 2014. 'It was different than any other part I've seen him play before, and he knocked it out of the park.'

TV has changed. Some of the finest writing is not in film but on the box, with shows such as *The Wire*, *House of Cards*, *Game of Thrones* and *Breaking Bad*. It used to be the case that once-popular film actors would only end up on TV if their careers had washed up, but nowadays actors of the calibre of McConaughey, Glenn Close and Kevin Spacey have turned their attention to TV because there are fewer restraints when it comes to the writing. Producer Richard Brown explained his view to *The Guardian*'s Edward Helmore: 'TV is made fast, but often lacks the tools of cinema. With *True Detective* we wanted to bring more cinema into TV – to find the sweet spot between film and TV.'

McConaughey read only the first two episodes of the series and he was committed. *True Detective* is planned as an anthology series with each series offering new storylines and characters. McConaughey signed a contract for the full eight episodes of the first series. Had it been a film it would have been a 450-page script.

'That was another way I got lucky,' said Pizzolatto to Sarah Hughes of *The Guardian*. 'When Matthew expressed an interest, it was right before his renaissance. I'd seen *Killer Joe* and knew he was one of the few actors who could say Rust's dialogue and make you believe it. With a lesser actor, the part would have had to be drastically rewritten.'

However, Pizzolatto also told Alan Sepinwall of *HitFix*: 'I was really excited about Matthew playing Cohle, but the truth is, Woody was already on a very short list of men we wanted to approach. He had just come off of *Rampart* and *Game Change*, which are two incredible performances and incredibly different performances. So we always had Woody in mind as someone to approach. And when Matthew asked if we considered him, we were like, "Yeah, of course, and maybe you could help with that, since you guys are friends."'

'The first conversation I had with Matthew on the phone,' director Fukunaga told *The Guardian*'s Paul MacInnes, 'I could tell he was a smart guy. The first time we met he brought some music that he thought would work for the show. Initially we had differences in how we envisioned Cohle, but in terms of where he came from, we 100 per cent agreed on that. It was up to Matthew to put the flesh on that, be it in his voice or the way he moves. I wasn't quite sure what he was going to do but I was very pleased with the results.'

Committed to just one season meant McConaughey didn't have to renew his contract after a year and go back. It worked well for him considering how his film career had been revitalised. Each day they filmed thirty-nine pages of script – which is a lot of work, involving hours of filming and long days. However, some fans feel cheated with anthology series because they get so close to the characters that by the end of the season they're left wanting more. Will viewers return for a second season? Will the scripts and actors be as good as season one? Vintage anthology series' such as *The Outer Limits* and *The Twilight Zone* have had a massive impact on science-fiction and fantasy, and *American Horror Story* is a successful modern anthology series that has run for four seasons with the possibility of a fifth, but in the main, anthology series don't have much of an impact – especially in an age of multiple channels, the internet, downloading and streaming.

'No more Rust Cohle, no more Marty Hart after eight episodes,' McConaughey said to late night US talk show host Jimmy Kimmel. 'They'll have another murder mystery to solve, but it will be all new detectives. Two of 'em, three of 'em, somewhere else.'

Pizzolatto expressed his thoughts on another season with McConaughey and Harrelson to Alan Sepinwall of *HitFix*: 'I love working with those guys, and we loved working together, and we're looking for things to do together in the future. I think for cinema actors, it's a very gruelling thing. It takes up half their year at least, when they might usually be able to make two movies, or make one movie and enjoy downtime with their family. I would be completely open to anything those guys would want to do. People have asked about them coming back and I just have to say I think that would completely depend upon our actors, and if they wanted to I would of course jump on board. I feel like watching them, it made me say, "Why hasn't anyone put these guys together before in a serious film?" They just play so well off each other. The highest compliment I can give their performances is I think it's impossible to imagine two other guys in these roles after you see them.'

McConaughey prefers to work with directors who understand him and his personal take on the character. Cary Joji Fukunaga knew what McConaughey was doing with his character, Cohle. McConaughey likes a nudge here and there, and a director with objectivity. The pair worked well together on set.

Pizzolatto wrote clear identities to the characters and tone of the series. McConaughey and Harrelson basically went off the source material as it was complex enough. McConaughey went inside his character's head to understand where he was coming from – why he is so obsessive, troubled and alone. Cohle is a realist living in a world that is not black and white. 'There's an ambiguity that is very existential in the guy,' McConaughey said to John Lopez of *Grantland*. 'He's very specific but you're like, "How many more things can you be like this about?" Which leads to what we were talking about earlier, the comedy comes from the exasperation of "Dude, shut up." "Well, you asked – you wanted to talk." But no one's selling.'

It's both interesting and challenging for McConaughey to get inside Cohle's head – to see what his character was like in 1995, a man who is going back on a homicide case, who is barely keeping everything together. And then go back to the character seventeen years later in 2012 when he's off the case and fallen off the rails. What happened in between? The storyline throughout the eight episodes fills in the gaps. The viewer slowly finds out what happened. It is an extraordinarily well written series; deep and immersive as it sucks the viewer into a complex web of plotlines. Cohle is certainly not a white knight. He's a deeply intense and complex man tormented by his own past.

'We usually have a shorthand in the way we work together but on this project a lot of what would be our shorthand didn't apply,' Harrelson told *Metro* about working with McConaughey on the set of *True Detective*. 'Usually, we finish each other's sentences but with this, Matthew was an island. He is one of the most gregarious guys I know but he is a little more method than me, and with this, he was fully in character and stayed in it.'

The 2014 HBO series *True Detective* won McConaughey rave reviews. Critics were stunned that the actor who'd been relatively lame in *The Wedding Planner*, *How to Lose a Guy in 10 Days*, *Failure to Launch*, *Fool's Gold* and *Ghosts of Girlfriends Past* could give such an alluring and grippingly dark performance. It was almost miraculous, really. Between 2001 and 2009 he'd hardly given any memorable film performances, but from 2010 onwards every performance he's given on screen is simply marvellous. McConaughey has since become one of the most watchable actors alive. A decade earlier, most critics couldn't stomach him.

David Wiegand of the *San Francisco Chronicle* wrote: 'The dialogue is rich, colourful and provocative, adding to the gothic sensibilities of the series. Director Cary Joji Fukunaga makes great use of the Louisiana location, giving it as much importance to the story as the characters of Cohle and Hart. All the performances are superb, but those of McConaughey and Harrelson are in a class by themselves.'

Benjain Secher of *The Daily Telegraph* wrote: 'In the rich, dense, intense *True Detective*, HBO has created as irresistible a way of killing time as you'll find on the small screen this year.'

The season finale, however, drew some negative complaints, but on the whole *True Detective* was hugely well received and will possibly go down as one of the truly great TV shows of the decade. 'Thought the series was great,' Alan Yuhas expressed in *The Guardian*, 'the finale was more than a little lacking. It's probably worth rewatching, though there were likely a few too many threads to tie up in eight episodes… In the end, *True Detective* finally flipped, and Marty and Rust discovered the good life again. They became the awkward buddy comedy we'd always wanted. I just wish the evidence were a little more convincing.'

McConaughey explained his fondness for his recent stream of outlaws, antiheroes and outcasts to *Entertainment Weekly*'s Jeff Labrecque: 'They're all characters who weren't placating to civilization or society, so I liked them. They've all been sort of fringe-y characters that I was able to define certain obsessions that they had. And as an actor, if I can grab a hold of an obsession or two, that's what I wanted to get drunk on.'

In June 2014, McConaughey was honoured with the Best Actor award at the fourth annual Television Critics' Awards for his role in *True Detective*. *Breaking Bad* picked up Best Drama. McConaughey praised television for 'raising the bar for character-driven drama.'

True Detective had begun the year in fine style and January also delivered a whole shelf of awards and accolades for McConaughey. It was awards season and McConaughey had both *The Wolf of Wall Street* and *Dallas Buyers Club* to his name, as well as *True Detective*, which is surely set for some recognition during the 2015 awards season. This period also gave McConaughey further chance to talk about *Dallas Buyers Club*, which he relished. He was presented with the 'Independent Spirit Award' at the annual Palm Springs International Film Festival on 4 January. Past actor recipients of the 'Independent Spirit Award' include Jeff Bridges, Bradley Cooper, Daniel Day-Lewis, Colin Firth, Jake Gyllenhaal, Sean Penn and Brad Pitt.

'Matthew McConaughey is the rare actor who effortlessly moves between cinematic genres. From drama to thrillers to romantic comedies, he captivates audiences with the depth and range of his performances,' said Harold Matzner, Chairman of the Palm Springs International Film Festival. 'In the acclaimed new movie *Dallas Buyers Club*, McConaughey plays real-life cowboy Ron Woodroof, who was diagnosed with HIV in 1985 and given a month to live – but fought for dignity, acceptance, and living life to the fullest. We are privileged to present Matthew McConaughey with an award that honours his extraordinary and versatile talent, the 2014 Desert Palm Achievement Award for acting.'

McConaughey was in fine company as the awards ceremony also presented honours to Meryl Streep, Tom Hanks, Julia Roberts, Sandra Bullock, director Steve McQueen, Bruce Dern, Lupita Nyong'o, Thomas Newman and the cast of *American Hustle*. McConaughey was presented with the award by the revered British actor Gary Oldman, who said McConaughey's performance in *Dallas Buyers Club* was fearless, sincere, honest and free. In his acceptance speech, McConaughey said: '*Dallas Buyers Club* was not an easy story to find. They don't come across our desk that often. It's been the best film in my career, that is for sure!'

McConaughey won a Golden Globe on 12 January. 'This film...Ron Woodruff's story was an underdog. For twenty years it was an underdog, turned down eighty-six times. Nobody wanted to put up money for it. We got the right people together five years ago, put some skin in the game, and here it is,' said McConaughey when he accepted the award at the star studded ceremony.

He added: 'Time like this makes me want to say thank you to my mother for a real reason. We were growing up, we weren't movie kids, we weren't TV kids, we weren't media kids... if it was daylight, you had to be outside playing. We'd go, "Why mom? Why can't I just watch 30 minutes of TV?" She goes, "Don't watch somebody on TV do it for you, get out there and do it for yourself." Now this many years later I'm like, "That's a pretty good recipe for an actor." Go be the subject of whatever you're doing.'

'How are you going to top that speech you made at the Golden Globes? It's untoppable,' Jimmy Kimmel said during an interview with McConaughey on his popular late night talk show on ABC. 'I feel like you wasted your A material on the

Golden Globes, and now you have a lot to live up to. Do you have anything in mind?'

McConaughey also won 'Best Actor' at the Screen Actors Guild Awards on 18 January where he gave a rather unusual speech, which involved Neptune and baffled everyone. He also bagged an Oscar for 'Best Actor' on 2 March 2014 (no Screen Actors Guild Award winner has failed to pick up an Oscar since 2003) for his role as Ron Woodroof.

He told the press (*Gossip Center*) that he sat down and spoke with his kids before the lavish Oscars ceremony: '"We're going out tonight because there's an award show. Remember when we were back in New Orleans and lived in that house? The work that dad did then, the work we all did, people are shining a light on it today, so if you do your best right now, it can have reciprocity later and come back and pay residuals." That's the lesson we're trying to get to them.'

The world's media watched the celebrities walk the red carpet in expensive tailor-made suits and dresses by some of the top names in fashion. McConaughey looked dapper in a handsome black and white tuxedo. Camila worked with Charlene Roxborough, hairstylist, Jasmin Robles and makeup artist Patrick DeFontbrune to create her dream Oscars look. Alves and Roxborough worked with designer Gabriela Cadena for her dress. 'I'm dressing for him [Matthew] and he does give input,' she said to ABC News. 'He likes to see me, not the dress taking over.'

With Kim Novak, star of Alfred Hitchcock's *Vertigo*, at his side McConaughey also delivered a trophy to *Frozen* for 'Best Animated Feature'.

McConaughey gave a detailed albeit rather baffling and pretentious thank-you speech, which included the following:

'There's a few things, about three things to my account that I need each day. One of them is something to look up to, another is something to look forward to, and another is someone to chase. Now, first off, I want to thank God. 'Cause that's who I look up to. He has graced my life with opportunities that I know are not of my hand or any other human hand. He has shown me that it's a scientific fact that gratitude reciprocates. In the words of the late Charlie Laughton, who said, "When you've got God, you got a friend. And that friend is you."'

The forty-four-year-old also thanked his family, friends and colleagues for the Oscar. There's no doubt that he was thrilled to finally get the coveted award. It's something that he'd always wanted to get his hands on. His co-star Jared Leto was also a winner, picking up 'Best Supporting Actor' – that meant that for the first time since 2003's *Mystic River* a single film had claimed both acting awards at the Oscars. McConaughey has also either won or been nominated for many film festival awards and regional film awards in North American and Europe.

'I just find that the more I wake up and find things to be appreciative about, they do reciprocate somehow,' McConaughey told Josh Elliott of ABC News backstage at the Oscars. 'Gratitude is a scientific fact. It fills me up to be thankful for things and I have a lot to be thankful for, always starting with just the fact that you get another day. We take that for granted.'

The Sun reported that McConaughey was eager to get home after winning the Oscar so he could celebrate with his wife. As reported in *The Sun*, he was allegedly overheard by one source saying: 'We won't stay at the after party long – I want to go home and make another baby!'

A source also said: 'Matthew wasn't worried about getting

drunk, he was more keen to get home with his beautiful wife, which he made quite clear in her ear... It was so lovely to see, though. It's clear how in love they are. They kissed and kissed and kissed.'

Winning an Oscar or an Emmy was not something that he was aiming for but he was extremely proud and happy to win them. 'I think that it's absolutely fair to judge art,' he told *RogerEbert. com*'s Susan Wloszczyna. 'I have opinions about things that are better than other things. If there was no gauge, you would say Shakespeare is the same thing as any junior-high girl's diary. I'm not really thinking about the result of it. But people are saying it to me. I don't know, we'll see. I like the film. I like the experience. I can talk about it for hours. And, if it translates in that way, great.'

Friends, family and fellow actors came out in support of McConaughey and spoke about how pleased they were for his success. His former onscreen lover Jennifer Lopez told *Para Todos* magazine: 'It was great working with Matthew. So proud of what he's accomplished over the last few years and I have fond memories of him on set.'

It's interesting to look at his spate of films post *The Lincoln Lawyer*: the characters are all defined by the predicaments that they find themselves in. Not every future venture will be an indie film but there does seem to be a link with auteur directors. These films have given him a newfound freedom as an actor. He doesn't feel tied down by genre or stereotype; he is free of all shackles. He's no longer interested in 'Saturday characters' as he refers to them. Once upon a time he'd been attracted to the lightness of the romantic-comedy, the fairy tale-like charm of them, but those roles were long over as more realistic characters came calling.

The first half of 2014 began extremely well for McConaughey and the second half of the year was no different, as it saw the release of the eagerly awaited science-fiction film *Interstellar*. The film, directed by *Batman Begins* and *Inception* director Christopher Nolan, tells the story of a group of space travellers who travel through a wormhole. The script by Jonathan Nolan, which had originally been set up for Steven Spielberg, had been undeveloped for years until his brother Christopher combined it with a separate idea of his own. In March 2013 Christopher had confirmed he was to direct the film, his first after he closed his *Batman* trilogy with *The Dark Knight Rises*. Matthew McConaughey and Anne Hathaway had been cast in April 2013.

'Matthew works from the inside out,' Nolan told *Variety's* Jenelle Riley. 'He approaches a character from a deep human understanding, refusing to take shortcuts to an emotional connection with the audience – all while never losing sight of the demands of the overall narrative.'

Interstellar sees McConaughey tackle the role of an engineer and pilot named Cooper who travels through time and space to find a new planet that is suitable for human inhabitation. Humanity's fate rests on Cooper's shoulders as Earth faces a crippling food shortage.

Nolan had seen *Mud* and was pleasantly surprised by McConaughey's performance. 'I admired him as a movie star and I knew he was a good actor, but I didn't know how much potential he had until I saw that early cut. It was a transformative performance,' Nolan said to Tom McCarthy of *The Hollywood Reporter*.

It was at an event when Nolan saw McConaughey and

approached him to tell him how impressed he was by the film. McConaughey was then asked to fly out to LA to meet Nolan. They had a two-hour chat at Nolan's house and not a word was uttered about *Interstellar*. McConaughey walked out unsure of what to think. McConaughey then received a call and was offered the role.

McConaughey likes the way Nolan works – straight to the point, on time and under schedule and with an indie sensibility. Nolan, after all, began his career making independent films such as *Following* and *Memento*.

The actor took his Airstream, one of three he now owns, to the set where he based himself during filming. On the door there is the now iconic aphorism: 'Just keep livin''.

'I'm a personal believer in faith and science,' McConaughey said to *Vulture*'s Jennifer Vineyard on the subject of faith versus science or science versus faith, as illustrated in *Contact* and *Interstellar*. 'I think the two can definitely co-exist. I'm always trying to make faith a science! But part of all of this is working with directors who have a really particular point of view. These independents that I'm getting acclaim for, let's remember – I could have given the same performance in crappy movies!'

The film features an ensemble cast of co-stars including Jessica Chastain, Bill Irwin, Ellen Burstyn, Michael Caine, Matt Damon, Casey Affleck, Topher Grace, John Lithgow, David Gyasi, Wes Bentley, Mackenzie Foy, David Oyelowo, Elyes Gabel, Leah Cairns and William Devane. The cast were sworn to secrecy.

The Bourne Identity and *Good Will Hunting* actor Matt Damon spoke to MTV News about working on the film with McConaughey and director Chris Nolan: 'All I can say is I don't have a big part. I was just thrilled to work with Christopher Nolan and I had a blast working with him… I really had so much fun. Matthew, he's the lead in the movie… talk about being in the zone, he's really just crushing everything right now and I think it's just going to be great.'

Interstellar was released in US and UK cinemas in November 2014.

*****

Who knows what projects McConaughey will choose after *Interstellar*. One idea that has yet to be green lit, but which McConaughey has spoken about for several years, is *The Grackle*. He plays a barroom fighter in New Orleans who hires himself out for $250 to settle arguments between folks who don't have to cash to pay for a lawyer. He planned to be generous with the casting as he told Tom Chiarella of *Esquire* back in 2011: 'Well, my company is developing it. So I'm figuring everyone who ever did me a favour, got me a ticket or a backstage pass, they're gonna be calling and asking to be extras. That's a lot of souls. Every bar in that movie is gonna be full of people I know.'

According to the industry website *The Wrap*, McConaughey had signed up for a role opposite Ken Watanabe in Gus Van Sant's drama *Sea of Trees*, though the actor had not announced it publicly at the time of writing. The script, which made the 2013 *Black List* (best unproduced scripts), was written by Chris Sparling (*Buried*). Gil Netter (*Life of Pi*) is set to produce, and it was to be Van Sant's first film since the Matt Damon, John Krasinski drama *Promised Land*. The film is about an American man who takes a venture into the Suicide Forest at the foothills of Mount Fuji with the aim of taking his life. However, a Japanese man intervenes and he has second thoughts about killing himself. He tries to find his way out of the forest, and both men begin a journey of reflection and survival. It is an existentialist story about faith in humanity.

When it looked as though McConaughey was destined to appear in romantic comedies and little-talked about dramas in the 1990s, he took a gamble and totally reinvented himself – so much so that by 2014 he was an Oscar-winning actor and back in the A-list elite of Hollywood stars. And in *Bernie, Killer Joe, Magic Mike, Mud* and *Dallas Buyers Club* he had a decent catalogue of recent critically acclaimed films under his belt. His performances were widely praised and rightly so; he is an incredibly talented and understated actor. Just when you think he has become a parody of himself he turns his career around and surprises audiences with stunning performances such as in the five films mentioned above. Here is an actor who had starred in reasonably acclaimed films as *Amistad* and *Contact*, but then sunk so low as to be cast in a series of forgettable romantic comedies such as *Fool's Gold* and *Ghosts of Girlfriends Past*. Critics and film buffs had written him off but he turned his career around and was cast in a number of highly praised films, as well as and one of the most talked about TV shows of the 2010s, which has been compared to HBO's critically acclaimed crime series, *The Wire*.

'Matthew is a bit of a vagabond,' said director Richard Linklater to *Vogue*'s John Powers 'He could live in a trailer and be just as happy. If he didn't have a family, he might not even have a house.'

Did anyone expect 2014 to be Matthew McConaughey's

year? It's highly doubtful. McConaughey is in a good place in 2014, both professionally and personally. He is a successful and revered actor, and an entrepreneur with a charity, clothes line and indie record label. He is happily married with three children (eldest son Levi Alves McConaughey, daughter Vida Alves McConaughey and youngest child Livingston Alves McConaughey), a beautiful home in West Texas – a 1,600-acre working ranch – and his career is going extraordinarily well. Family is very important to him.

'They eat, they crap, they sleep and if they're crying they need to do one of the three and they're having trouble doing it. Real simple,' he once admitted to late night talk show host Jay Leno.

In 2014 they planned an eleven-day trip to Brazil to see Camila's family and they made a rule: they'd each carry a backpack and stay holed up in one room together. It goes back to his family tradition in Texas growing up: there are always stories to tell and adventures to take. He keeps a diary; one for each film and one for each time he travels. Being married to a busy working actor can be tough but they are a team.

'The best education I've had in my life is to travel,' McConaughey told *IndieLondon* in 2008, 'and that's what we get to do in this job. My kid's going to travel, and I've got a goal to fill that passport pretty early in his or her life. That'll be its own challenge, but that's going to be fun. I want to bring my kid to the set, to the locations that I go to. Some of the greatest people that I've met in my life, the most creative people I've met, are in this circus, this carnival of people who get together and go and make a movie.'

Having children changed everything for him. He knew he wanted to be a father even before he chose what career he wanted to pursue. For McConaughey, being a father reminds him of the great things in life. It helps him approach things with more significance and has changed acting for him. You pass down your knowledge and experience to your children. He doesn't want to rush his children; he allows them to grow up on their own time and enjoy childhood.

'Being a father is the one thing I always knew I wanted to be,' McConaughey confessed to *The Daily Telegraph*'s Tom Shone. 'Looking around at my own life, I said to myself, "Man, what I'm doing in my own life is more interesting than my work." I was like, "That's OK. Better be that way than the other way around. At least you're getting something out of life. You're going to work and you're enjoying it. You're finding ways to get challenged, McConaughey." You do the work, it pays the bills, but boy my life was vital. The way I'm loving, the way I'm expressing my anger, either I'm mad as hell or I'm laughing harder at that joke than anyone else does.'

McConaughey is a loyal man; he stays loyal to his family and friends. In fact, he's had the same friends for a long time. His loyalty is a trait he wants to pass on to his children. 'I guess the other things are how much do you decipher between what's just DNA and what's the culture and environment they're going to be raised in,' he explained to *IndieLondon*. 'The way I was raised, the one thing we knew no matter what was that Mom and Dad loved us. That made it easy for us to adapt even when you're getting your butt whupped or you're getting in trouble. It was the old: "I love you but I don't like you right now," so you always knew you had that.'

His mother Kay, who had self-published a book called *I Amaze Myself* in 2008 and is an active member of The Children's

Advocacy Centre and Family Outreach, was asked by Donna White of *Austin Daze* if she was a traditional all-American milk and cookies sort of grandma to which she replied: 'NO! Not at all! But, I mean, they don't try me. They're very respectful to me and I can't imagine them talking back to me. But they're always happy to see me because I do the fun stuff. Levi (Matthew's son) loves to role-play and he's only three. I say, come on let's go, and he says, "Is the big black car gonna pick us up?"'

As with Kay's own children, her three boys, she loves to tell stories to her grandkids. Her book was all the stories she used to tell and how she wanted them to be passed down through the generations. She's happy to be herself and enjoys life to the max and is both a good mother and grandmother. She's had a fun life; she's made mistakes but learned along the way. She's treated well by her youngest son who allows her to travel with him sometimes to far away and exotic places such as Italy and Africa. She does, however, get frustrated when the family is disturbed by journalists or members of the public who ask for autographs or photographs because of his celebrity status. Details of some of his personal habits became popularised: he uses Kiehl's face lotion every day; when he dresses up in a suit he uses Clarisonic and puts on his signature scent, 'The One'; and his everyday scent is fresh-cut St. Augustine grass which is grown in his home state of Texas.

Winning an Oscar and riding on the back of a handful of revered films, McConaughey has become a target for the paparazzi and entrainment gossip journalists. He had also become a darling of the critics. On 20 February, he appeared on *Inside The Actor's Studio* with presenter James Lipton. McConaughey was snapped at LA airport on 25 March with his mother having arrived from a flight from Rome, Italy.

Gossip Center reported: 'An Italian eyewitness told press that McConaughey treated his mom to only the best cuisine while overseas, including dinner at Antica Pesa. [The witness said:] "They looked adorable. His love for his mom was evident, and he treated her like a queen. You can tell he is such a southern gentleman, and they looked happy to be spending time together."'

McConaughey was in Italy for work while Kay was travelling around Europe, but they still found time for each other over dinner. They enjoyed a variety of appetisers including *crudo e bufala*, tuna carpaccio and some vegetables. For the main course, they tried *cacio e pepe* and amatriciana pastas, followed by beef cheek braised with Sangiovese wine reduction, orange foam and seared radicchio.

Only days earlier – on the Saturday – he was snapped at LAX catching a flight. McConaughey is now a fully-fledged celebrity – not that he had never been one before but his status had faded somewhat – although he is not getting the sort of attention that was given to him on the back of *A Time to Kill* in the mid-1990s.

Other celebrity news surrounding McConaughey's recent burst of popularity circulated around the world as the hat, which he had worn in *Dallas Buyers Club*, sold at auction for a staggering $12,956. The starting price was $3,000 and three bids were made. The LA based auctioneer Nate D. Sanders had originally bought the hat for $1,291 at the SAFG auctions, but he felt it had the 'potential for much more' and indeed it did.

One Upper East Side coffee shop (DTUT) played an April's fool's joke when they offered customers a chance to 'Meet Matthew McConaughey' only to discover it's the name of the shop's goldfish. Needless to say some people who turned up did not find the joke funny at all.

McConaughey was also given the opportunity to induct Willie Nelson and Stevie Ray Vaughan & Double Trouble into the Austin City Limits Hall of Fame on 26 April. Director Richard Linklater also wrote a piece on him for *Time* magazine's '100 Most Influential People' special, which included McConaughey.

There are three distinct phases to his career just like there are so many stories of his seemingly oddball lifestyle. When he started out he was touted as the next Paul Newman. That phase lasted a few films and then he became the actor Hollywood went to for romantic comedies. Finally phase three came about as he relaunched his career so very successfully in 2010 and 2011.

'I didn't actually go out and grab all those things – some of them came to me – but I did put the brakes on some other things I was doing for about a year and a half and decided I was going to wait,' explained McConaughey about his career facelift to the *Yorkshire Post* in 2013. 'I said to myself, "I don't know exactly what it is I want to do but I want to wait until something comes in that really intrigues me."'

Then there are stories of Airstream trailers, playing golf barefooted, push-ups on the beach, lost flip-flops, shirtless afternoons, playing the bongos naked, brushing his teeth while driving and random trips to far off places, and naming his dog Miss Hud (named after the Paul Newman film, *Hud*, one of McConaughey's favourite movies since his teenage years). There's certainly something unconventional about him. He's just a humble kid from Texas who did his parents proud.

'I do have less time for friends now,' he admitted to *Details'*

Adam Sachs. 'My close friends have had to come to understand that I can't just throw on a backpack and say, "We'll be back in four days."'

Life is an adventure and McConaughey has always wanted to live every day as though it is his last. He has played real-life heroes, but who are his influences and inspirations? 'In the eighties, Steve Biko's story, in apartheid South Africa,' he admitted to *Stylist*'s Susan Riley. 'Thomas Merton, a Benedictine monk who was a real rebel and then died from an electric shock in a monastery. [Stunt rider] Evel Knievel – talk about a will to live. Those are a few people who've been an inspiration.'

Similarly to his character Mud, McConaughey knows how to survive; he's become wiser as he's gotten older. When he's been hurt he's learned not to get hurt again and he's experienced heartbreak, which he doesn't want to repeat. He believes in innocence, in the dream. 'Well, I have still inside of me a lot of innocence,' he admitted to *Total Film*. 'I'm not nearly as naïve as I used to be, thankfully, but you know they say as you grow older you grow wiser, you should know better, and you know well there's some things that you know worse. There's some things that you don't want to [know], life teaches you some lessons that can kind of creep in and break that dream a little bit. Pragmatism does that. And all of a sudden, the avenue between here and here becomes using a one-way street from the head down.'

His company Just Keep Livin has grown from strength to strength over the years. Originally there was just McConaughey and his childhood buddy and business partner Gus Gustawes, before they employed more staff. A website – MatthewMcConaughey.com – was set up which the actor was really proud of. They then spent time funding and making their first finished production *Surfer, Dude,* before expanding the company into music, clothing and charity.

The days when he appears with his shirt off on the cover of *People* magazine are seemingly long gone, and leading roles in fluffy romantic comedies are equally a thing of the past. He's a different actor now because he is a different man. He has evolved. He is a thinker, a dreamer; a deep man often waxing philosophical ideas. Sure, there is more than a hint of pretentiousness to him but he is nevertheless an interesting individual, far more interesting than some have been led to believe. McConaughey is a calm individual. He usually finds his Zen through diet, exercise and a healthy lifestyle. His family is massively supportive and they help, too, especially during busy periods of his life. Coming from a Methodist background, he is also religious and takes a minute or two timeout to thank God. Religion and family give him perspective and reassurance. Religion also connects him to his past and gives him an understanding of where his future lays.

'…responsibility is when you create your own weather,' he once said, as quoted on *Cinema.com.* 'Whether it's the people you hang out with, the places you choose to go, the things you choose to do, you have to be responsible to it, and the more responsible you are, the more Lady Luck shines on you. It's circular. It keeps coming back, and regurgitates.'

McConaughey spoke to John Lopez of *Grantland* about religion and its place in his life: 'I do believe in God, but I think it's very healthy for a believer to spend time in the pragmatism of agnosticism, and I think God appreciates agnostics trying to make a science of it and going, "I will not believe any further than that." I enjoy that kind of engineering mind. In no way did it ever feel blasphemous to me as a man of faith. And what was I like at home? I was a pretty good explainer to the kids about things. I got pretty good at breaking down – if/then, this/that.'

McConaughey has learned that you may not get everything in life but that you can get everything you need and be appreciative of what you have. He'll wake up in the morning and find things to be grateful for and learn that they do, somehow, reciprocate. He knows to be thankful for what he has and to enjoy life. Like a travelling circus, the McConaughey's split their time between homes in Malibu and Austin. 'I have a very healthy relationship with time,' he said to Dennis Lim of *The New York Times* in 2012. 'It's a very unimpressed town because it has an identity.'

McConaughey is enjoying acting and wants to be an actor for hire. Finally, he is getting noticed. He wants roles that are going to scare him a little, that take him out of his comfort zone. He's also looking to gain more experiences as more scripts come his way.

There's no question that McConaughey will from now on be careful about which projects he chooses. As with the resurrection of the once flagging career of Robert Downey Jr's post-*Iron Man*, McConaughey can now command millions of dollars per film and star in some of the most talked about and popular Hollywood films. Careers constantly rise and fall in Hollywood. Nicolas Cage, a once popular and respected actor who often starred in unconventional, on the edge roles, has seen his career flagging in recent years due to poor decision-making. Lindsey Lohan wasn't helped by a seemingly bad attitude and an overindulgent personal life; films like *Herbie: Fully Loaded* didn't help her either. McConaughey can now be spoken in the same breath as Leonardo DiCaprio, Denzel Washington and Sean Penn, with a string of great performances and fantastic films to his name. It will perhaps be the critics who will continue to be surprised by McConaughey more than anyone else. They'd once written him off but are now praising him to high heaven. Such is the fickle nature of the industry.

He's a character actor as well as a movie star nowadays, but it took twenty years for people to find how just how talented an actor he is. The wave of movies – *Killer Joe*, *Magic Mike*, *The Paperboy*, *Mud* and *Dallas Buyers Club* – were all part of an idea that McConaughey had about getting some first-time experiences. He wanted to be excited. He wanted to be scared. He was having much better results than with any of period of his career. His career had been turned around by those bold choices.

Since his turn of fortunes, McConaughey has begun to impress fellow thespians. 'When he started making choices that were less based on his looks and had artistic integrity, a lot of young actors became very impressed,' Laura Gardner, an actress and instructor at the Howard Fine Acting Studio in NYC, said to *The New York Times*' Brooks Barnes. 'McConaughey has demonstrated a commitment to his art, to finding that truth in his characters.'

In terms of professional pursuits, McConaughey isn't interested in anything but acting at the moment. He doesn't want to produce or direct, even though he has expressed a keen interest in doing so in the past. He wants to choose the right role, make the film and then a year or so later go out there and talk about it, sell it and promote it. That's his main concentration now. He's learned how to survive in Hollywood. A cesspool of failed dreams, tragedy and lost hope, and yet also a land of glamour, fantasy and incredible wealth. He knows how to navigate his way around the industry and govern his career by his own set of rules and standards. He doesn't allow Hollywood to direct him. It's the other way around.

'I'm getting much more of an array of stuff,' McConaughey admitted to *Deadline*'s Christy Grosz. 'It's not of one specific genre. That's what's really fun now. I'm getting to choose. People are going, "OK, so you want to do dramas?" Yeah, I'm enjoying the dramas, but keep that comedy coming! That stuff's fun, man!'

Matthew McConaughey has the option to do whatever he pleases and whatever he does he will no doubt surprise himself and his fans. McConaughey has learned to say yes to roles because he feels lucky. He is thankful but he is now being more selfish. There is room for evolution because every aspect of his life is in the ascendant.

He just keeps livin'.

FILM CREDITS

FILM

Dazed and Confused (1993)

My Boyfriend's Back (1993)

Angels in the Outfield (1994)

Texas Chainsaw Massacre: The Next Generation (1994)

Boys on the Side (1995)

Glory Daze (1995)

Lone Star (1996)

A Time to Kill (1996)

Larger than Life (1996)

Scorpion Spring (1996)

Contact (1997)

Amistad (1997)

The Newton Boys (1998)

EDtv (1999)

U-571 (2000)

The Wedding Planner (2001)
Thirteen Conversations About One Thing (2002)
Frailty (2002)
Reign of Fire (2002)
How to Lose a Guy in 10 Days (2003)
Tiptoes (2003)
Sahara (2005)
Two for the Money (2005)
Failure To Launch (2006)
We Are Marshall (2006)
Fool's Gold (2008)
Tropic Thunder (2008)
Surfer, Dude (2008)
Ghosts of Girlfriends Past (2009)
The Lincoln Lawyer (2011)
Bernie (2011)
Killer Joe (2012)
Magic Mike (2012)
The Paperboy (2012)
Mud (2013)
Dallas Buyers Club (2013)
The Wolf of Wall Street (2013)
Interstellar (2014)

SHORT FILMS

Submission (1995)
Judgement (1995)
Making Sandwiches (1998)
The Rebel (1998)

DOCUMENTARIES
Freedom: A History Of US (2003)
Magnificent Desolation: Walking on the Moon 3D (2005)

TV
Unsolved Mysteries (1992)
King of the Hill (1999)
Bonne Nuit (1999) *(TV Movie)*
Sex and the City (2000)
Eastbound & Down (2010-2012)
True Detective (2014)

MUSIC VIDEOS
Trisha Yearwood – 'Walkway Joe' (1992)
Butch Walker and The Black Widows' – 'Synthesizers' (2003)

NOTE: Release dates are from IMDB not Wikipedia.

SOURCES AND ACKNOWLEDGEMENTS

PRINT

The Austin Chronicle
Boston Phoenix
Empire
Huffington Post
The Independent
The Los Angeles Times
The New York Times
Orlando Sentinel
Para Todos
San Francisco Chronicle
USA Today
Variety

ONLINE

http://abcnews.go.com
http://www.aintitcool.com
http://au.lifestyle.yahoo.com
http://cinema.com
http://collider.com
http://thefilmexperience.net
http://thefilmstage.com
http://grantland.com
http://insidemovies.ew.com
http://movies.about.com
http://movieline.com
http://moviesblog.mtv.com
http://tech.mit.edu
http://variety.com
www.austindaze.com
www.bbc.co.uk
www.beliefnet.com
www.bullz-eye.com
www.chud.com
www.cinemablend.com
www.thecinemasource.com
www.clarionledger.com
www.crazedfanboy.com
www.thedailybeast.com
www.deadline.com
www.denofgeek.com
www.details.com
www.dvdtalk.com
www.elle.com

www.empireonline.com

www.esquire.com

www.ew.com

www.express.co.uk

www.filmcomment.com

www.filmjournal.com

www.goldderby.com

www.gq.com

www.gwhatchet.com

www.hitfix.com

www.hollywood.com

www.huffingtonpost.com

www.iamrogue.com

www.independent.co.uk

www.ivillage.com

www.interviewmagazine.com

www.kpbs.org

www.latimes.com

www.mensfitness.co.uk

www.mirror.co.uk

www.movieweb.com

www.newsweek.com

www.npr.org

www.people.com

www.phase9.tv

www.popmatters.com

www.redeyechicago.com

www.reelfilm.com

www.rogerebert.com

www.rollingstone.com

www.sbs.com.au
www.scotsman.com
www.slate.com
www.standard.co.uk
www.starnewsonline.com
www.starpulse.com
www.stylist.co.uk
www.terra.com
www.texasmonthly.com
www.timeout.com
www.totalfilm.com
www.townsvillebulletin.com.au
www.usatoday.com
www.villagevoice.com
www.vogue.com
www.vulture.com
www.washingtonpost.com
www.wwwd.com
www.yorkshireeveningpost.co.uk

Thank you to the following journalists whose work was integral in the making this book:
Beth Accomando, Derek Adams, David Ansen, Michael Atkinson, Helen Barlow, Brooks Barnes, Steven Beard, Bart Blasengame, Peter Bradshaw, Simon Braund, Xan Brooks, Dave Calhoun, Alec Cawthorne, Sandie Angulo Chen, Tom Chiarella, Mike Clark, Rich Cline, Jason Cohen, Jason Coleman, Robbie Collin, Dave Davies, Phillip Duncan, Roger Ebert, David Edelstein, Eric Eisenberg, Josh Elliott, Devin Faraci, Phillip

SOURCES AND ACKNOWLEDGEMENTS

French, Caroline Frost, Cynthia Fuchs, Christian Ghigliotty, Owen Gleiberman, Phil & Sue Godsell, Bill Graham, Terry Gross, Christy Grosz, Jason Guerrasio, Edward Guthmann, Stephen Harrigan, Will Harris, Edward Helmore, Christopher Hemblade, Stephen Holden, Skip Hollandsworth, Desson Howe, Sarah Hughes, Evan 'Mushy' Jacobs, Dan Jolin, Mark Kermode, Kimberley Jones, Tina Jordan, Simon Kinnear, Robert Koehler, Jeff Labrecque, Christy Lemire, Emanuel Levy, Allison C. Lewis, Dennis Lim, John Lopez, Frank Lovece, Brian Lowry, Beth Anne Macaluso, Paul MacInnes ,Geoffrey MacNab, Derek Malcolm, J.P. Mangalindan, Andrea Mandell, Caitlin Martis, Janet Maslin, Tim Masters, Todd McCarthy, Jenny McCartney, Andy Metzger, Charlie Mihelich, Holly Milea, Nell Minow, Elvis Mitchell, Roger Moore, James Mottram, Mr. Beaks, Ian Nathan, Rob Nelson, Lisa Nesselson, David Nusair, Helen O'Hara, Lesley O'Toole, Ann Oldenburg, Daniel Ordona, Dominic Patten, Garth Pearce, James Peaty, George Perry, Jami Philbrick, John Powers, Jessica Pressler, Andrew Pulver, Joe Queenan, Nathaniel R., Christina Radish, Jenelle Riley, Susan Riley, Tim Robey, Brenda Rodriguez, Kelly Rondeau, Adam Sachs, Michael Sauter, Mary Kaye Schilling, Lisa Schwarzbaum, A.O. Scott, Benjain Secher, Alan Sepinwall, Ramin Setoodeh, David Sexton, Caroline Shoard, Tom Shone, Anna Smith, Michael A. Smith, Michael Snyder, John Spong, Peter Stack, Natasha Stoynoff, Kevin P. Sullivan, Amy Taubin, Ella Taylor, Luke Y. Thompson, Michael Thomson, Charles Thorp, Scott Tobias, Chris Tookey, Fred Topel, Peter Travers, Andrea Tuccillo, Jennifer Vineyard, Mike Voorheis, Andy Warhol, Joe Warner, Billy Watkins, Glenn Whipp, Donna White, David Wiegand, Jessica Winter, Susan Wloszczyna and Alan Yuhas.

Thank you also to Chris Mitchell and the staff at John Blake Publishing.

Apologies if I have missed out any names; it was not intentional.

Visit my website: www.neildanielsbooks.com.